The Academic Profession in Europe: New Tasks and New Challenges

The Changing Academy – The Changing Academic Profession in International Comparative Perspective 5

Scope of the series

As the landscape of higher education has in recent years undergone signifi cant changes, so correspondingly have the backgrounds, specializations, expectations and work roles of academic staff. The Academy is expected to be more professional in teaching, more productive in research and more entrepreneurial in everything. Some of the changes involved have raised questions about the attractiveness of an academic career for today's graduates. At the same time, knowledge has come to be identifi ed as the most vital resource of contemporary societies.

The Changing Academy series examines the nature and extent of the changes experienced by the academic profession in recent years. It explores both the reasons for and the consequences of these changes. It considers the implications of the changes for the attractiveness of the academic profession as a career and for the ability of the academic community to contribute to the further development of knowledge societies and the attainment of national goals. It makes comparisons on these matters between different national higher education systems, institutional types, disciplines and generations of academics, drawing initially on available data-sets and qualitative research studies with special emphasis on the recent twenty nation survey of the Changing Academic Profession. Among the themes featured will be:

1. Relevance of the Academy's Work
2. Internationalization of the Academy
3. Current Governance and Management, particularly as perceived by the Academy
4. Commitment of the Academy

The audience includes researchers in higher education, sociology of education and political science studies; university managers and administrators; national and institutional policy-makers; offi cials and staff at governments and organizations, e.g. the World Bank.

For further volumes:
http://www.springer.com/series/8668

Barbara M. Kehm • Ulrich Teichler
Editors

The Academic Profession in Europe: New Tasks and New Challenges

 Springer

Editors
Barbara M. Kehm
University of Kassel
INCHER
Kassel
Germany

Ulrich Teichler
University of Kassel
INCHER
Kassel
Germany

ISBN 978-94-007-9498-6   ISBN 978-94-007-4614-5 (eBook)
DOI 10.1007/978-94-007-4614-5
Springer Dordrecht Heidelberg London New York

Springer is part of Springer Science+Business Media (www.springer.com)

Contents

About the Authors

Dominik Antonowicz is a higher education researcher, policy analyst and policy maker. He has solid academic background in both social sciences (MA, University of Toruń) and public management (Msc, University of Birmingham). His research interests focus on transformation of higher education systems in transitional countries, globalization of higher education and university governance. He has obtained his PhD from Toruń University in Poland and spent one year as a fellow research at Centre of Higher Education Policy Studies at University of Twente in Netherlands. He is an author or co-author of 2 books and approximately 30 articles in the field of higher education. He also served as a full-time strategic adviser to the Minister of Science and Higher Education in Poland (Prof. Barbara Kudrycka) and now sits in the board of the Committee for Evaluation of Research Units (KEJN) in Poland.

Gülay Ates studied sociology and educational studies in Heidelberg and graduated at the University at Vienna in sociology. Currently she is a PhD candidate and young researcher at the University of Klagenfurt and the University of Vienna. She is a sociologist specialising in Higher Education Research, Migration and Integration Research with a keen interest in empirical methods (mixed-methods approach). She is also a lecturer at the University of Vienna. Her PhD-thesis focuses on structured and semi- (non-)structured PhD programmes. Gülay Ates is a member of the Eurodoc survey expert team and president of the Austrian association doktorat.at. Recently she published as a co-author "Eurodoc Survey I: The First Eurodoc Survey on Doctoral Candidates in Twelve European Countries" (2011).

Cristina-Corina-Bentea is a lecturer at the Department of Teacher Training from "Dunarea de Jos" University of Galati, Romania. She is Bachelor in Psychology, M.S. in Social Psychology and Doctor in Psychology (Educational) at Romanian Academy—Institute of Philosophy and Psychology, Bucharest, Romania (2007). Her domains of interest are educational psychology, psychology of personality and self, developmental and social psychology. The research topics are cooperation and competition in educational groups, the relationships between personality traits and cognitive performances and the development of personality and identity in adolescence. She is author and co-author of 4 books and handbooks and more than 80 book chapters and scientific articles in journals, university annals and conference proceedings. Also, she has more than 50 paper presentations on international and national conferences and congresses of Psychology and Educational sciences. In her professional service, she has been working in activities, programs and projects focused on initial and continuous human resources training in educational domain.

Dr. Marie Clarke is a lecturer in Curriculum Studies, History of Education, and Educational Research Methods in the School of Education, University College Dublin. She is an elected member of UCD Governing Authority and served as Head of the School from September 2007 until August 2011. She was a member of UCD, University Management Team; UCD Academic Council, UCD Academic Council Committee on Academic Centres and UCD College of Human Sciences Executive. She was appointed Chair of UCD Academic Council Working Group on Bonus CAO points for Leaving Certificate Mathematics and was also a member of UCD Evaluation and Interview Panel for the President's Teaching Award.

Marie is a lead investigator on a range of research projects, which include teacher education, higher education, and development education and is published in each of these areas. She is a reviewer for a number of international journals, and is an evaluator for the European Science Foundation.

Marie was a visiting scholar to Teachers College, Columbia University, New York during the academic year 2007. She is a member of the Executive of the Association of Teacher Educators in Europe (ATEE). She was elected President of the Irish Federation of University Teachers for a two-year term 2011–2013. She was appointed by the Minister for Education and Skills as a member of the Student Grants Appeals Board, which was established under the Student Support Act (2011).

Bojana Ćulum is a junior researcher and higher teaching assistant at the University of Rijeka, Department of Education. She graduated with a degree in Pedagogy and Computer Science at the University of Rijeka (2003), defended her MSc thesis (2009) and PhD thesis (2010) in the field of higher education at the University of Rijeka. She took part in several research projects at the national and international levels, with academics and non-academic practitioners and experts. In addition, she has initiated and collaborated with civil society organizations, institutions and local authorities on numerous projects in the local community.

Her main research interests have been in the field of higher education and civil society, particularly the university civic mission and its role in local community development. Her teaching follows service-learning pedagogy, and covers themes in education, didactics, and qualitative methodology, particularly qualitative research. She authored and co-authored several books and book chapters in these fields, as well as several articles.

She has been a member of the National Committee for Volunteering Development from 2007, appointed by the Croatian Government. She has initiated the membership of the University of Rijeka in the Talloires Network, and has been appointed as a university representative. She is one of the co-founder of The Association for Higher Education Development "Universitas" and has been engaged in several national and international professional and civil society organizations.

Jonathan Drennan is a lecturer at the School of Nursing, Midwifery and Health Systems, University College Dublin (UCD). He holds a PhD and master's degree in education from UCD, a postgraduate diploma in statistics from Trinity College Dublin and a bachelor's degree in nursing from the University of Ulster. He has published a number of papers on higher education in leading international journals including: *Studies in Higher Education, Journal of Advanced Nursing, Advances in Health Sciences Education and Assessment and Evaluation in Higher Education.* In total Dr. Drennan has published over 60 academic papers and book chapters. His specialization is on the impact and outcomes of the master's degree for health professionals. He has extensive experience of large-scale research projects having worked as principal investigator and co-applicant on a number of nationally and internationally funded studies. Currently he is the co-principal investigator in a European Science Foundation/Irish Research Council for the Social Sciences funded programme of research entitled: *The Academic Profession in Europe: Responses to Societal Change.*

Tatiana Fumasoli is research associate at the Centre for Organisational Research (CORe), University of Lugano, Switzerland. She holds a doctorate from the same university on strategy in higher education institutions. Her areas of specialisation also include university management and governance. She has published in Higher Education and contributed to several projects for the European Science Foundation, European Union, Council of Europe and Swiss National Science Foundation.

Gaële-Goastellec is a sociologist, assistant professor (MER) and head of the politics and organizations of higher education research unit at the Observatory Science, Policy and Society, University of Lausanne, Switzerland. She leads comparative research on higher education systems and social inequalities, as well as on academic labour markets. She has been a Fulbright New Century Scholar fellow 2005–2006 and a Lavoisier fellow 2004–2005. Amongst her latest publications (2012, eds), with Benninghoff M., Fassa F. and Leresche J-P., *Inégalités sociales et enseignement supérieur,* Bruxelles, De Boeck Editions (2011), *Egalité et Mérite à l'Université,* Sarrebruck, Editions Universitaires Européennes, (2010, eds) *Understanding Inequalities in, through and by higher education,* Rotterdam, SensePublishers.

Ester Ava Höhle is a researcher of sociology and higher education research affiliated to the International Centre for Higher Education Research (INCHER) at the University of Kassel in Germany. Her areas of research include student careers, careers of PhD holders, risk of science and technology, gender and the academic profession. She works theoretically as well as empirically, mainly in greater quantitative surveys but has done qualitative work as well.

She spent one year as a student in PA, USA and obtained her Master's Degree at the University of Stuttgart in Germany. In recent years she worked in different sociological projects at the University of Stuttgart, University of Hohenheim and the Technical University of Munich. She published a number of articles about the topics risk perception of climatic change, freshman study phase in STEM disciplines under gender aspects, and several articles about different aspects of the academic profession using the German as well as the international CAP and EUROAC data. Concurrently she is co-editing the second volume of the series about the international survey in twelve countries in the EUROAC project.

Abbey Hyde is an Associate Professor at the School of Nursing, Midwifery & Health Systems, University College Dublin (UCD) in Ireland. She was formerly Head of Teaching & Learning (Post-graduate Studies) at the School and is currently Director of Graduate Studies there. She is a graduate of University College Cork (sociology and social administration) and later obtained her PhD in gender studies from Trinity College Dublin. She has been the principal investigator of a number of nationally-competitive research awards, has published over 80 articles in leading journals of international standing, and has co-authored 2 books. She has published on aspects of higher education in journals such as Assessment and Evaluation in Higher Education; Advances in Health Sciences Education; Innovations in Education and Teaching International, and Reflective Practice: International and Multidisciplinary Perspectives. She is a member of the Editorial Board of the journal Nurse Education Today: International Journal for Healthcare Education.

Professor Marek Kwiek is the founder (2002) and director of the Centre for Public Policy Studies, a research unit of Poznan University, Poland. A higher education researcher and higher education policy analyst, with strong background in political philosophy and political sciences. His research interests include university governance, globalization and education, supranational and European educational policies, welfare state and public sector reforms, transformations of the academic profession, and academic entrepreneurialism.

He has published about 100 papers and 9 books, most recently *University Transformations. Institutional Change and the Evolution of Educational Policies in Europe* (2010, in Polish) and *The University and the State: A Study into Global Transformation* (2006). His *Knowledge Production in European Universities: the State, Market, and Academics* and *The Modernization of European Universities* (with A. Kurkiewicz) are forthcoming.

He has been a higher education policy expert to the European Commission, USAID, OECD, the World Bank, UNESCO, OSCE, the Council of Europe, UNDP, as well as governments and academic institutions in numerous transition countries. Apart from about 20 international higher education policy projects, he has participated in about 20 international (global and European) research projects, funded by the European Commission, European Science Foundation (ESF), Ford, Rockefeller and Soros foundations, German and Norwegian research foundations in the last ten years. Most recently, he has been a partner in *EDUWEL—Education and Welfare* (2009–2013, EU 7th Framework Programme), *WORKABLE—Making Capabilities Work* (2009–2012, EU 7th Framework Programme), *EUROAC—The Academic Profession in Europe* (2009–2012, ESF), 6th Framework Programme project *EUEREK: European Universities for Entrepreneurship* (2004–2007), *GOODUEP—Good Practices in University—Enterprises Partnerships* (2007–2009, an EU LLL Multilateral Project). He serves as an advisory board member in "Higher Education Quarterly" and "European Educational Research Journal" and is a general editor of a book series Higher Education Research and Policy (Peter Lang).

Jasminka Ledić is a tenured professor at the University of Rijeka's Department of Education. She was also one of the founders and the first president of Universitas, Association for Higher Education Development and was Fulbright Scholar at the Indiana University School of Education, Educational Leadership and Policy Studies Department (1994/1995). She was engaged in academic administration (vice-dean for academic affairs) at the Faculty of Humanities and Social Sciences. She also took part in commissions ad working groups concerning higher education policy at national level. The Croatian Parliament awarded her in 2003 for the contributions in the field of higher education.

Her main research interests have been in the field of higher education and civil society. She took part in several research projects at the international level and was project leader of research projects funded by the Croatian Ministry of Science (*"University and its Environment in the Context of European Integration Process"* *"Preconditions for the Quality Assurance System in Higher Education"*, *"The Quality of Teaching in Higher Education: Criteria, Present State and University Staff Development "Culture of Quality" Model"*, *"The Presumptions and the Criteria of University Teaching Efficiency"*). Recently, her main research interests are directed in making links between these two fields. She authored and co-authored several books in these fields, as well as numerous articles.

Simona Marin is a professor of Pedagogy and she is the Head of Teacher Training Department at the University Dunarea de Jos of Galati. Her areas of interest include educational management, organizational development, initial and continuous forming of education human resources, quality assurance and management of higher education, competences and qualifications in higher education.

During the last five years, she does work about psycho-pedagogical and social research, and also interdisciplinary studies regarding the relevance and impact of different types of socio-economic changes on the educational politics and strategies used in the field of training the human resources. On this topic, she has carried research for the Romanian Ministry of Education aims to increase the quality in initial and continuous training of the didactic personnel, to make a comparative presentation of other educational systems and of their adaptation mechanisms to the new social demands and changes, and also to elaborate educational policies to improve the academic communities by quality and professional management.

She is currently working on large research analyzing the organization of academic markets in a comparative perspective: ESF-EuroHesc research, "EUROAC", The Academic Profession in Europe: Responses to Societal Challenges. These research articulate quantitative and qualitative methods, and provide an in-depth understanding of academic market (re)organization, from doctoral/junior researcher training to full professorship and human resources development.

She has served or is serving as member of scientific board for international/national conferences, scientific reviewer of the international journals and as member of Romanian Agency for Quality Assurance in Higher Education.

Simona Marin's publication output consists of 2 books authored (The Methodology of the Educational Research, The „Dunărea de Jos" Universitary Foundation Press, Galați, 2005 and The Development of the School Organization. The Project Management, The Didactic and Pedagogic Press, Bucharest, 2007), 4 books co-authored and more than 50 book chapter and journal articles. She has carried out or is carrying out several projects for the Romanian Research Council.

Nadine Merkator is researcher at the International Centre for Higher Education Research (INCHER-Kassel) at the University of Kassel in Germany. Her areas of specialisation include (higher) education research, empirical methods, higher education professionals and university as organisation. She obtained her Magister Artium (German pre-Bologna equivalent to master's degree) in sociology, education science and psychology at Kassel University in Germany. For her PhD she does research on professionalization of student counselling services at German universities. Recent publications (in German only) are on disciplinary approaches to the field of higher education research, higher education professionals and differentiation of the academic profession.

Luminita Moraru is a professor of Physics at Faculty of Science and Environment and she is the Head of Quality Assurance in Higher Education Board at the University Dunarea de Jos of Galati. Her areas of interest include methods and techniques for evaluation and quality assurance of higher education and management in HE; active preparation and implementation of institutional assessment criteria and self-evaluation in Quality Assessment of HE; develop the methodology for accreditation of programs and higher education providers and reports to assess its own operational quality.

During the last five years, she also does work about Quality assurance in Higher Education which covers all stages of higher education: bachelor, master and doctoral studies. On this topic, she has carried research for the Romanian Ministry of Education aims to increase the quality in initial training of the personnel of doctoral schools through transnational partnerships based on the development of scientific and managerial capacity of the target group members and improving supervision of doctoral activity. She is currently working on large research analyzing the organization of academic markets in a comparative perspective: ESF-EuroHesc research, "EUROAC", *The Academic Profession in Europe: Responses to Societal Challenges*. These research articulate quantitative and qualitative methods, and provide an in-depth understanding of academic market (re)organization, from doctoral/junior researcher training to full professorship and human resources development.

She has served or is serving as member of scientific board for international/national conferences, scientific reviewer of the international journals and as permanent member of Romanian Agency for Quality Assurance in Higher Education.

Luminita Moraru's publication output consists of 6 books (authored and co-authored) and more than 130 book chapter and journal articles. She has carried out or is carrying out several projects for the Romanian Research Council, the European Commission and the Council of Europe.

Nicolas Pekari is a researcher affiliated to FORS—Swiss Centre of Expertise in the Social Sciences hosted by the University of Lausanne. His areas of expertise include quantitative research, survey methodology, and public policy. He has worked in the areas of higher education, electoral behavior, and political participation. He has a Master's degree in Work Psychology from the University of Neuchâtel in Switzerland, as well as a Master's degree in Public and Social Policies from the Pompeu Fabra University in Barcelona, Spain.

Yurgos Politis is a Post Doctoral researcher at the School of Education in University College Dublin (UCD) in Ireland. He obtained his undergraduate Physics degree from the National University of Athens, Greece. He then received his MA in Education and PhD in Physics Education from University College Dublin (UCD). His primary area of expertise is Physics Education and has developed an interest in the areas of Development Education and Higher Education. He is a member of the Institute of Physics (IoP), and is involved with the Steering Committee for Development Education and the Early Career Higher Education Researchers Network (ECHER Net). He has published 2 journal articles till date.

Mirela Praisler is a professor of Physics at Faculty of Science and Environment and she is Vice Rector responsible for the Scientific Research and International Affairs at the "Dunarea de Jos" University of Galati. Her areas of interest include statistical methods and techniques for the quantitative evaluation of the trends in quality assurance and management in HE; development and implementation of institutional assessment criteria in HE; development of methodologies for the program evaluation and reports to assess the internal and external operational quality of universities.

During the last five years, her work also included studies about Quality assurance in Higher Education, especially at doctoral level. On this topic, she has carried out international research to increase the quality of the doctoral school of "Dunarea de Jos" University of Galati. She is currently involved in an extensive study regarding the organization of the academic markets in a comparative perspective: ESF-EuroHesc research, "EUROAC", *The Academic Profession in Europe: Responses to Societal Challenges*. These research articulate quantitative and qualitative methods, and provide an in-depth understanding of academic market (re)organization, from doctoral/junior researcher training to full professorship and human resources development.

She has been member of the scientific board of an important number of international and national conferences, scientific reviewer of the international journals and project evaluator in the programs of the Education, Audiovisual and Culture Executive Agency, European Community.

Mirela Praisler's publication output consists of 10 books (authored and co-authored) and more than 148 articles published in major scientific journals. She has been the coordinator of major research projects for the Romanian National Agency for Scientific Research and the European Commission.

Carole Probst is a post-doc researcher at the Centre for Organisational Research at the Faculty of Economics, University of Lugano (USI), Switzerland. She holds a PhD from the Faculty of Communication sciences at USI, based on a dissertation entitled "Serving Different Masters. The Communication Doctorate in the Knowledge Society" (2009). Her main research interests include the academic profession, academic careers, the doctorate, as well as indicators on and evaluation of research and higher education institutions and bibliometrics. She has been collaborating in several projects concerning the academic profession, the construction of indicators for measuring research performance or the use of institutional databases for evaluative and descriptive purposes in the academic environment. Her publication list contains several papers in peer-reviewed journals in the area of higher education, research policy, bibliometrics and communication studies. Since end of 2011, she is employed as a "higher education professional" at a university of applied sciences.

Nena Rončević is a higher teaching assistant at the University of Rijeka, Department of Education. She graduated with a degree in Sociology at the University of Zagreb (2002) and defended her MSc thesis (2009) and PhD thesis (2011) in the field of education at the University of Rijeka. From 2003–2007 she worked at the Primorsko-goranska County, The County Institute for Sustainable Development and Town and Country Planning, first as a trainee and later as a professional associate— sociologist, where she has been involved in different regional and local research projects in the field of sustainable development.

Her main research interests are theoretical and empirical research in the field of higher education and education for sustainable development/sustainability. She co-authored two books in these fields, as well as several articles. Her teaching interests also covers fields of methodology of social sciences and quantitative methodology. She is a member of Croatian Sociological Association and Universitas, Association for Higher Education Development.

Christian Schneijderberg is researcher at the International Centre for Higher Education Research (INCHER-Kassel) at the University of Kassel in Germany. He directs the research unit "Innovation and Transfer" at INCHER-Kassel. His areas of specialisation include higher education research, transfer and innovation studies, transfer of knowledge and technology, higher education professionals, university as organisation, doctoral education and training, academic careers and academic disciplines, especially social sciences and humanities. He obtained his *Magister Artium* (German pre-Bologna equivalent to master's degree) in sociology and political sciences at Albert-Ludwigs-University Freiburg in Germany. For his PhD he does research on the decomposition of doctoral education and training comparing sociology, political sciences and economics in Austria, Germany, and Switzerland. He is serving in the Executive Committee of the German Association for Higher Education Researchers. Recent publications (in German only) are on disciplinary approaches to the field of higher education research, higher education professionals, differentiation of the academic profession, and transfer of knowledge and technology.

Kevin Toffel holds a master in Sociology from the Free University of Brussels.

About the Editors

Barbara M. Kehm is a professor of higher education research affiliated to the International Centre for Higher Education Research (INCHER) at the University of Kassel in Germany. Her areas of specialisation include internationalisation of higher education and new form of governance in higher education. In recent years she also done work about the implementation of the Bologna Process, changes in doctoral education, and the emergence of new higher education professionals. She has obtained her PhD from Bochum University in Germany and spent three years as lecturer at the School of European Studies at Sussex University in the UK. Barbara M. Kehm is member of the editorial board of four international journals. She has served or is serving in the Executive Committee of EAIR, CHER and the German Association for Higher Education Researchers. She is also a member of the International Advisory Board of the University of Helsinki (Finland) and of the Board of Governors of the University of Siegen (Germany). Barbara M. Kehm's publication output consists of more than 20 books (authored, co-authored and edited) and more than 200 book chapters and journal articles. She has carried out several large-scale projects for international organisations such as UNESCO, the OECD, the European Commission, and the Council of Europe. Her publications include more than 20 monographs and more than 200 journal articles and book chapters. Among her recent publications in English, she has edited the volumes: *Reforming University Governance. Changing Conditions for Research in Four European Countries* (with U. Lanzendorf) (2006), *Looking Back to Look Forward. Analyses of Higher Education Research after the Turn of the Millennium* (2007), *The European Higher Education Area: Perspectives on a Moving Target* (with J. Huisman and B. Stensaker) (2009), and *University Rankings, Diversity and the New Landscape of Higher Education* (with B. Stensaker; 2009).

Ulrich Teichler is professor and former director of the International Centre for Higher Education Research, University of Kassel (INCHER-Kassel), Germany. Born in 1942, he was a student of sociology at the Free University of Berlin and a researcher at the Max Planck Institute for Educational Research Berlin. His doctoral dissertation was on higher education in Japan. He has had extended research periods in Japan, the Netherlands and the USA. For a period each, has was professor on part-time/short-term basis at the Northwestern University (USA), College of Europe (Belgium), Hiroshima University (Japan), and Open University (UK) and other teaching assignments in Argentina, Austria, Germany and Norway. Key research areas include higher education and the world of work, comparison of higher education systems, and international mobility in higher education. Ulrich has more than 1,000 publications to his name. He is a member of the International Academy of Education and the Academia Europaea, former chairman of the Consortium of Higher Education Researchers, former president and distinguished member of EAIR, honoured with the Comenius Prize of UNESCO and Dr. h.c. of the University of Turku (Finland).

Introduction

Barbara M. Kehm and Ulrich Teichler

This book is the first in a series of three volumes reporting on the results of a comparative analysis of the academic profession in Europe and its responses to societal challenges. The analysis, which includes eight European countries (namely Austria, Croatia, Finland, Germany, Ireland, Poland, Romania, and Switzerland), focuses on the question of how the profession is being shaped by changing conditions and contradictory expectations.

The study is funded by the respective national research councils of the countries involved and is supported by the European Science Foundation (ESF) in the framework of its programme titled "European Higher Education and Social Change" (EUROHESC). It emerged from a forward-looking exercise (Brennan et al. 2008) initiated by the ESF which examined:

> higher education and research within a wider context of social science research ... to address some of the larger questions concerning the changing relationship between higher education and society and to develop research agendas that would be relevant both to researchers and to policy makers and practitioners. (Brennan et al. 2008, p. 5)

The study of the academic profession in Europe used as its starting point the observation that since the 1990s, the pace of change affecting this profession in sometimes contradictory ways has been accelerated by the emergence of the 'knowledge society'. At the same time, and related to this, there have been substantial changes in the organisational fabric of higher education systems and institutions. Both developments are connected to an increasing diversity in higher education that also affects the academic profession. New settings for the tasks and functions of the academic role have emerged, career patterns as well as employment and working conditions are changing, and new forms of division of work and cooperation

B. M. Kehm (✉) · U. Teichler
International Centre for Higher Education Research Kassel (INCHER-Kassel),
University of Kassel, Moenchebergstr. 17, 34109 Kassel, Germany
e-mail: kehm@incher.unikassel.de

U. Teichler
e-mail: teichler@incher.unikassel.de

B. M. Kehm, U. Teichler (eds.), *The Academic Profession in Europe: New Tasks and New Challenges,* The Changing Academy – The Changing Academic Profession in International Comparative Perspective 5, DOI 10.1007/978-94-007-4614-5_1, © Springer Science+Business Media Dordrecht 2013

between the academic profession and other professionals within higher education institutions are being developed.

However, there is as yet little evidence to indicate whether these changes in social contexts and institutional settings are sufficiently powerful to affect the values, attitudes, and professional practices of the academic profession. Obviously, the academic profession is embedded in a changing institutional context that is likely to leave its imprint on the profession as a collective and on its individual members. However, the interests and preferences of the academics and the social norms they consider important will mediate and influence these effects. In studying the impacts of institutional change on the academic profession, we assume that institutional change matters and that it is interrelated with professional attitudes and practices but not necessarily due to a universal and direct causality between institutional change and professional change.

The focus of the study is therefore on how the academic profession in various European countries perceives, interprets, and interacts with changes in the socio-economic environment and in the organisational fabric of higher education systems and institutions; i.e. how do academics view major developments around and within higher education as potentially relevant for them, and how do they interpret and eventually shape their professional roles under the given circumstances? Concerning socio-economic developments, attention is paid to three key issues: the relevance of knowledge, diversification of higher education systems, and internationalisation. Concerning changes in the institutional fabric attention is also paid to another five key issues: governance, management, evaluation, academic career setting, and professionalisation.

This volume documents extensive and explorative literature reviews of state of the art research into changes in higher education governance, changes in academic careers, and new forms of professionalisation within higher education institutions that are related to the changing environment in higher education and the resulting socio-economic challenges and expectations. The focus is on how institutional settings are changing and how these changes might influence the perception of academic roles by the academic profession itself. Further volumes to be published in the framework of this study will present the results of a major survey of the academic profession and a comparison of the eight countries involved based on the outcomes of interviews with representatives of the institutional management, the academic profession, and the new higher education professionals (for the last group cf. Chap. 4).

The volume consists of eight literature reviews carried out by researchers involved in the study on the academic profession in Europe. All of the reviews are the result of team work, sometimes involving researchers from more than one country. There now follows a brief summary of each chapter, highlighting the key issues around which the study as a whole currently revolves.

The second chapter on professional identity in higher education was written by the Irish team. *Clarke, Hyde and Drennan* point out that this is as yet an under-researched area and that it is influenced by personal attributes, early socialisation experiences, and contextual factors. Apart from the fact that gendered identity patterns continue to exist in higher education, the authors also point out that a change in the

identity formed at doctoral and early career stages occurs in mid-career. With growing and multiple responsibilities at this latter career stage, a blurring of boundaries
can be observed between the academic identity of teacher and researcher within a
given discipline and a professional identity as manager and entrepreneur. Thus, expectations and challenges arising from the socio-economic environment have to be
integrated into the work of the academic profession just as much as academic work
has to demonstrate its relevance for the wider society.

The third chapter by *Höhle and Teichler* from the German team focuses on the
academic profession in the light of comparative surveys. The authors summarise the
main results of the first internationally comparative study of the academic profession initiated by the US-based Carnegie Foundation at the beginning of the 1990s
and involving 15 countries from all continents. Though the relevance and a certain
degree of prestige of the academic profession was not called into question at that
time, changing societal expectations and the changing nature of knowledge for and
in society indicated a growing sense of crisis characterised by a loss of status, tighter resources, loss of power of the academic guild, and culpability for not providing
the services expected. More than a decade later, another internationally comparative
study on the changing academic profession was carried out in 18 countries around
the world which had some surprising results. In particular, the sense of crisis had
abated and overall job satisfaction had increased. While the academic profession
had accepted the expectations to deliver socially relevant results, it did not see this
as a threat to the pursuit of knowledge for its own sake. Interestingly, the results of
these comparative studies confirm the trend towards blurring boundaries in academic identities at mid-career stages pointed out by Clarke, Hyde and Drennan.

In the following chapter, again written by the Irish team, the focus is extended
from academic identities to the interaction between the academic profession and the
institutional management of higher education. A few recent studies as well as the
second chapter in this volume have pointed out that—often in mid-career—many
academics take over managerial roles within higher education institutions, be it for
a limited or unlimited term of office. We do not really know much about the management styles of academics who have moved into managerial positions, but the
rise of managerialism in higher education is a well-researched topic and American
experts (e.g. Rhoades 1998, 2007) have come to the conclusion that the academic
profession is increasingly becoming a managed profession characterised by managerial control over its work and loss of professional power. However, in this literature review *Clarke, Hyde and Drennan* focus on the impacts of new managerialism
on the nature of academic work and on the extent to which managerial values may
clash with academic values. Interestingly, the general picture emerging from the
research literature is again one of a profession in crisis and of managerial values
superseding collegial ones. However, the picture is no longer very clear. Not only
do academics themselves frequently take over managerial roles without necessarily
losing their academic values, but there are also different degrees of managerialism
as well as some degree of adaptation by the academic profession to the new ways
of governing higher education institutions. These, in particular, are issues which
require further research and empirical evidence.

The fifth chapter again broadens the focus and bridges two of the central issues of the study as a whole; namely governance and management on the one hand and professionalisation on the other. *Schneijderberg and Merkator*, members of the German team involved in another though similar research project, focus on the emergence of a group of higher education professionals within higher education institutions which are occupying a "third space" (Whitchurch 2008) between the core business of teaching and research and central-level management. This group offers special services, prepares background information for top-level management decisions or supports their implementation in departments and faculties. The authors trace the emergence of this group which has been studied in a variety of countries over the last 10 years or so, and make an in-depth attempt to define and clarify the concept of higher education professionals in the light of existing research literature from various European countries, Australia, and the USA. Part of this attempt entails a closer look at how the relationships between the academic profession and the new higher education professionals have been described. Do they provide services for various hierarchical levels within the institution? Do they try to relieve the academic profession of the burden of administrative and bureaucratic tasks? Or do they implement top-level decisions on the shop floor in order to circumvent resistance? Does the emergence of this group constitute just another dimension in the process of de-professionalisation of academics? Or is it rather the other way round, namely that by cooperating with each other and finding new forms of division of labour both groups, academics and higher education professionals, experience a thrust towards further professionalisation? The authors conclude that in order to accomplish their work, the higher education professionals have to base what they do on academic rather than managerial or bureaucratic values, which then opens up the field for research on identity and its link to the changing functions and roles of higher education professionals and the academic profession. A first tentative hypothesis in this respect is that of an academic and administrative overlap institutionalising hybrid professional roles in higher education.

The next chapter, written jointly by members of the Swiss and the Austrian team, picks up the third focus of the study on the academic profession in Europe, namely the issue of changing academic careers. In particular, the authors ask how academic markets and academic careers are related to each other. The team of *Goastellec, Park, Ates and Toffel* begin with a historical perspective of research on academic markets and recruitment procedures in order to delineate changes from a comparative perspective. They identify prestige, performance, and a certain degree of inbreeding as central dimensions in the analysis and understanding of academic labour markets. The authors then proceed to describe stages of academic careers until tenure or a professorship is achieved. In the final part of this review of existing research, the authors argue that academic labour markets are based on national career path structures which have increasingly become an object of supra-national policy making in Europe and—from the perspective of the individual academic—of career management in the last few years. The aim is to create an attractive European labour market for academics and draw the best talent from all over the world. This challenges the traditional structure of academic career paths in a rather fundamental way.

The seventh chapter, produced by *Probst and Goastellec* from the Swiss team, is a logical sequel to the previous one. The authors look at the internationalisation of academic labour markets, which is a development particularly supported by the European Commission. This chapter focuses first on the macro-level in terms of the international composition of academic staff within higher education institutions, mobility flows of academics including the issues of brain drain and brain gain, and finally on the practices and rules of higher education institutions when attracting and recruiting international staff. A second perspective is that of the individual academic. Again three dimensions are discussed by the authors: mobility patterns within the careers of academics, individuals' perceptions of the outcomes and benefits of mobility, and finally the strategies of individual academics as regards mobility and the underlying motives or rationales. The authors conclude by developing further proposals for research questions to be included in the study on the academic profession.

Chapter 8 takes a broader look at the new challenges with which the academic profession is confronted and how these challenges impact on the academics' satisfaction with their work. The authors, *Moraru, Praisler, Marin and Bentea*, are members of the Romanian team and they focus on three issues: quality assurance, governance, and relevance. While insisting that universities should be models for a democratic society and professional integrity, there is also no denying that new hierarchies and greater managerial control demonstrate a loss of trust in the work of academics. In addition, the new challenges in terms of quality, relevance and emphasis on research demand that many members of the academic profession—especially in the central and eastern European countries—change their work routines. In the face of low salaries and under-funding of higher education institutions, it is hard to confront these challenges in a positive and productive way. The authors conclude that the impacts of these new challenges on the academic profession require new forms of organisation of academic work with which not every academic might be satisfied.

The ninth chapter, written by the Croatian team, focuses on the civic mission of the university and what this means for the academic profession. The authors, *Ćulum, Rončević, and Ledić*, point out the growing importance of the universities' third mission and that the academic profession is challenged to contribute something in fulfilment of this mission. This challenge impacts on the work of academics and there is an ongoing debate about the need to broaden the view of scholarship to include "services". However, there is actually no real consensus about what exactly defines the universities' third mission and the services expected of the academic profession. For some it is the call for relevance to economic development, for others it entails all kinds of community service, and a third group tries to integrate public, private, and non-profit cooperation into the third mission. The authors identify a variety of third-mission discourses and models and reflect on their relationships with the core business of the academic profession, namely teaching and research. As an example they use the idea of education for sustainable development, and report on studies that analysed the driving forces as well as the barriers in implementing this type of education which clearly presents an extension of traditional ideas of teaching and requires new priorities, in particular, a closer interaction between higher education and the community and society at large.

It would be premature to draw final conclusions at this point, but the literature review of state of the art research on the academic profession and ongoing changes vis-à-vis societal challenges of today has demonstrated that it has become a rather broad and complex issue for analysis. The various literature studies in this book provide an insight into the many interfaces with other topics of research in the field of higher education which gives the issue of the academic profession a rather 'fuzzy' and multi-dimensional character. But this 'fuzziness' is also an indicator of a growing importance of the role and self-understanding of the academic profession and related career paths within it. Not only is the academic profession confronted with new challenges and tasks, but it is also challenged to be good at these new tasks. This of course implies a further professionalisation or a further division of labour, possibly both at the same time. Simply teaching and doing research is no longer sufficient. New competences are needed for outreach and interaction with society, for awareness of new standards of quality in teaching, for competitiveness and success in attracting funding for research, for strategic thinking in terms of output and publications, for project management, and for work in larger, often interdisciplinary or even international teams. Looking at the diversity of career paths and the multitude of qualifications required to progress on the career ladder, we might even ask whether we can still speak of a unified profession. The empirical part of the project, the results of which will be published in two future volumes, will have to provide evidence of the ongoing trends and their direction. By now the academic profession has certainly stepped out of its secluded and privileged space and has become more interactive with society in general and higher education stakeholders in particular. Whether recent developments lead to de-professionalisation or to more pathways for professionalisation and what that implies for possible careers must remain an open question here, though it is one that will be answered in the near future.

References

Brennan, J., Enders, J., Musselin, C., Teichler, U., & Välimaa, J. (Eds.). (2008). *Higher education looking forward: an agenda for future research*. Strasbourg: European Science Foundation.

Rhoades, G. (1998). *Managed professionals: unionized faculty and restructuring academic labor*. Albany: State University Press.

Rhoades, G. (2007). The study of the academic profession. In P. J. Gumport (Ed.), *Sociology of higher education. Contributions and their contexts* (pp. 113–146). Baltimore: Johns Hopkins University Press.

Whitchurch, C. (2008). Beyond administration and management: reconstructing the identities of professional staff in UK higher education. *Journal of Higher Education Policy and Management, 30*(4), 375–386.

Professional Identity in Higher Education

Marie Clarke, Abbey Hyde and Jonathan Drennan

1 Introduction

Research in higher education has concentrated on a number of areas, which include the values and collective identities of academic faculty, their role in higher
education governance, faculty norms and socialisation processes, and the impact of
change in higher education on academic roles (Rhoades 2007). While many authors
advocate the types of research methodology that should be used in such investigations, few question how academics come to possess the constructs and ideas that inform their professional identity. Academic identity generally relates to teaching and
research activities that are subject or disciplined based (Deem 2006, p. 204). While
the academic department (or a sub-unit of it) is usually the main one for academic
staff, faculty members also operate within research, curriculum development, or
teaching programme teams (Trowler and Knight 2000). Discipline-based cultures
are the primary source of faculty members' identity and expertise and include assumptions about what is to be known and how tasks to be performed, standards for
effective performance, patterns of publication, professional interaction, and social
and political status (Becher 1989). Each discipline has its own concept of success
as a vehicle for prestige. Despite these differences, the academic profession pos-
sesses a set of common values across disciplinary and institutional boundaries, such
as "academic freedom, the community of scholars, scrutiny of accepted wisdom,
truth seeking, collegial governance, individual autonomy, and service to society
through the production of knowledge, the transmission of culture, and education
of the young" (Kuh and Whitt 1986, p. 76). In the same vein, reward structures
in the academic profession across disciplines are based on prestige and symbolic

M. Clarke (✉) · A. Hyde · J. Drennan
University College Dublin,
Dublin, Ireland
e-mail: marie.clarke@ucd.ie

B. M. Kehm, U. Teichler (eds.), *The Academic Profession in Europe: New Tasks and
New Challenges,* The Changing Academy – The Changing Academic Profession
in International Comparative Perspective 5, DOI 10.1007/978-94-007-4614-5_2,
© Springer Science+Business Media Dordrecht 2013

recognitions such as publications and awards. Faculty members learn the academic culture according to their discipline and specific department through a socialisation process (Mendoza 2007, p. 75). However, changes in higher education have added a further complexity to identity formation within higher education.

Professional identity is not a stable entity; it is complex, personal, and shaped by contextual factors. Rhoades (2007) points to the fact that there is a lack of sufficient case studies to facilitate an understanding about the conditions and experiences of those working in the higher education system. The concept of professional identity is complicated by competing definitions. Rhoades (2007) suggests that in order to understand higher education, the relationships and interactions among the multiple professions within the organisation must be considered. A number of categories have been identified that seek to explain the various professional identities that exist within the higher education context. Whitchurch (2009a) suggests four: (1) bounded professionals who perform roles that are clear and prescribed; (2) cross boundary professionals who perform translational functions and contribute to institutional capacity building; (3) unbounded professionals who contribute to broad based projects across the university, and (4) blended professionals who straddle both professional and academic areas. Against this background, this chapter will explore the following areas: professional identity as a construct; the different ways in which professional identity is viewed; the relationship between identity and professional socialisation in higher education; and the role played by networks and their impact on identity formation. This chapter will also consider gender; midlife career academics; the emergence of mixed identities; and the development of new professional boundaries within higher education.

2 Professional Identity Formation

Identity formation is a process involving many knowledge sources, such as knowledge of affect, human relations, and subject matter (Beijaard et al. 2004). Gee et al. (1996) suggests that as people acquire discourses they form the social self in new ways. Given the complex interweaving of values, social forms, linguistic forms, beliefs, and roles which comprise a discourse in which people feel at home (Lundell and Collins 2001, p. 58) and without giving it much critical reflection people acquire values, world views, and perceptions of others. These perceptions are acquired within the same contexts as peoples' sense of what is right, what is wrong, and how the social world is modelled. In that way, people construct their social selves within the everyday realities that they inhabit (Lundell and Collins 2001).

Zizek (1989) uses the theoretical framework of symbolic and imaginary identification developed by the psychoanalyst Lacan (1977, 1979) to explore the manner in which identity is formed within the teaching profession. According to Zizek (1989), the theory of symbolic and imaginary identifications is central to professionals who require a mandate for the position that they occupy and the manner in which they carry out their prescribed tasks (Zizek 1989, p. 105). Symbolic identification within this theory concerns the way in which people perceive themselves within and in relation to the 'symbolic order' of language, ritual, custom, and representation. Zizek (1989) argues that this symbolic identification is effectively an identification with the 'place' (within the symbolic order) from which people are observed. He suggests that the 'interplay' between these two forms of identification, 'constitutes the mechanism by means of which the subject is integrated in a given socio-symbolic field' (Zizek 1989, p. 110). Both Gee and Zizek map out, in a conceptual framework, the manner in which people create and embrace identities within which they feel comfortable and that have been influenced by many factors from their early socialisation experiences. Equally, the influence of the structural features of the social world (Bourdieu 1993) plays an important role in identity formation. Many struggle within the boundaries of those structures and struggle to legitimately enter that social world (Deem 2006). It is also within the social field that people struggle to accommodate and maximise symbolic capital (Deem 2006). Participation in this struggle also impacts upon the development of both academic and professional identity.

Professional identity is viewed as an on-going process of interpretation and re-interpretation of experiences (Beijaard et al. 2004; Day 1999; Kerby 1991). It does not answer the question of whom I am at the moment but who I want to become (Beijaard et al. 2004). Henkel (2000) argues that key concepts of academic identity encompass the distinctive individual who has a unique history, who is located in a chosen moral and conceptual framework, and who is identified within a defined community or institution by the goods that she or he has achieved. These three elements of individual identity are what make an academic an effective professional. Kogan (2000, p. 210) argues that these elements are strengthened and matured through the processes of professional education and experience. He suggests that the distinctive individual is also an embedded individual and is a member of communities and institutions which have their own languages, conceptual structures, histories, traditions, myths, values, practices, and achieved goods. The individual has roles, which are strongly determined by the communities and institutions of which he or she is a member. Thus, Kogan (2000) asserts that the concept of professional identity, is both individual and social, so that people are not only stronger because of their expertise and their own moral and conceptual frameworks, but also performing a range of roles which are strongly determined by the communities and institutions of which they are members (Kogan 2000, p. 210). Interestingly professional identity is an area that has not been researched in any great depth among the professions let alone in higher education. Some studies exist in the teaching profession and these provide some interesting insights into the area of professional identity that serve as a useful starting point for understanding this area in higher education.

3 Professional Identity—How it is Viewed

Beijaard et al. (2004, p. 108) looking at professional identity in teaching, argue that the concept of professional identity is used in different ways. In the 22 studies reviewed by those authors in the period 1998–2000, the concept of professional identity was defined differently or not defined at all (Beijaard et al. 2004). Three categories of study dominate this field of research: (1) studies that focused on teachers' professional identity formation, (2) studies which focused on the identification of characteristics of teachers' professional identity, and (3) studies where professional identity was represented by teachers' stories (Beijaard et al. 2004, p. 107). Goodson and Cole (1994), Coldron and Smith (1999), Dillabough (1999) and Samuel and Stephens (2000) presented some interesting findings in relation to teacher identity.

Goodson and Cole (1994) found in their study that the broader institutional context played an important role in facilitating the realisation of teachers' personal and professional potential (Beijaard et al. 2004, p. 110). Connelly and Clandinin (1999) found that institutional stories are crucial influences on professional identity, particularly, in the context of programme and curricula change, where teachers in their study experienced a loss of their sense of self. Their study also found that teachers responded differently to those institutional stories and matters of professional identity which were interwoven with the spatial and temporal borders of the professional landscape (Beijaard et al. 2004, p. 120).

Coldron and Smith (1999) found that the professional identity of teachers reflected the landscape that the teacher was a part of and that professional identity was manifested in classroom practice and was unique. They also found a tension between agency (the personal dimension in teaching) and structure (the socially given). Reynolds (1996) found that what surrounds a person, what others expect from the person, and what the person allows to impact on him or her greatly affected his or her identity as a teacher. She pointed out that teachers' workplace is a 'landscape' which can be very persuasive, very demanding, and, in most cases, very restrictive (Beijaard et al. 2004, p. 113). Dillabough (1999) suggests that the teaching self is also an 'embedded self' which makes professional identity a complex and multifaceted entity. The findings from the Samuel and Stephens (2000) study supported the view that there is a tension between hope and ambition about what the teacher can achieve. This is reflected in the many competing influences on teachers' roles and identities in a changing world context.

Bullough (1997) and Sugrue (1997) sought to identify the most formative personal and social influences on student teachers' professional identity by deconstructing their lay theories. These theories are the ones that student teachers brought with them prior to taking teacher education courses. Sugrue analysed interview transcripts of nine beginning student teachers for emerging themes. From his research, he found that lay theories begin with the student teachers' personalities, were significantly shaped by immediate family, significant others or extended family, apprenticeship of observation, atypical teaching episodes, policy context, teaching traditions, cultural archetypes, and tacitly acquired understandings. He argues that lay theories are tacit or unarticulated and lead to forms of professional identity formation that differ from forms of professional identity formation derived from research-based theories of teaching. What has emerged in Beijaard et al.'s (2004) study on teacher identity is that much of the research has concentrated on teachers' personal practical knowledge and few studies actually made explicit the relationship between this knowledge and professional identity. They suggest that future research on teachers' professional identity should devote attention to the relationship between relevant concepts such as self and identity, the role of context in professional identity formation, and the employment of research perspectives other than those within the cognitive tradition (Beijaard et al. 2004, p. 107). This is a useful starting point in studying the area of professional identity and socialisation in higher education.

4   Identity and Professional Socialisation in Higher Education

Weidman et al. defined socialisation as "the process by which persons acquire the knowledge, skills, and dispositions that make them more or less effective members of their society" (2001, p. 4). They argue that throughout the socialisation process, graduate students acquire necessary information by way of communication strategies to aid in their transition to an academic profession.

Authors including Austin and McDaniels (2006), Gardner (2007), Golde (1998), and Lovitts (2001) discussed the various stages of socialisation that occur at the doctoral level which prepare students for academic careers. Organisational socialisation has received substantial research attention as a means of understanding how organisational newcomers come to identify and understand the norms and expectations of their new environment and future profession (Austin and McDaniels 2006).

Tierney and Rhoads defined organisational socialisation as a "ritualized process that involves the transmission of culture" (1993, p. 21) through a mutually adaptive process between the organisation and individuals. In Tierney and Rhoads' framework, faculty socialisation consists of two stages: anticipatory and organisational. Anticipatory socialisation occurs during graduate school, where individuals learn attitudes, actions, and values about the faculty group in their discipline and the profession at large. During anticipatory socialisation, "[a]s young scholars work with professors, they observe and internalize the norms of behaviour for research as well as supporting mechanisms such as peer review and academic freedom" (Sweitzer 2009, p. 4; Anderson and Seashore Louis 1991, p. 63). The organisational stage occurs as faculty members embark upon their academic careers and build upon the anticipatory socialisation. During the organisational stage, faculty face extraordinary challenges to gain membership into the profession. However, this stage is usually framed by the experiences during anticipatory socialisation, because individuals learn during their training what it means to be a member of an organisation (Sweitzer 2009). This learning process might be at odds with what the individual ultimately finds at the chosen institution. Thus, the organisational socialisation stage might reaffirm what a new faculty member learned during anticipatory socialisation if his or her graduate school and entering setting hold similar cultures and structures; otherwise, the entering organisation will try to modify the new faculty member's qualities (Tierney and Rhoads 1993). It should also be remembered that individuals bring a multitude of experiences to work and academic contexts that are likely to influence the ways they make sense of socialisation experiences (Trice 1993). Their development is also linked to their access to both professional and social networks.

5 Networks and Identity

Research has shown that individuals' networks influence career outcomes including job satisfaction and attainment (Podolny and Barron 1997), promotion and advancement (Burt 1992), and overall career success (Sweitzer 2009, p. 4; Guiffe 1999; Hansen 1999). Recently, social network scholars have begun to explore the possibility that individuals' social networks may serve as identity-construction mechanisms (Ibarra et al. 2005).

Operating under the assumption that individuals construct their identities through their developmental networks, Dobrow and Higgins (2005) studied the extent to which individuals' developmental relationships enhanced the clarity of their professional identity. They employed two developmental network characteristics: high and low developmental network range (social relationships from multiple contexts or from a single context) and density (access to redundant or non-redundant sources of information). Their research suggested that as developmental network density increased (i.e. less access to non-redundant sources of information), the clarity of one's professional identity decreased (Sweitzer 2009, p. 6). However, the authors noted that more longitudinal research is needed that examines the content and help-giving interactions of relationships and why and how developmental networks change over time (Sweitzer 2009, p. 6).

Resources that individuals invoke from networks of "weak ties" are forms of social capital important to success in professional labour markets. Such ties can provide information regarding perceptions of job candidates' social skills, personality, and ability to "fit in" with colleagues (Lin 1999). Having used informal methods to gain professional employment signals access to influential networks that can be beneficial to subsequent career success, including mobility opportunities (Burt 1992). The prestige of the undergraduate institution also captures the effect of family socio-economic background, the quality of training received at the institution and academic achievement, or some combination of these effects (Kay and Hagan 1998). Research conducted by McBrier (2003, p. 1212) concluded that the prestige of the undergraduate university or college has been found to have a positive effect on obtaining tenure-track law teaching positions at higher status law schools.

While an individual may be new to a particular organisation, that person may not be new to a given field or to being a professional (Wulff et al. 2004). Sweitzer (2009) argues that the expectations of the faculty career are changing in many fields and across institutional types. Pressures for promotion and tenure such as "A-level" (top-tier) publications in top academic journals, procurement of external funding, and earning a reputation for being the best among one's peers are becoming overwhelming (Sweitzer 2009, p. 21). Gender differences are important in relation to access to networks. For women in academic life, professional networks have remained highly gendered, with women experiencing greater difficulty than their male colleagues in establishing and maintaining high-level network ties (Rogers 2000).

6   Identity and Gender in Higher Education

Waddoups and Assane (1993) suggest that, given current high levels of job segregation within traditionally male professions, women and men in the professions tend to be stratified by disparate placement across jobs with different mobility structures and opportunities, where women are more likely than men to be initially hired into secondary jobs within professions. In much of this research, sex differences in mobility are assumed to result primarily from women's over-representation in jobs that have fewer prospects of mobility for both women and men in such positions (McBrier 2003, p. 1203).

Geographic mobility is of paramount importance in many professional labour markets, especially in academia. Some argue that geographic mobility among academics signals commitment to career over personal life (Kauffman and Perry 1989). On average, academic women are more likely than academic men to place geographic limits on their careers, suggesting an indirect nature of the negative effect of geographic constraints on women's versus men's career mobility. Family responsibility or husbands' careers could constrain the geographic mobility of married academic women (Bielby and Bielby 1992), and unmarried women may be geographically constrained relative to men as well, preferring to stay in a particular location because of family or social ties (Rosenfeld and Jones 1987).

It has been argued that the norms which are assumed to operate in academia, suggest that promotion and mobility opportunities should accumulate more quickly for the most productive workers in terms of contribution to the discipline's body of knowledge, one of the most important measures being research productivity (Long et al. 1993). Although the gap appears to be closing, women have tended to publish less than their male colleagues (Zuckerman 1987). McBrier (2003) suggests that part of this publication gap could be due to women's heavier domestic responsibilities; to job segregation that disproportionately places women in jobs, such as skills-related teaching, with high teaching demand but fewer publishable topics; to more time spent by women than men on class preparation; and/or to female teachers' greater service-related labour for schools, including service on committees as well as in their capacity as unofficial counsellors to students (Apel 1997). It is also possible that although female academics produce fewer articles, these articles are published in higher status journals than those of male academics (Sonnert 1995). While many factors impact upon gendered patterns of identity within academia, age and length of service also contribute to issues of professional identity in higher education.

7 Identity and Midlife Career Academics

Baldwin et al. (2005) suggest that mid-career is the longest and, in most cases, the most productive phase of academic life; it covers as much as 15–25 years of one's professional career. During this period, most faculties teach a majority of their students, produce the bulk of their scholarship and publications, and serve their institution, disciplines, and society in a variety of expert and leadership roles. Furthermore, faculty in the middle years represent the largest segment of the academic profession. They argue that for these reasons alone, mid-career deserves the interest and attention of academic leaders, policymakers, and higher education researchers (Baldwin et al. 2005, p. 98). Issues of definition bedevil the mid-career phase of academic life. There are several ways to distinguish "faculty in the middle" from their colleagues. Levinson (1986) tentatively segments middle adulthood into the years between 40 and 65 with distinctive sub-stages and developmental tasks falling within this lengthy period. Cytynbaum and Crites (1982) define midlife faculty as "men and women in their late 30s to mid- or late-50s who are consciously or unconsciously confronting midlife tasks", such as revising career goals, seeking balance between personal and professional life. A second way to look at "faculty in the middle" is to separate faculty by total years of teaching in higher education. Williams and Fox (1995) report that another way to define mid-career is based on the duration of an occupation.

Hall defines mid-career as "the period during one's work in an occupational (career) role after one feels established and has achieved perceived mastery and prior to the commencement of the disengagement process" (1986, p. 127). According to this definition, mid-career is a variable phenomenon that arrives once a person advances beyond novice status and becomes a full-fledged member of his or her profession and institution. Mid-career continues until disengagement begins in anticipation of retirement or a major career transition. Most faculty need several years in the occupation to advance beyond novice status and become established professionals. Based on this perspective, mid-career faculty would be seasoned professionals past the probationary stage of their careers but not yet nearing retirement. Years of teaching at the same institution is another way to identify faculty in the middle. If mid-career is indeed a variable phenomenon, the perception of mid-career may be stronger for faculty who spend many years of their professional life in one institution, fulfilling essentially the same basic duties in the same environment than for faculty who have moved numerous times and had repeatedly learnt the procedures, mores, and cultures of new settings (Baldwin et al. 2005).

Hall's (1986) model of organisational career stages portrays mid-career as a complex phase where the career advancement or establishment stage (approximately ages 30–45 years) can lead to a less predictable stage of career maintenance, growth, or stagnation (approximately ages 45–65 years). Hence, mid-career can either be a stable phase of work life with adequate performance but not much change or, in contrast, a period marked by dramatic shifts in attitudes and work activities. Career routines, usually well established by mid-career, often inhibit experimentation and career revision. However, Hall (1986) contends that various "triggers" in the individual, work environment, or organisation can disrupt the career routine and stimulate a new cycle of exploration, transition, and establishment. Whenever this occurs, mid-career becomes more dynamic and less predictable. Hall's organisational career model lends further support to the notion that mid-career deserves more empirical investigation in the context of the academic profession.

Baldwin et al. (2005) suggest that today's mid-career faculty are living through a period of unprecedented change in higher education. Greater student diversity, new educational applications of technology, for-profit education competitors, and increased use of part-time and term-contract appointments are some of the developments transforming faculty work and careers. In this changed context, it is important to know how the large middle component of the academic profession is adapting to changed work demands and performance expectations while, simultaneously, they are serving critical instructional, leadership, administrative, and mentoring roles within their programmes and institutions. Baldwin et al. (2005, p. 104) suggest that teaching and administration begin to take larger portions of faculty time while time devoted to research, service, and professional development decreases supporting the view that faculty work during midlife and beyond has a perceptibly different character than the work distribution of early-life faculty. The authors found in their study, the percentage of time faculty devoted to administration was highest in the middle years with lower levels of faculty engagement from the middle years onward in key roles and activities such as research, service, and professional development. This may result as faculty move into career maintenance or a career plateau where habitual patterns take hold and less new professional ground is broken. This is an area that requires more in-depth research and analysis.

While some forms of productivity (e.g. articles and presentations) peak in the early or middle years of faculty life, books and book chapters increase in a linear pattern across the career. It is logical that forms of scholarly productivity requiring longer gestation periods would be somewhat more common during the middle and later years of the faculty career. The findings from the Baldwin et al. (2005) study reveal that some forms of scholarly productivity (e.g., articles, presentations) follow a downward pattern from some point in the middle of the academic life cycle.

Baldwin et al. (2005) sought to measure levels of dissatisfaction by years at the institution. They found that a downward linear pattern of dissatisfaction emerged. When they employed life stage and total years of teaching as the metrics, early midlife and mid-career faculty exhibited slightly higher levels of dissatisfaction on several key variables than did their peers at other points in faculty life. They concluded that the added administrative burdens common among midlife and mid-career faculty may account for some of their dissatisfaction. The process of life and career re-examination that frequently characterises the midlife and mid-career periods may also contribute to the somewhat elevated dissatisfaction identified (Baldwin et al. 2005, p. 115). To understand the overlooked middle years of academic life, scholars need to design research focusing specifically on faculty in the middle years (Baldwin et al. 2005, p. 117). Linked to this is the issue of peer review and anonymity. Di Leo (2008, p. 64) suggests that dialogue in academe involves the free exchange of ideas and opinions but that rarely happens. Differing ideas and differences of opinion make the academy a vibrant, living, organic entity. He argues that knowledge of the identity of the participants allows for proper and relevant questions to be asked—it also allows for questioners and answerers to be accountable for their dialogical acts. Di Leo (2008) argues that part of the problem with academia today is a fear and avoidance of critical judgment. He goes on to suggest that anonymity breaks down the critical dialogue that brings academics together into a unified profession in search of answers to questions—and questions to answers (Di Leo 2008, p. 72). Equally important to this discussion is the fact that higher education is now populated by many different types of professionals, which poses a number of challenges to the understanding of the complexity of identity within higher education.

8   Mixed Identities in Higher Education

Bourdieu (1988) has suggested that career routes for academics may be based on quite different attributes and dispositions depending on whether or not they pursue a scientific or academic or administration and management pathway. Whitchurch (2008) has addressed the complexity of identity in higher education by focussing on the mixed identities that have emerged within the sector. Traditionally, activity in higher education institutions has been viewed in binary terms: of an academic domain, and an administrative or management domain that supports this. While some academic staff retain a balanced teaching and research portfolio, others focus on one or the other (Whitchurch 2008). Although there has begun to be recognition in the literature of movements within and across academic and management domains (Rhoades and Sporn 2002; Gornitzka and Larsen 2004; Gornitzka et al. 2005), Whitchurch (2008) argues there has, hither to, been little empirical work on crossovers that are occurring. While considerable attention has been paid to the implications of a changing environment for academic identities (Henkel 2000, 2007; Becher and Trowler 2001; Barnett 2005; Kogan and Teichler 2007; Barnett and di Napoli 2008), there has been less recognition of the impact on professional staff or on the emergence of increasingly mixed identities (Whitchurch 2008, p. 378; Deem 2006, p. 204). Kehm (2006, p. 169) points to the development of a new environment within higher education, where new roles have emerged that focus on institutional development though this fact is not always acknowledged.

Whitchurch (2008) contends that due to the blurred nature of professionalism within higher education rather than drawing their authority solely from established roles and structures, professionals in higher education increasingly build their credibility on a personal basis, via lateral relationships with colleagues inside and outside the university. In particular, new forms of blended professional are emerging, with mixed backgrounds and portfolios, dedicated to progressing activity comprising elements of both professional and academic domains. As professional staff who work across and beyond boundaries, they are re-defining the nature of their work (Whitchurch 2008, p. 394) and also contribute to the changes in working patterns in higher education (Whitchurch 2009b, p. 417). They are expected to work with a range of colleagues, internal and external to the university, and to develop what Whitchurch (2009b, p. 417) describes as "new forms of professional space, knowledge, relationships and legitimacies associated with broadly based institutional projects such as student life, business development and community partnership". She concludes that both academic and professional staff "are adopting more project-oriented approaches to their roles, and that portfolio-type careers are becoming more common" (Whitchurch 2010, p. 630). This also impacts on the development of identity through the interface of multiple professional boundaries.

9 Identity and Professional Boundaries

Over the last 20 years, governments internationally have fostered cooperation between industries and universities in order to cope with funding gaps and global competitive markets by introducing a number of laws and programmes that allow universities to patent their research and to engage in collaborations with the private sector towards opportunities in the new economy (Slaughter et al. 2004). Under this scenario, research universities have become a source of national wealth development through applied research rather than primarily a means for liberal education of undergraduates and warfare research (Slaughter and Rhoades 2005). At the turn of the twenty-first century, Mendoza (2007) argues that these initiatives have fostered entrepreneurialism through a variety of interdisciplinary centres and partnerships with the private sector around new technologies derived from disciplines such as biotechnology, materials science, optical science, and cognitive science. This entrepreneurialism in certain fields is based on the premise that faculty have the primary responsibility for obtaining their own research funds and running their own laboratories (Mendoza 2007, p. 71).

Mendoza's (2007) study found that the scientists and engineers in the sample had a clear sense of changing boundaries. They thought the way industry was valued by the academic community had changed. In the past, involvement with industry was "dirty" or polluting; in the present, federal grants continued to be regarded highly, but funding was increasingly valued regardless of its source. Faculty members still saw basic research as important but no longer saw the basic/applied division as demarcating the boundary between academe and industry. Many thought that applied work on "interesting" and "broad" problems was commensurate with "basic" research (Slaughter et al. 2004, p. 160). The issues which professors faced at the boundaries between academe, industry, and universities focused on publishing versus patenting, secrecy versus openness, and contests over ownership of intellectual property. Faculty members generally resolved the publishing versus patenting problem by publishing and patenting, accommodating industry's concerns with protecting knowledge by sequencing their publications, but not giving up publishing. In the case of secrecy versus openness, professors sanitised data, thus, accommodating industry, but continued to publish.

At the same time that faculty members had to accommodate industrial requests for secrecy, they had to negotiate university administrators' increased pressures to patent, pressures, which reinforced accommodations such as sequencing and sanitising their research (Mendoza 2007). When faculty members entered the market directly through start-up companies, boundary negotiations and difficulties multiplied. They wrestled with issues surrounding the loss of control of their technology; the manner in which corporations represented the discoveries they had patented; the use of graduate student labour; conflicts of interest and commitment; and what they considered they owed the public. Most of the respondents in that study have resolved to continue to work with industry. Mendoza (2007) also found that institutional administrators were actively working to make the boundaries between academe and industry more permeable.

10 Summary

This chapter has considered a number of important and complex issues that inform academic and professional identity in higher education. This is an area that has been under-researched and is influenced by personal attributes, early socialisation experiences, and contextual factors at both doctoral and initial career level. Research has demonstrated that gendered patterns of identity exist within higher education and professional boundaries are becoming blurred between higher education and other areas of professional life. An overlooked aspect of this issue is the change that occurs in identity between the early and mid-career stages. The changes that have occurred in higher education entail multiple responsibilities and new job descriptions have also lead to new perceptions of professional identity within higher education. These are key areas that are fundamental to understanding how academics come to possess the constructs and ideas that inform their professional identity.

References

Anderson, M. S., & Seashore Louis, K. (1991). The changing locus of control over faculty research: from self-regulation to dispersed influence. In J. C. Smart (Ed.), *Higher education: handbook of theory and research* (Vol. 7, pp. 57–101). New York: Agathon.

Apel, S. B. (1997). Gender and invisible work: musings of a woman law professor. *University of San Francisco Law Review, 31,* 993–1016.

Austin, A. E., & McDaniels, M. (2006). Preparing the professoriate of the future: graduate student socialization for faculty roles. In J. C. Smart (Ed.), *Higher education: handbook of theory and research* (pp. 397–496). The Netherlands: Springer.

Baldwin, R. G., Lunceford, C. J., & Vanderlinden, K. E. (2005). Faculty in the middle years: illuminating an overlooked phase of academic life. *The Review of Higher Education, 29*(1), 97–118.

Barnett, R. (2005). Re-opening research: new amateurs or new professionals? In R. Finnegan (Ed.), *Participating in the knowledge society* (pp. 263–278). New York: Macmillan.

Barnett, R., & Napoli, R. di. (2008). *Changing identities in higher education: voicing perspectives.* Abingdon: Routledge.

Becher, T. (1989). *Academic tribes and territories: intellectual enquiry and the culture of disciplines.* Bristol: SRHE/Open University Press.

Becher, T., & Trowler, P. (2001). *Academic tribes and territories: intellectual enquiry and the culture of disciplines.* Buckingham: SRHE/Open University Press.

Beijaard, D., Meijer, P. C., & Verloop, N. (2004). Reconsidering research on teachers' professional identity. *Teaching and Teacher Education, 20,* 107–128.

Bielby, D. D., & Bielby, W. T. (1992). I will follow him: family ties, gender role beliefs, and reluctance to relocate for a better job. *American Journal of Sociology, 97,* 1241–1267.

Bourdieu, P. (1988). *Homo Academicus* (trans: Collier, P.). Stanford: Stanford University Press.

Bourdieu, P. (1993). *The field of cultural production.* Cambridge: Polity.

Bullough, R. V. (1997). Becoming a teacher: self and the social location of teacher education. In B. J. Biddle, T. L. Good, & I. F. Goodson (Eds.), *The international handbook of teachers and teaching* (pp. 79–134). Dordrecht: Kluwer.

Burt, R. S. (1992). *Structural holes: the social structure of competition.* Cambridge: Harvard University Press.

Coldron, J., & Smith, R. (1999). Active location in teachers' construction of their professional identities. *Journal of Curriculum Studies, 31*(6), 711–726.

Connelly, F. M., & Clandinin, D. J. (1999). *Shaping a professional identity: stories of education practice.* London: Althouse.

Cytynbaum, S., & Crites, J. O. (1982). The utility of adult development theory in understanding career adjustment process. In M. Arthur, D. Hall, & B. Lawrence (Eds.), *Handbook of career theory* (pp. 66–88). Cambridge: Cambridge University Press.

Day, C. (1999). *Developing teachers, the challenge of lifelong learning.* London: Falmer.

Deem, R. (2006). Changing research perspectives on the management of higher education: can research permeate the activities of manager-academics? *Higher Education Quarterly, 60*(3), 203–228.

Di Leo, J. R. (2008). Anonymity, dialogue and the academic. *Symploke, 16*(2), 61–73.

Dillabough, J. A. (1999). Gender politics and conceptions of the modern teacher: women, identity and professionalism. *British Journal of Sociology of Education, 20*(3), 373–394.

Dobrow, S. R., & Higgins, M. C. (2005). Developmental networks and professional identity: a longitudinal study. *Career Development International, 10*(6/7), 567–583.

Gardner, S. K. (2007). I heard it through the grapevine: doctoral student socialization in chemistry and history. *Higher Education, 54,* 723–740.

Gee, J. P., Hull, G., & Lanshear, C. (1996). *The new work order: behind the language of the new capitalism.* St. Leonards: Allen & Unwin.

Golde, C. M. (1998). Beginning graduate school: explaining first-year doctoral attrition. In M. S. Anderson (Ed.), *The experience of being in graduate school: an exploration* (pp. 55–64). San Francisco: Jossey-Bass.

Goodson, I. F., & Cole, A. L. (1994). Exploring the teacher's professional knowledge: constructing identity and community. *Teacher Education Quarterly, 21*(1), 83–105.

Gornitzka, A., & Larsen, I. M. (2004). Towards professionalisation? Restructuring of administrative workforce in universities. *Higher Education, 47*(4), 455–471.

Gornitzka, A., Kyvik, S., & Stensaker, B. (2005). Implementation analysis in higher education. reform and change in higher education. In A. Gornitzka, M. Kogan, & A. Amaral (Eds.), *Analysing policy implementation* (pp. 35–36). Dordrecht: Springer.

Guiffe, K. A. (1999). Sand piles of opportunity: success in the art world. *Social Forces, 77,* 815–832.

Hall, D. T. (1986). Breaking career routines: midcareer choice and identity development. In D. T. Hall (Ed.), *Career development in organizations* (pp. 20–59). San Francisco: Jossey-Bass.

Hansen, M. T. (1999). The search-transfer problem: the role of weak ties in sharing knowledge across organization subunits. *Administrative Science Quarterly, 44,* 82–111.

Henkel, M. (2000). *Academic identities and policy change in higher education.* London: Kingsley.

Henkel, M. (2007). Shifting boundaries and the academic profession. In M. Kogan & U. Teichler (Eds.), *Key challenges to the academic profession* (Werkstattberichte, Vol. 65, pp. 191–204). Kassel: International Centre for Higher Education Research Kassel (INCHER-Kassel) and UNESCO Forum on Higher Education, Research and Knowledge.

Ibarra, H., Kilduff, M., & Tsai, W. (2005). Zooming in and out: connecting individuals and collectivities at the frontiers of organizational network research. *Organization Science, 16*(4), 359–371.

Kauffman, D. R., & Perry, F. J. (1989). Institutionalized sexism in universities: the case of geographically bound academic women. *National Women's Studies Association Journal, 1,* 644–659.

Kay, F. M., & Hagan, J. (1998). Raising the bar: the sex stratification of law-firm capital. *American Sociological Review, 63,* 728–743.

Kehm, B. M. (2006). Strengthening quality through qualifying mid-level management. In M. Fremerey & M. Pletsch-Betancourt (Eds.), *Prospects of change in higher education. Towards new qualities and relevance: Festschrift for Matthias Wesseler* (pp. 161–171). Frankfurt a. M.: IKO-Verlag.

Kerby, A. (1991). *Narrative and the self.* Bloomington: Indiana University Press.

Kogan, M. (2000). Higher education communities and academic identity. *Higher Education Quarterly, 54*(3), 207–216.

Kogan, M., & Teichler, U. (Eds.). (2007). *Key challenges to the academic profession.* (Werkstattberichte, Vol. 65). Kassel: International Centre for Higher Education Research Kassel (INCHER-Kassel) and UNESCO Forum on Higher Education, Research and Knowledge.

Kuh, G. D., & Whitt, E. J. (1986). *The invisible tapestry: culture in American colleges and universities* (ASHE-ERIC Higher Education Report, No. 1). Washington: The George Washington University.

Lacan, J. (1977). *Ecrits.* London: Tavistock.

Lacan, J. (1979). *The four fundamental concepts of psychoanalysis.* London: Penguin.

Levinson, D. J. (1986). A conception of adult development. *American Psychologist, 41,* 3–13.

Lin, N. (1999). Social networks and status attainment. *Annual Review of Sociology, 25,* 467–487.

Long, J. S., Allison, P. D., & McGinnis, R. (1993). Rank advancement in academic careers: sex differences and the effects of productivity. *American Sociological Review, 58,* 703–722.

Lovitts, B. E. (2001). *Leaving the ivory tower: the causes and consequences of departure from doctoral study.* New York: Rowman & Littlefield.

Lundell, D., & Collins, T. G. (2001). Towards a theory developmental education: the centrality of discourse. In D. Lundell & J. L. Higbee (Eds.), *Theoretical perspectives in developmental education* (pp. 3–20). Minneapolis: Centre for Research on Developmental Education and Urban Literacy, General College, University of Minnesota.

McBrier, D. B. (2003). Gender and career dynamics within a segmented professional labor market: the case of law academia. *Social Forces, 81*(4), 1201–1266.

Mendoza, P. (2007). Academic capitalism and doctoral student socialization: a case study. *The Journal of Higher Education, 78*(1), 71–96.

Podolny, J. M., & Barron, J. N. (1997). Relationships and resources: social networks and mobility in the workplace. *American Sociological Review, 16,* 18–21.

Reynolds, C. (1996). Cultural scripts for teachers: identities and their relation to workplace landscapes. In M. Kompf, W. R. Bond, D. Dworet, & R. T. Boak (Eds.), *Changing research and practice: teachers' professionalism, identities and knowledge* (pp. 69–77). London: Falmer.

Rhoades, G. (2007). The study of the academic profession. In P. J. Gumport (Ed.), *Sociology of higher education. Contributions and their contexts* (pp. 113–146). Baltimore: The Johns Hopkins University Press.

Rhoades, G., & Sporn, B. (2002). New models of management and shifting modes and costs of production: Europe and the United States. *Tertiary Education and Management, 81,* 3–28.

Rogers, J. K. (2000). *Temps: the many faces of the changing workplace.* New York: ILR.

Rosenfeld, R. A., & Jones, J. A. (1987). Patterns and effects of geographic mobility for academic women and men. *Journal of Higher Education, 58,* 493–515.

Samuel, M., & Stephens, D. (2000). Critical dialogues with self: developing teacher identities and roles—a case study of South Africa. *International Journal of Educational Research, 33*(5), 475–491.

Slaughter, S., & Rhoades, G. (2005). Markets in higher education: students in the seventies, patents in the eighties, copyrights in the nineties. In P. G. Altbach, R. O. Berdahl, & P. J. Gumport (Eds.), *American higher education in the twenty-first century: social, political, and economic challenge* (pp. 486–516). Baltimore: The Johns Hopkins University Press.

Slaughter, S., Archerd, C. J., & Campbell, T. I. D. (2004). Boundaries and quandaries: how professors negotiate market relations. *The Review of Higher Education, 28*(1), 129–165.

Sonnert, G. (1995). What makes a good scientist? Determinants of peer evaluation among biologists. *Social Studies of Science, 25,* 35–55.

Sugrue, C. (1997). Student teachers' lay theories and teaching identities: their implications for professional development. *European Journal of Teacher Education, 20*(3), 213–225.

Sweitzer, V. (2009). Towards a theory of doctoral student professional identity development: a developmental networks approach. *The Journal of Higher Education, 80*(1), 2–30.

Tierney, W. G., & Rhoads, R. A. (1993). *Enhancing promotion, tenure and beyond: faculty socialization as a cultural process.* Washington: The George Washington University.

Trice, H. M. (1993). *Occupational subcultures in the workplace.* New York: IRL.

Trowler, P., & Knight, P. T. (2000). Coming to know in higher education: theorising faculty entry into New Work contexts. *Higher Education Research and Development, 19*(1), 27–42.

Waddoups, J., & Assane, D. (1993). Mobility and sex in a segmented labor market: a closer look. *American Journal of Economics and Sociology, 52,* 399–412.

Weidman, J. C., Twale, D. J., & Stein, E. L. (2001). *Socialization of graduate and professional students in higher education: a perilous passage* (ASHE-ERIC Higher Education Report 28(3)). Washington: Association for the Study of Higher Education.

Whitchurch, C. (2008). Shifting identities and blurring boundaries: the emergence of third space professionals in UK higher education. *Higher Education Quarterly, 62*(4), 377–396.

Whitchurch, C. (2009a). The rise of the blended professional in higher education: a comparison between the United Kingdom, Australia and the United States. *Higher Education, 58,* 407–418.

Whitchurch, C. (2009b). Progressing professional careers in UK higher education. *Perspectives, 13*(1), 2–9.

Whitchurch, C. (2010). Some implications of 'public/private' space for professional identities in higher education. *Higher Education, 60,* 627–640.

Williams, S. L., & Fox, C. J. (1995). Organizational approaches for managing mid-career personnel. *Public Personnel Management, 24,* 351–363.

Wulff, D. H., Austin, A. E., Nyquist, J. D., & Sprague, J. (2004). The development of graduate students as teaching scholars: a four-year longitudinal study. In D. Wulff & A. Austin (Eds.), *Paths to the professoriate: strategies for enriching the preparation of future faculty.* San Francisco: Jossey-Bass.

Zizek, S. (1989). *The sublime object of ideology.* London: Verso.

Zuckerman, H. (1987). Persistence and change in the careers of men and women scientists and engineers. In L. S. Dix (Ed.), *Women: their underrepresentation and career differentials in science and engineering* (pp. 127–156). Washington: National Academy Press.

The Academic Profession in the Light of Comparative Surveys

Ester Ava Höhle and Ulrich Teichler

1 The Academic Profession in Focus

In recent decades, conviction spread that knowledge is becoming more and more the key resource for ensuring technological progress, economic growth, societal advancement and cultural enrichment. All over the world, universities and other institutions of higher education are viewed as the institutions responsible to generate, retain, and disseminate knowledge through research and through the teaching of students. The scholars active at these institutions, with the professors at the apex of the career ladder, can be viewed as the "key profession" (Perkin 1969), i.e. those persons whose activities consist of research and teaching. They are the most superior carriers of knowledge in all disciplines and thereby also shape the knowledge of the experts working in influential positions in the various professional areas; as a consequence, high prestige in society characterises the academic profession.

Three features characterise the academic profession all over the world, even though the conditions might vary considerably among countries. First, the *process of learning and maturation* until being eventually considered a full-fledged member of the academic profession is *very long*. While in other occupational areas, university graduates might become fully competent professionals mostly after 1–3 years after graduation, academics often concurrently learn and do productive academic work for a period of 10–15 years after graduation. Only those in senior positions are acknowledged as fully competent personnel. Second, academic careers are *highly selective*; it is accepted as a matter of prestige that rigorous examinations such as those linked to the award of a doctoral degree or other assessment prior to entering professorial positions are narrow-entry gates. More of those who aim at becoming an academic might have to leave the academic profession after a while that is

E. A. Höhle (✉) · U. Teichler
International Centre for Higher Education Research Kassel (INCHER-Kassel),
University of Kassel, Moenchebergstr. 17, 34109 Kassel, Germany
e-mail: hoehle@incher.uni-kassel.de

U. Teichler
e-mail: teichler@incher.uni-kassel.de

B. M. Kehm, U. Teichler (eds.), *The Academic Profession in Europe: New Tasks and New Challenges,* The Changing Academy – The Changing Academic Profession in International Comparative Perspective 5, DOI 10.1007/978-94-007-4614-5_3, © Springer Science+Business Media Dordrecht 2013

customary in most other intellectually demanding occupations. Third, the academic profession enjoys a higher degree of freedom in determining its work tasks than other professions do. "Academic freedom" is the key notion concept for the exceptionally high degree of professional disposition; it is considered necessary in order to generate new knowledge and in order to prepare students for indeterminate work tasks. In many countries, "academic freedom" is reinforced by a high degree of institutional "autonomy", whereby academics used to have influence on administrative matters of the institution as a whole.

In most countries of the world, the most creative institutions of higher education ensure that their academics are responsible both for teaching students and for independent research. In Europe, the term "university" usually is confined to institutions where teaching and research are closely linked. The close tie between research and teaching, most impressively advocated by Wilhelm von Humboldt in the process of the foundation of the University of Berlin at the beginning of the nineteenth century, tends to be regarded as a key characteristic of the modern university. The close tie is expected to stimulate research through communication in teaching and learning and to make sure that teaching is undertaken on the intellectually most demanding level and is based on the most recent state of knowledge.

Many historians point out that the concepts of modern institutions of higher education, which became dominant at the beginning of the nineteenth century, remained the dominant concepts till today (see, for example Perkin 1991). However, there is an agreement among experts as well that higher education has changed dramatically after World War II (see Ben-David 1977; Rüegg 2011). *Expansion, diversity* and *knowledge society* are key terms in the discourse about dramatic changes in recent decades. In economically advanced countries, the rate of new student entries among the corresponding age group increased from less than 5 % on average around 1950 to more than half on average in the first decade of the twenty-first century; the coining of the words "elite, mass and universal higher education" by the American higher education researcher Martin Trow (see Trow 1974) had an outreaching impact on the public debate and contributed to the fact that this process of expansion of student numbers was accompanied in many countries by increased diversity of tasks and functions of the institutions of higher education and the scholars; in many countries, the proportion of higher education institutions grew which have only a limited research function or no official task of research at all. Therefore, reputational differences between institutions increased in many countries as well. An enlarging number of institutions opted for specific profiles in order to serve the growing diversity of motives, talents, and job prospects of students (Trow 1974; see also Burrage 2010). Finally, the term "knowledge society" spread since the 1970s and emphasises how the diffusion, creation, dissemination, and use of information and knowledge has gained increased importance in all societal fields and became a serious counterpart to what used to be the most relevant resources: work, raw material, and financial capital (cf. Drucker 1969; Bell 1973; Stehr 1994; Knorr-Cetina 1998; Bindé 2005). As *the* knowledge creating institution, higher education has an increasing potential to serve society. On the one hand, more experts are needed on the labour market because the breadth and depth of available knowledge has expanded rapidly. More highly qualified employees are needed since highly specified and knowledge-intensive sectors have expanded their share of the overall economic production. Knowledge has become an important resource in a market of scientification. On the other hand, higher levels of formal education have become increasingly expected even where high degrees were usually not demanded in former times, thus carrying the meaning of a symbolic expertise rather than disciplinary qualification (Enders 2001c).

The expansion and increasing relevance of higher education, in principle, could enhance the status and reputation of the core profession in academia: working as scholars could be expected to be more prestigious, and perceived as relevant for the progress of society. It could be better paid and more satisfying than ever before. However, a closer look revealed that expansion and increasing relevance did not automatically mean paradise. There were a number of signs that the rising role of systematic knowledge concurrently leads to a decline of the social exclusiveness of the academic profession in various respects. In the public debates within various countries about the future developments of societies, academics by no means seem to play a more important role. Surveys of the reputation of professions show a declining position of the professoriate in many countries (Jacob and Teichler 2011, p. 9; Altbach and Lewis 1996, p. 45). In some countries, scholars' salaries show a loss of exclusiveness as well (Karpen and Hanske 1994, p. 42). Last but not least, professors in various countries feel more restrained as far as academic freedom and their power in shaping their institutional environment are concerned. The key literature on the academic profession in the 1980s and early 1991 indicates a growing sense of crisis around the academic profession (see Clark 1987, various articles in European Journal of Education 1983, *18*(3); Finkelstein 1984; Bowen and Schuster 1986; Altbach 1991). Even though the relevance and a certain degree of prestige by no means was called into question, the view spread that the changing nature of knowledge in society is accompanied by changes in higher education that are a mixed blessing for the academic profession (see Enders and Teichler 1997).

2   The Carnegie Study 1991–1993

2.1   The Initiative and the Design of the Study

Entry rates to higher education beyond 10 %, years later beyond 20 %, and eventually beyond 30 % were reality in the United States of America substantially earlier than in European countries. Moreover, activities of analysing developments of higher education systematically emerged in the United States earlier and more forcefully than in other countries. Already in 1969, the Carnegie Foundation for the Advancement of Teaching started the first survey of the academic profession. The survey addressed the attitudes, values, and professional orientations of the professoriate, reviewed the working and employment situation as well as chronicled its changing demographic profile. In the 1980s, various literature studies, surveys, and expert analyses of the Carnegie Foundation, guided by its President Ernest L. Boyer, stirred up lively debates in the United States about the state of higher education—notably, as these studies made clear that the public debate often had focused too much on the sector of the prestigious research universities and had overlooked the changes of the overall system in the process of rapid expansion and changing social functions.

Ernest L. Boyer took first steps for the preparation of a comparative study already in 1990. He was convinced that the US audience would benefit from knowing whether issues of the academic profession were similar across the globe. Since social changes in the academy were perceived worldwide and issues of the academic profession came out to be global, while in other respects it was obvious that nations had different traditions and different policies, it became apparent that an international comparison was necessary. Moreover, the professoriate had developed more and more international communication and collaboration, colleagues across the countries benefitted from the exchanges, and these exchanges seemed to enrich knowledge production and the world's reservoir of knowledge. The Carnegie Foundation approached possible research partners in different countries of the world, provided funds for partners from middle-income countries to undertake national surveys and volunteered to take the lead for joint data processes and for the analysis of results.

In 1990, researchers of different countries gathered at the headquarters of the Carnegie Foundation in Princeton, New Jersey (United States) to plan the first international study about the academic profession. A subsequent preparatory conference in 1991, addressing the diversity of the higher education systems and the situation of the academic profession in the various countries participating, made clear that there was a sufficiently broad range of common issues to consider such a comparative study as valuable. However, immense activities of developing a joint questionnaire were needed beyond the most recent US predecessor survey (Carnegie Foundation for the Advancement of Teaching 1989, see Boyer 1990) in order to cover the key issues and the key conditions for a large number of countries.

Actually, the first international survey of the academic profession (commonly called Carnegie Survey of the Academic Profession) was undertaken in 1991–1993. Information was collected about the demographic facts of the profession, the employment and work situation, time spent on various activities, attitudes towards teaching and learning and actual activities in these areas, the governance of academic institutions, and on morale. Scholars from 15 countries (more precisely 14 countries and one "territory") from all continents participated in surveying their academics: Australia; the Asian countries of South Korea, Japan, and Hong Kong; the Latin American countries of Brazil, Chile, and Mexico; the United States; the European countries of United Kingdom, Germany, the Netherlands, Sweden, and Russia; and also Egypt and Israel from the Middle East. However, scholars from Egypt and Russia had initially participated, but eventually did not succeed in gathering a representative overview of the academic profession in their country; their data was only included in part in national reports eventually published and was not included in the international data set.

As already pointed out, the questionnaire was loosely based on the Carnegie's questionnaire for the previous survey of the American scholars. The new questionnaire, comprising about ten questions with frequent long lists of response items, was adapted in a collaborative process to the topics and interests of the various countries. It was modified to be relevant to the international context and to focus on the topics that were particularly salient to the members of the research group. "The very process of designing the questionnaire was itself a revealing exercise, as differences in priorities of the professoriate, and even in the meaning of basic concepts, were discussed, debated, and ultimately resolved. The questionnaire was carefully translated into the languages of the countries involved" (Altbach and Lewis 1996, pp. 5–6). For the actual surveying, a common methodology was used to select institutions and individuals. A representative sample of academics teaching and researching at institutions providing programmes at least on the Bachelor's level was constructed. The questionnaire was mailed in 1992 and 1993 to altogether more than 40,000 persons. Response rates varied from about 70 % to less than 30 %, and altogether 19,161 respondents provided the information for the comparative analysis (see Altbach and Lewis 1996; Enders and Teichler 1995b, pp. 5–8; cf. the slightly varying report in Whitelaw 1996).

2.2   Major Results of the Carnegie Study

A first, relatively short overview of the results of this first comparative study was published by the Carnegie Foundation itself in 1994 (Boyer et al. 1994). The major publication, made available 2 years later, was a collection of country reports supplemented by a comparative analysis on the part of two US scholars who had not been involved in the comparative project at the time the joint questionnaire had been developed (Altbach 1996). Scholars involved in the project published various national and comparative data analyses, among them substantial reports in Japan (Arimoto and Ehara 1996) and Germany (Enders and Teichler 1995a, b). Finally, several reports about the project contributed to a major conference of the Academia Europaea held in 1996, the proceedings of which were published in the same year (Maassen and van Vught 1996), and articles were published in a special issue of the journal "Higher Education" in 1997 (Welch 1997).

The first comparative report (Boyer et al. 1994) underscored a broad range of findings. In most countries, the academic profession had remained more strongly male dominated than in the United States in those days, and the proportion of youth considered as well equipped for study in higher education was rated smaller than in the United States. Across countries, scholars felt most closely affiliated to their discipline, but the sense of affiliation to their university varies substantially as well as the role they attribute to research in their overall activities; across countries, the authors observed a relatively low degree of satisfaction as regards the prevailing modes of evaluation. Salaries in most countries were regarded as high or acceptable, the overall satisfaction seemed to be high, and the overall academic climate was rated positively. Views varied more strongly across countries as regards the assessment of working conditions, and many academics in some countries considered their profession as a source of personal strain. Across all countries, academics expressed dissatisfaction with the prevailing conditions of governance. In most countries, academics felt the academic profession to be sufficiently protected, while the views varied, whether academics play and should play an active role in society. Finally, the majority of academics all over the world believed that international ties were highly important for the academic professions, whereby the actual activities of international collaboration and mobility seemed to differ strikingly. The analysis concludes "Scholars everywhere, while maintaining national distinctions, acknowledge common concerns—not just intellectually but professionally as well. And in the century ahead, three critical issues will influence profoundly the shape and vitality of higher learning around the world" (Boyer et al. 1994, p. 21): student access and the balance of access and excellence, governance ("How can the university reorganise itself to achieve both efficiency and collegiality?") as well as the relationships between teaching, research, and services (rewards and increased contribution to public good).

In the major publication of the Carnegie Study, Altbach and Lewis (1996, pp. 47–48) summarise the findings of the country reports as follows:

> One cannot but be struck by the many similarities among the scholars and scientists in the diverse countries. It is with regard to those working conditions most affected by local political and cultural customs and policies that international differences are most apparent. The professoriate worldwide is committed to teaching and research, and in varying degree to service. While there is a feeling that higher education faces many difficulties and that conditions have deteriorated in recent years, most academics are committed to the profession and to its traditional values of autonomy, academic freedom, and the importance of scholarship, both for its own sake and for societal advancement. Academics are not especially supportive of senior administrators, yet they express remarkable loyalty to the profession and to other academics. They seem prepared to respond to the call that higher education contribute more tangibly to economic development and social well-being. They believe that they have an obligation to apply their knowledge to society's problems.

After pointing to some differences between countries, the authors continue:

> Resiliency, determination, and a focus on the core functions of higher education characterise the academic profession in these 14 countries. While the vicissitudes experienced by the profession in recent years have been considerable, the professoriate is by no means demoralised. In all but three countries, 60 % or more agree that this is an especially creative and productive time in their fields. Professors are generally satisfied with the courses they teach, and with few exceptions are pleased with the opportunity they have to pursue their own ideas. The intellectual atmosphere is good; faculty do not regret their career choices and are generally happy with their relationships with colleagues.
>
> This portrait of the professoriate depicts a strong, but somewhat unsettled profession. Academics around the world are inspired by the intellectual ferment of the times. The intrinsic pleasures of academic life obviously endure. Academe is facing the future with concern but with surprising optimism. (Altbach and Lewis 1996, p. 48)

In the overview of the major results of the Carnegie Study, Teichler (1996) makes two strategic choices from the outset. First, he concentrates the analysis on six economically advanced countries, thereby underscoring the quite different conditions academics face in middle-income countries. Second, data are presented separately for university professors, junior academic staff at universities and academics at other institutions of higher education, thereby pointing out that the academic profession is distinctively sub-divided by status and function.

In summarising the findings of the Carnegie Survey, Teichler (1996, p. 59) points out, first, that the academic profession "is more satisfied with their profession than the prior public debate suggested". He underscores, though, that satisfaction is higher among university professors than the other two groups, and that the areas for which dissatisfaction is expressed vary substantially by country.

Second, a clear link between teaching and research has persisted for university professors. "Neither is research endangered because of teaching and administrative loads nor is teaching put aside due to research-oriented motives and research-oriented assessment." (Teichler 1996, p. 60). However, individual options vary strikingly among university professors, and the link between teaching and research is less obvious for large proportions of junior staff and, as one could expect, for academics at other higher education institutions.

Third, the author notes surprising commonalities among university professors across disciplines, notably "in their value judgements about the university administration, about the role higher education is expected to play and about the views on how higher education is perceived and estimated in the public" (Teichler 1996, p. 60). In contrast, the author notes substantial differences between senior and junior academics at universities as well as between academics at universities and other institutions of higher education in many respects.

Fourth, more than the other authors Teichler points out differences. Among others, "the English senior academics at universities consider themselves more strongly a profession under pressure than their colleagues in other European countries" (Teichler 1996, p. 61). According to the author, the country differences are striking

> as regards the role foreign languages and international relationships play for their academic life. Sweden belongs to those countries, where a view prevails which I would call 'internationalise or perish'. Germany belongs, as also Japan, to those countries which I would call 'two-arena countries': scholars might opt whether they more strongly prefer national or international involvement and visibility. Actually, the Dutch scholars seemed to be closer on average to their Swedish than to their German colleagues in this respect. Finally, many English scholars, though to a lesser extent than their US-American colleagues, seem to take 'internationalisation through import' for granted. (Teichler 1996, p. 61)

Fifth, junior academics at universities are more heterogeneous groups than professors as far as priorities and actual time spent on various functions are concerned. On average, they assess their working conditions favourably, but are clearly less satisfied than university professors, though they are similar to them with respect to academic values.

Sixth, not surprisingly, views and activities of academics at other institutions of higher education are clearly shaped by the dominance of teaching. They tend to be less satisfied with their overall professional situation than academics at universities.

Seventh, the administration is assessed by academics on average neither positively nor negatively. Most academics do not see any significant infringement as regards their academic work though some point out visible restrictions.

Eighth, finally, Teichler points out as well that academics, though in the majority clearly defending the right to pursue research for its own sake, do not present themselves as an 'ivory tower profession'. Rather they expect research and teaching to help resolve basic social problems.

Altogether, the international comparative study undertaken in 1991–1993 does not depict an academic profession as suffering from status loss, resource restrictions, or adverse administrative conditions. Critique of the conditions for academic work is by no means infrequent, but the academic profession seems to be in the position to opt for activities which they favour and shape their job role themselves in a predominantly satisfactory way.

2.3   Subsequent Years

This does not mean, however, that the Carnegie Study was successful to change the perception of the situation of the academic profession substantially. In depicting the public debate a few years afterwards, Enders—actually a team member of the Carnegie Study who knew its results very well—pointed out that the academic profession continued to be viewed to be under pressure: rapid loss of status, tighter resources, loss of power of the academic guild, and being blamed for not providing the services expected. "Furthermore, one fears a decline in the faculty morale, disillusionment of their mission, seeing themselves as academic workers who are merely doing routine jobs and who are no longer strongly committed to the traditional norms and values of the profession". (Enders 2001b, p. 2). Similarly, Altbach (2000b, p. 1) notes a "deterioration of the academic estate". An even wider range of challenges is listed by Welch (2005a, p. 1) for the academic profession "in uncertain times".

Moreover, some subsequent analyses paid more attention to the situation of junior academics. Notably in European countries, the long process of concurrent learning and productive work and the high selectivity of the profession is often combined with a long period of unsecure employment and reduced access to resources (see Altbach 2000a; Enders 2001a; Enders and de Weert 2004; Welch 2005b; Teichler 2006); but also junior academics in other countries faced similar problems (cf. Schuster and Finkelstein 2006).

It is difficult to judge whether the public debate overrates adverse contexts and underrates the ability of the academics to benefit from the potentials and partly set aside the adverse conditions, or whether in fact the conditions became harsher after the Carnegie Study had been conducted. A question like this could be answered more convincingly on the basis of a comparative study on the academic profession that was undertaken some years later.

3 The CAP Study

3.1 *The Approach*

More than a decade later, researchers from various countries initiated a second comparative study on the academic profession. On the one hand, they noted that the crisis mood in a variety of issues has persisted. The academic profession still worried about a loss of exclusiveness, both as status and as a loss of the oligopoly of the "knowledge profession" are concerned, about a possible relative decline of the employment and work conditions, and finally about a possible loss of power and even of academic freedom. Therefore, it was seen as worthwhile to explore whether in fact the perception of the employment and work situation, the values and the academic activities had changed since the early 1990s, and this was reflected in the title of the new project: "The Changing Academic Profession" (CAP). On the other hand, the scholars initiating the new project were convinced that three additional themes had gained momentum and therefore should be extensively treated in the new survey which played only a moderate role in the early 1990s, but now might have a pervasive influence on the academic profession: a higher expectation of relevance, a growing internationalisation, and a substantially increased managerial power in higher education. These "three key challenges" were formulated at the outset of the CAP project as follows (see Kogan and Teichler 2007b, pp. 10–11, cf. more detailed explanations in Cummings 2006, Brennan 2006, 2007):

Relevance: Whereas the highest goal of the traditional academy was to create fundamental knowledge, what has been described as the 'scholarship of discovery', the new emphasis of the knowledge society is on useful knowledge or the 'scholarship of application'. This scholarship often involves the pooling and melding of insights from several disciplines and tends to focus on outcomes that have a direct impact on everyday life. One consequence is that many future scholars, though trained in the disciplines, will work in applied fields and may have options of employment in these fields outside of the academy. This provides new opportunities for more boundaryless forms of academic career and knowledge transfer while it may also create recruitment difficulties in some places, and especially in fields such as science, technology and engineering.

There are strong interdependencies between the goals of higher education, the rules for distributing resources, and the nature of academic work. The changes associated with movement from the 'traditional academy' with its stress on basic research and disciplinary teaching to the 'relevant academy' are largely uncharted and are likely to have unanticipated consequences. The task of the project is therefore to understand how these changes influence academic value systems and work practices and affect the nature and locus of control and power in academe.

Internationalisation: National traditions and socio-economic circumstances continue to play an important role in shaping academic life and have a major impact on the attractiveness of jobs in the profession. Yet today's global trends, with their emphasis on knowledge production and information flow, play an increasingly important role in the push towards the internationalisation of higher education. The international mobility of students and staff has grown, new technologies connect scholarly communities around the world, and English has become the new lingua franca of the international community.

The economic and political power of a country, its size and geographic location, its dominant culture, the quality of its higher education system and the language it uses for academic discourse and publications are factors that bring with them different approaches to internationalisation. Local and regional differences in approach are also to be found. Therefore, questions are raised about the functions of international networks, the implications of different access to them and the role of new communication technologies in internationalising the profession.

Management: In academic teaching and research, where professional values are traditionally firmly woven into the very fabric of knowledge production and dissemination, attempts to introduce change are sometimes received with scepticism and opposition. At the same time, a greater professionalisation of higher education management is regarded as necessary to enable higher education to respond effectively to a rapidly changing external environment. The control and management of academic work will help to define the nature of academic roles—including the division of labour in the academy, with a growth of newly professionalised 'support' roles and a possible breakdown of the traditional teaching/research nexus. New systemic and institutional processes such as quality assurance have been introduced which also change traditional distributions of power and values within academe and may be a force for change in academic practice. The project will examine both the rhetoric and the realities of academics' responses to such managerial practices in higher education.

A number of views can be discerned about recent attempts at the management of change in higher education and the responses of academics to such changes. One view would see a victory of managerial values over professional ones with academics losing control over both the overall goals of their work practices and their technical tasks. Another view would see the survival of traditional academic values against the managerial approach. This does not imply that academic roles fail to change, but that change does not automatically mean that interests and values are weakened. A third view would see a 'marriage' between professionalism and managerialism with academics losing some control over the goals and social purposes of their work but retaining considerable autonomy over their practical and technical tasks. The desirability of these three different positions is also subject to a range of different views. (Kogan and Teichler 2007b, pp. 10–11)

Finally, the initiators of the CAP study pursued higher ambitions as regards the theoretical and methodological basis of analysis. A closer cooperation between the participating researchers from different countries was envisaged.

3.2 The Design of the CAP Study

In contrast to the Carnegie Study, the CAP study could not rely on substantial funds from a single research-promoting source. In 2004, William Cummings, professor at George Washington University (Washington DC, USA), invited higher education researchers from various countries to collaborate in a new comparative study on the academic profession and to raise funds from their respective national sources. In the framework of five meetings held from 2004 to 2006 in Paris (France), London (United Kingdom), Stockholm (Sweden), Hiroshima (Japan), and Kassel (Germany), the state of research on the academic profession was carefully analysed, the conceptual base of the new project was developed, the methodological approach was specified, and the questionnaire was formulated (see Research Institute for Higher Education, Hiroshima University 2006; Kogan and Teichler 2007a; Locke and Teichler 2007).

Scholars from 18 countries (more precisely: 17 countries and one "territory") succeeded in raising funds to participate in the survey in 2007 and 2008. Half of them had participated in the Carnegie Study and thus provided the basis for the analysis, how the situation and the views of the academic profession have changed over time: Australia, Brazil, Germany, Hong Kong, Japan, Korea, Mexico, the United Kingdom, and the United States. Nine countries were newly included: Argentina, Canada, China, Finland, Norway, Italy, Malaysia, Portugal, and South Africa. In 2010, the Netherlands conducted the CAP survey as well; data from this country were included in the comparative analysis undertaken from 2011 onwards. Some countries included in the Carnegie Study did not succeed in participating in the CAP Study (Chile, Egypt, Israel, Russia, and Sweden).

The CAP Study was coordinated by William Cummings. Major decisions were taken by a "concepts commission" chaired by John Brennan (Centre for Higher Education Research and Information of the Open University), located in London (United Kingdom) and by a "methods commission" chaired by Martin J. Finkelstein (Seton Hall University, South Orange, NJ, USA). The data coordination was undertaken by Ulrich Teichler (International Centre for Higher Education Research, University of Kassel, Kassel, Germany).

The questionnaire was similar in length and in some parts identical or similar to the questionnaire of the previous study. The individual countries undertaking the survey were successful in calculating the number of persons to be addressed in such a way that the actual number of respondents was between 800 and 1,200 in most of the countries. The total number of responses was more than 23,000 in the 19 countries participating. However, the response rates varied substantially by country, and they were very low in some countries where academics were sent an online questionnaire only (not a paper and pencil version or an e-mail version).

Team members wrote analyses on selected themes on the occasion of a dozen joint conferences held from 2007 to 2010 in Argentina, Australia, Canada, Finland, Italy, Japan, Mexico, Norway, and the United States. Some results were published in conference proceedings (Research Institute for Higher Education, Hiroshima University 2008, 2009, 2010; Diversification of Higher Education and the Academic Profession 2010), and national studies of the academic profession in comparative perspective were published in some countries (Bentley et al. 2010; Jacob and Teichler 2011). The major results of the study, however, are expected to be published in 2011 and 2012 in the book series "The Changing Academy" published by Springer (see the first volume: Locke et al. 2011). In addition to a general overview on the results, specific studies are envisaged on academic careers, job satisfaction and its determinants, the internationalisation of the academic profession as well as on the academic profession in emerging countries.

3.3 First Results

The second comparative study, the CAP Study, suggests—as the Carnegie Study— that respondents in most countries do not consider the academic profession to be in a major crisis. Surprisingly, even the resources for academic work are assessed more positively in many countries in 2007–2008 than in 1991–1993. Also, overall job satisfaction has slightly increased over the years on average of the countries for which information is available at both points of time.

The academics surveyed observe strong expectations to deliver socially relevant results; most of the respondents, however, believe that efforts to care for academic creativity and pursuit of knowledge for its own sake are not endangered by the growing pressures for relevance. A growth of evaluation activities and an increasing managerial power is noted, but most academics surveyed do not consider their academic work to be subordinated or overtly controlled. The most obvious exception is the United Kingdom, where many academics consider themselves as losing the typical academic life due to managerial pressures.

In various countries, research shapes the daily life of scholars even more strongly than in the past, but this is not a consistent trend across all countries. Junior academics in most countries characterise their situation and their views somewhat similarly than they had done previously. Academics at institutions of higher education primarily in charge of teaching are quite distinct from those at universities with major research responsibilities in some countries, but quite similar in other countries.

One should bear in mind, though, that the first publications on the results of the CAP study often focus on a single theme and the respective findings for a single or only a few countries. Thus, it might be possible that the more thorough and the more comparative analysis expected to be available in the near future will lead to other conclusions than those presented here after a first glance.

4   Subsequent Comparative Studies

The CAP Study triggered two subsequent comparative studies on the academic profession: A study on the academic profession in Europe comprising a larger number of countries, and a follow-up study on the academic profession in Asia.

In Europe, Ulrich Teichler who had coordinated the German CAP study, initiated a research consortium comprising a larger number of European countries. In the study "The Academic Profession in Europe—Responses to Societal Challenges" (EUROAC), funded by the European Science Foundation (ESF) and national research promotion agencies and undertaken in 2009–2012, scholars from six additional European countries (Austria, Croatia, Ireland, Poland, Romania, and Switzerland) undertook a questionnaire survey in 2010 which in most parts was identical to the CAP questionnaire. Through a merger of these data with those of the European countries of the CAP survey, a comparison can be undertaken of 13 European countries; this is based on the assumption that no dramatic changes have occurred between 2007 and 2011. This will provide an opportunity to analyse the extent to which the academic profession faces similar conditions and harbours similar views, as some of the visions of the "European Higher Education Area" and the "European Research Area" suggest, or whether different traditions and different recent policies continue to put their stamp on the academic profession. Moreover, the EUROAC study foresees interviews in eight countries (the above named as well as Finland and Germany) in order to undertake an in-depth analyses on issues related to those addressed in the CAP survey: the links between the academic profession and "higher education professionals", the service function of higher education, the situation of junior academics and career trajectories, etc.

The Japanese researchers involved in the CAP project initiated a new study on The Academic Profession in Asia (2011) and invited to a preparatory conference held in February 2011. Contrary to the EUROAC study, this project, scheduled for 2011–2012, aims to measure changes within a few years, i.e. from 2007–2008 to 2012. Similarly to the EUROAC study, the Asian study strives to broaden the thematic range beyond the CAP study and to analyse the extent to which variety between countries in Asia is prevailing or whether some common features are visible.

The emergence of these new studies suggests that the comparative analysis of the academic profession does not remain anymore only an occasionally addressed theme of higher education research. Also, the number of countries seems to grow where the quality of systematic information on the academic professions tends to increase.

5   A Final Observation

In reviewing the state of research and of public discourse on the academic profession, Enders (2006, p. 19) ends with a sentence which looks cryptic at first glance: "Overall, the fate of the academic profession may lie solely in how it responds to changes that impact on universities and higher education systems worldwide in the coming years". The comparative studies on the academic profession lead to similar conclusions: The academic profession—possibly more strongly than in the past—is exposed to substantial expectations and pressures, but these expectations and pressures are not enforcing ways how the scholars view their situation and how they act; they have to respond, but they have leeway for interpretation and action.

References

Altbach, P. G. (1991). The academic profession. In P. G. Altbach (Ed.), *International higher education: an encyclopedia* (pp. 23–45). New York: Garland.

Altbach, P. G. (Ed.). (1996). *The international academic profession: portraits of fourteen countries*. Princeton: Carnegie Foundation for the Advancement of Teaching.

Altbach, P. G. (Ed.). (2000a). *The changing academic workplace: comparative perspectives*. Boston: Boston College, Center for International Higher Education.

Altbach, P. G. (2000b). The deterioration of the academic estate: international patterns of academic work. In P. G. Altbach (Ed.), *The changing academic workplace: comparative perspectives* (pp. 1–23). Boston: Boston College, Center for International Higher Education.

Altbach, P. G., & Lewis, L. S. (1996). The academic profession in international perspective. In P. G. Altbach (Ed.), *The international academic profession: portraits of fourteen countries* (pp. 3–48). Princeton: Carnegie Foundation for the Advancement of Teaching.

Arimoto, A., & Ehara, T. (Eds.). (1996). *Daigaku kyôjushoku no kokusai hikaku* [International comparison of the academic profession]. Tokyo: Tamagawa University Press.

Bell, D. (1973). *The coming of post-industrial society*. New York: Basic Books.

Ben-David, J. (1977). *Centers of learning: Britain, France, Germany, United States*. New York: McGraw-Hill.

Bentley, P., Kyvik, S., Vaboe, A., & Waagene, E. (2010). *Forskningsvilkar ved norske universiteter I et internasjonalt perspektiv* [Research conditions at Norwegian universities from a comparative perspective] (Rapport, 8/2010). Oslo: NIFU STEP.

Bindé, J. (2005). *Towards knowledge societies*. Paris: United Nations Educational.

Bowen, H., & Schuster, J. (1986). *American professors: a national resource imperiled*. New York: Oxford University Press.

Boyer, E. L. (1990). *Scholarship reconsidered: priorities of the professoriate*. Princeton: Carnegie Foundation for the Advancement of Teaching.

Boyer, E. L., Altbach, P. G., & Whitelaw, M. J. (1994). *The academic profession: an international perspective*. Princeton: Carnegie Foundation for the Advancement of Teaching.

Brennan, J. (2006). The changing academic profession: the driving forces. In RIHE (Ed.), *Reports of changing academic profession project workshop on quality, relevance, and governance in the changing academia: international perspectives* (pp. 37–44). Hiroshima: Research Institute for Higher Education, Hiroshima University.

Brennan, J. (2007). The academic profession and increasing expectations of relevance. In M. Kogan & U. Teichler (Eds.), *Key challenges to the academic profession* (pp. 19–28). Kassel: International Centre for Higher Education Research Kassel (INCHER-Kassel).

Burrage, M. (Ed.). (2010). *Martin Trow: twentieth-century higher education*. Baltimore: Johns Hopkins University Press.

Carnegie Foundation for the Advancement of Teaching. (1989). *The condition of the professoriate: attitudes and trends: a technical report*. Princeton: Carnegie Foundation for the Advancement of Teaching.

Clark, B. R. (Ed.). (1987). *The academic profession: national, disciplinary and institutional settings*. Berkeley: University of California Press.

Cummings, W. K. (2006). The third revolution of higher education: becoming more relevant. In RIHE (Ed.), *Reports of changing academic profession project workshop on quality, relevance, and governance in the changing academia: international perspectives* (pp. 209–222). Hiroshima: Research Institute for Higher Education, Hiroshima University.

Diversification of Higher Education and the Academic Profession (special issue). (2010). *European Review, 18*(1).

Drucker, P. F. (1969). *The age of discontinuity*. New York: Harper & Row.

Enders, J. (Ed.). (2001a). *Academic staff in Europe: changing contexts and conditions*. Westport: Greenwood.

Enders, J. (2001b). Between state control and academic capitalism: a comparative perspective on academic staff in Europe. In J. Enders (Ed.), *Academic staff in Europe: changing contexts and conditions* (pp. 1–23). Westport: Greenwood.

Enders, J. (2001c). *Karriere mit Doktortitel* [Career with a doctorate?]. Frankfurt a. M.: Campus.

Enders, J. (2006). The academic profession. In J. F. Forest & P. G. Altbach (Eds.), *International handbook of higher education* (pp. 1–21). Dordrecht: Springer.

Enders, J., & Teichler, U. (1995a). *Berufsbild der Lehrenden und Forschenden an Hochschulen* [The professional image of those teaching and undertaking research at institutions of higher education]. Bonn: Bundesministerium für Bildung, Wissenschaft, Forschung und Technologie.

Enders, J., & Teichler, U. (1995b). *Der Hochschullehrerberuf im internationalen Vergleich* [The academic profession in international comparison]. Bonn: Bundesministerium für Bildung, Wissenschaft, Forschung und Technologie.

Enders, J., & Teichler, U. (1997). A victim of their own success? Employment and working conditions of academic staff in comparative perspective. *Higher Education, 34*(3), 347–372.

Enders, J., & Weert, E. de. (Ed.). (2004). *The international attractiveness of the academic workplace in Europe*. Frankfurt a. M.: Gewerkschaft Erziehung und Wissenschaft.

Finkelstein, M. J. (1984). *The American academic profession: a synthesis of social scientific inquiry since World War II*. Columbus: Ohio State University Press.

Jacob, A. K., & Teichler, U. (2011). *Der Wandel des Hochschullehrerberufs im internationalen Vergleich: Ergebnisse einer Befragung in den Jahren 2007/08* [Change of the academic profession in international comparison: results of the survey of the years 2007–2008]. Bonn: Bundesministerium für Bildung und Forschung.

Karpen, U., & Hanske, P. (1994). *Status und Besoldung von Hochschlullehrern im internationalen Vergleich* [Status and remuneration of professors in an international comparison]. Baden-Baden: Nomos.

Knorr-Cetina, K. (1998). Sozialität mit Objekten. Soziale Beziehungen in post-traditionalen Wissensgesellschaften [Sociality with objects. Social relations in post-traditional knowledge-societies]. In W. Rammert (Ed.), *Technik und Sozialtheorie* [Technology and social theory] (pp. 83–120). Frankfurt a. M.: Campus.

Kogan, M., & Teichler, U. (Eds.). (2007a). *Key challenges to the academic profession* (Werkstattberichte, Vol. 65). Kassel: International Centre for Higher Education Research Kassel (INCHER-Kassel) and UNESCO Forum on Higher Education, Research and Knowledge.

Kogan, M., & Teichler, U. (2007b). Key challenges of the academic profession and its interface with management: some introductory thoughts. In M. Kogan & U. Teichler (Eds.), *Key challenges to the academic profession* (Werkstattberichte, Vol. 65, pp. 9–15,). Kassel: International Centre for Higher Education Research Kassel (INCHER-Kassel) and UNESCO Forum on Higher Education, Research and Knowledge.

Locke, W., & Teichler, U. (Eds.). (2007). *The changing conditions for academic work and careers in select countries* (Werkstattberichte, Vol. 66). Kassel: International Centre for Higher Education Research Kassel (INCHER-Kassel).

Locke, W., Cummings, W. K., & Fisher, D. (Eds.). (2011). *Changing governance and management in higher education*. Dordrecht: Springer.

Maassen, P. A. M., & Vught, F. A. van. (Eds.). (1996). *Inside academia: new challenges of the academic profession*. Utrecht: De Tijdstroom.

Perkin, H. (1969). *Key profession: a history of the association of university teachers*. London: Routledge/Palmer.

Perkin, H. (1991). History of universities. In P. G. Altbach (Ed.), *International higher education: an encyclopedia* (pp. 169–204). New York: Garland.

Research Institute for Higher Education, Hiroshima University. (Ed.). (2006). *Reports of changing academic profession project workshop on quality, relevance and governance in the changing academia: international perspectives* (COE Publication Series, Vol. 20). Hiroshima: RIHE.

Research Institute for Higher Education, Hiroshima University. (Ed.). (2008). *The changing academic profession in international comparative and quantitative perspectives* (RIHE International Seminar Reports, Vol. 12). Hiroshima: RIHE.

Research Institute for Higher Education, Hiroshima University. (Ed.). (2009). *The changing academic profession over 1992–2007: international, comparative and quantitative perspectives* (RIHE International Seminar Reports, Vol. 13). Hiroshima: RIHE.

Research Institute for Higher Education, Hiroshima University. (Ed.). (2010). *The changing academic profession in international comparative and quantitative perspectives: a focus on teaching & research activities* (RIHE International Seminar Reports, Vol. 15). Hiroshima: RIHE.

Rüegg, W. (Ed.). (2011). *A history of the university in Europe. Volume IV: universities since 1945*. Cambridge: Cambridge University Press.

Schuster, J., & Finkelstein, M. J. (2006). *The American faculty: the restructuring of academic work and careers*. Baltimore: Johns Hopkins University Press.

Stehr, N. (1994). *Knowledge societies*. London: Sage.

Teichler, U. (1996). The conditions of the academic profession: an international, comparative analysis of the academic profession in Western Europe, Japan and the USA. In P. A. M. Maassen & F. A. Vught van (Eds.), *Inside academia: new challenges of the academic profession* (pp. 15–65). Utrecht: De Tijdstroom.

Teichler, U. (Ed.). (2006). *The formative years of scholars*. London: Portland.

Trow, M. (1974). *Problems in the transition from elite to mass higher education. Policies for higher education* (pp. 51–101). Paris: OECD.

Welch, A. (Ed.). (1997). Special issue on the academic profession. *Higher Education, 34*(3), 323–345.

Welch, A. (2005a). Challenge and change: the academic profession in uncertain times. In A. Welch (Ed.), *The professoriate: profile of a profession* (pp. 1–19). Dordrecht: Springer.

Welch, A. (Ed.). (2005b). *The professoriate: profile of a profession*. Dordrecht: Springer.

Whitelaw, M. J. (1996). The international survey of the academic profession, 1991–1993: methodological notes. In P. G. Altbach (Ed.), *The international academic profession: portraits of fourteen countries* (pp. 669–678). Princeton: Carnegie Foundation for the Advancement of Teaching.

The Changing Role of Academics and the Rise of Managerialism

Abbey Hyde, Marie Clarke and Jonathan Drennan

1 Introduction

In this review, we situate the changing role of academics within existing national and international literature on the topic. We consider how the traditional model of a university has evolved in the light of recent shifts in the character of higher education institutions under the influence of the private business-sector model. Whilst higher education has arguably always been in transition, this business-like model, known as managerialism, has been the subject of scholarly debates in educational discourse and is linked to wider societal shifts and political ideologies such as the rise of neo-liberalism and the Evaluative State, concepts that will be clarified in the course of this review. In particular, a genre of theoretical and empirical work has emerged that considers the implications of managerialism on academic activities, particularly the diversification of academic work, changes in the control over academic work and the loss of professional power of academics, as well as the impact of managerialism on the nature of teaching and research. At a discursive level, as will become clear as the chapter unfolds, there is a sense of crisis in academia. However, the manner in which academics have actually responded to the alleged crisis, and how they make sense of recent changes as captured in empirical 'micro' studies in specific social locations will also be considered.

2 The Traditional Model of a University

At the heart of the debate about the loss of autonomy of academics are notions about the purpose of a university education. The central functions of the university, broadly agreed upon in the literature, are to educate (knowledge transfer), to undertake

A. Hyde (✉) · M. Clarke · J. Drennan
University College Dublin, Dublin, Ireland
e-mail: abbey.hyde@ucd.ie

B. M. Kehm, U. Teichler (eds.), *The Academic Profession in Europe: New Tasks and New Challenges,* The Changing Academy – The Changing Academic Profession in International Comparative Perspective 5, DOI 10.1007/978-94-007-4614-5_4,
© Springer Science+Business Media Dordrecht 2013

research (knowledge production), and to provide a service to the community (using the knowledge base for the greater good of the society; Smeenk et al. 2009). Although universities are generally acknowledged to be amongst the most stable and change-resistant institutions in industrially developed societies with a long history dating back to the medieval period (Smeenk et al. 2009), recent transformations are in progress that share a number of recognisable features.

Whilst it is important not to oversimplify how universities operated in the period prior to the advent of managerialism, they are broadly viewed as having been democratic institutions governed by academics and were protected from direct state regulation (Olssen 2002). Drawing on the writings of John Stuart Mill (1965), Olssen notes that as representative institutions, part of their role was to keep check on central state authority, to foster active citizenship, and to encourage diversity of opinion in an open and transparent environment (Olssen 2002, p. 16). Olssen (2002) reflects on John Stuart Mill's (1965) notion that a representative democracy not alone permits types of participation in public discourses that are educative, but also, at the level of institutions, guards against the negative effects of centralism.

Traditionally, academics were regulated through collegial governance, and according to some commentators, had a particular style of conducting their affairs and making decisions that contrasts with that associated with the private business sector (Scott 2002). Scott describes this as allowing for "… more give and take, more discussion, more commitment to the exchange of ideas, and more respect for differences" (p. 4). The process of interaction is underpinned by deliberation rather than speed, she notes. The scientific capital (wherewithal that enables an individual to make noticed achievements; Bourdieu 2004) deriving from their intellectual endeavours has meant that academics have traditionally not been an easy lot to manage, and as Dearlove (2002, p. 267) has observed, they "recognise no boss …" and have shown little interest in collective action as they "grumble about the demands [the wider university] makes on 'their' time and the problem of parking".

3   Towards Managerialism in Higher Education: The Rise of Neo-Liberalism and the Evaluative State

There is a general consensus in the literature that at a broad level, European universities have increasingly begun to adopt a working culture and ethos traditionally found in the private business sector, a development that has had a longer tradition in the USA (Smeenk et al. 2009). Whilst Smeenk et al. (2009) date the arrival of the market model of Higher Education in Europe to the late 1990s, in some countries aspects of the model were rolling out much earlier; indeed, Enders and Musselin (2008) note that the extra-scientific relevance of academic research, for example in industry and healthcare, have always been part of the academic world, but that entrepreneurial academic work has become more prevalent since the 1960s. Furthermore, Neave (1988) notes that a concept referred to as the Evaluative State—a precursor to the market model in universities—has been circulating in educational scholarship since the late 1980s. Thus, whilst there is broad agreement that third level institutions are experiencing a new kind of scrutiny, the reasons why this arose and the pace of its roll-out across Europe has varied. Neave (1998) roots the genesis of the Evaluative State primarily to European political ideas in the case of France, Sweden, and Belgium, and later in Spain, and by contrast, largely to the influence of US economic discourses in the case of Britain and the Netherlands.

Reasons for this shift from the traditional model to a managerialist one in the higher education (HE) sector have been well documented and include fiscal restraints, increasing emphasis on quality and accountability, the 'massification' of HE, and its decentralisation (Smeenk et al. 2009). This trend is not unique to HE, being also a feature of public sector areas such as the health services (McDonnell et al. 2009, p. 51), and is associated with 'New Public Management' (NPM), a concept strongly linked to 'neo-liberalism' and 'economic rationalism' (see Olssen 2002). The move towards managerialism has also been linked to the concept of the Evaluative State referred to earlier. Let us explore these notions of neo-liberalism and the Evaluative State as they apply to changes in higher education.

Olssen (2002) notes that whilst neo-liberal theories purport to safe-guard the freedom and agency of the individual whilst limiting the power and control of the state, in reality, they operate in a contradictory manner. Whilst they attempt to rescind the welfare state and position themselves within anti-statist discourses, nonetheless, neo-liberal practices are contemporaneously prescriptive and controlling in their activities. In addition, a defining feature of neo-liberalism is that markets are invoked as a control mechanism through state power and envelop traditionally non-economic spheres (Olssen 2002). Mayo (2009) identifies neo-liberal tenets in the European Union (EU) discourse on higher education over the past number of years as evidenced in a number of communiqués and associated documentation, although he notes that these have been invoked at various paces in different countries. Mayo's analysis suggests that the adoption of neo-liberal policies within Europe is driven by competitiveness and the EU aspiration to improve its economic position vis-à-vis the United States and Asia and achieve a dominant position in the 'knowledge economy' (p. 89). An aspect of the means to achieve 'a much desired supremacy in the global knowledge economy' (Mayo 2009, p. 9) is to get European academics working together towards this common goal. Thus, the 'social Europe' of student and faculty exchanges through programmes such as Erasmus, Leonardo, and Socrates that ostensibly contrast with the detachment and self-serving motives associated with neo-liberalism are, Mayo suggests, a smokescreen for the real objective of consolidating European power in the global economy. This 'Europeanisation' differs from another concept in recent EU discourse on higher education, namely 'internationalisation'. The latter concerns attracting high-calibre non-EU students who in many instances bring with them substantial fees and facilitate European universities to increase their rankings in the international league tables such as the QS World University Rankings, particularly relative to their US rivals. Another related aspect of EU discourse on higher education, Mayo purports, is the imperative to enhance partnerships between higher education and the business sector. The implications of this for the type and status of knowledge developed will be taken up in a later section.

The Evaluative State refers to a complex set of ideologies and the shift from the historic 'routine and maintenance modes of evaluation' (Neave 1998, p. 267), to a more strategic type of evaluation focused on the appraisal of outcomes. Thus, the product rather than the process is subjected to scrutiny, and higher education 'steered' in line with national economic priorities (1988, p. 10). However, this shift does not represent a simple top-down direct imposition of state power; how the state exercises its power within the higher education sector is complex, because as Neave (1998) argues, it "[also] steers *by directly manipulating or adjusting the responsibilities assigned to intermediary bodies* and, in certain instances, abolishing or creating agencies of surveillance [italics in original]" (1998, p. 281). An ironic complexity of the Evaluative State is that individual institutions enjoy increased levels of self-regulation and institutional autonomy but are pitted in competition with other institutions to secure the limited resources available.

4 The Changing Role of Academics with the Advent of Managerialism

Managerialism, encompassing discourses and practices established in the private market such as corporate modes of speech, professional administrators, line management, and competition for resources, is now a feature of the entrepreneurial governance of the higher education sector in countries across Europe (see Kolsaker 2008). Additional features of this model are "a hierarchical differentiation of research funding, the increased importance of private funding, and students having to pay a significant share of their tuition" (Smeenk et al. 2009, p. 591).

Managerialist ideology may also be dissected further by considering its position on quality compared with that of a traditional academic perspective (Findlow 2008). As Findlow notes, managerial-audit constructions of quality prioritise "saleability, strategy, demonstrable usefulness of outcome … and conformity to pre-set, transferable standards" (p. 321) whilst according to the liberal academic perspective, quality was judged in terms of "truth, engagement, accuracy and depth in relation to diverse contexts". The industrialisation of academic work is exemplified by Musselin (2007) in the case of E-learning: with E-learning, she argues, teaching that was previously the personal exercise of an individual academic and amenable to adjustments according to the needs of specific student groups involves the co-operation of various individuals (academics and technicians) who produce set and standardized products and are separated from the learners. The need to translate operative processes into measurable outcomes and to facilitate harmonisation across Europe through mechanisms such as the Bologna process, Mayo (2009) proposes, have resulted in an increasing shift in power from the academic sector to the bureaucratic sector. Whilst the two ideologies, traditional and managerialist, are frequently contrasted and defined in opposition to one another, Fanghanel (2007) has noted that the two have more recently appeared in official British government texts as complementary rather than contradictory educational aspirations. This, she argues, is evident in the repetitive use of the collocation of the terms 'social and economic' in official texts on tertiary education as though they were collectively un-problematic. We will revisit the extent to which degrees of traditionalism and managerialism co-exist when considering empirical studies of academics a little further on. First though, we consider the changing role of academics in relation to the increasing diversification of their work; the increasing control over their activities and loss of professional power; and the impact of increased managerialism on teaching innovation and the substance of their disciplinary knowledge.

4.1 The Increasing Diversification of Academic Work

To varying degrees, depending on the country and institution, academic tasks in general have become increasingly diverse (Musselin 2007). Whilst it might be argued that academics have always engaged in a range of activities including academic administration, Musselin notes that, in the past, academic tasks might crudely be divided into teaching and research, and even if the emphasis on one or other gave rise to two different career pathways, the central activities of academics constituted teaching in classrooms and writing in academic journals. Whilst many were also involved in additional endeavours as 'outside' activities, these were optional and not seen as part of their work. However, in the current period, management skills have become part and parcel of the expectation of the role and diverse activities characterise the role. The requirement now is that senior academics engage in activities such as proposal writing, bidding for funding, seeking collaborative partners, and arranging patents and technology transfers (Musselin 2007). Promotion to senior posts increasingly requires not just evidence of academic writing (the merits of which are increasingly being judged by quantitative ratings of impact rather than their inherent level of scholarship), but also evidence of leading research teams and organising the activities of others. 'Teaching' has also become more diverse and includes embracing teaching technologies and arranging student placements as aspects of that role. Musselin also draws attention to 'third mission' aspects of the revised role of academics, a mission that concerns making links with various bodies and decision makers at national and international levels, networking with other academics, engaging in public discourses, and dovetailing with public policy.

Musselin (2007) links the diversification of tasks within academia to the specialisation of academic work. Within scientific disciplines, a division of labour has emerged, with early-career scientists engaged in laboratory work whilst their senior (and particularly professorial) colleagues do less actual science and more strategic work, namely, writing proposals, securing bids, processing contracts and so forth. One consequence of the specialisation of academic work in countries such as the *one or the other*

United States, the UK, and Holland, is the trend towards the fissuring of the professoriate into posts that are either teaching or research. This constitutes a move away from the Humboldtian tradition of the integration of teaching and research towards a more differentiated arrangement whereupon research and teaching are socially organised as two separate activities (see Mayo 2009). In addition to a division of labour according to one's location on the career trajectory, Musselin also identifies the trend towards allocating work according to contractual status, with teaching duties often assigned to part-time or contractual staff. In addition, she observes a trend towards employing mixed competency individuals (with both high-calibre research and management/administrative skills) to staff those realms that straddle academia and management such as technology transfer offices.

4.2 The Increasing Control over Academic Work and Loss of Professional Power

Identifying what characterises a profession is problematic, and various characteristics or 'traits' have been mooted over the years that attempt to capture what constitutes a profession and what distinguishes professionals from others. 'Trait theory', to which it is referred, has given way to more diverse ways of examining occupations, particularly in the wake of criticisms about the power and elitist position of the so-called higher professions and criticisms of the apparent objectivity of their scientific knowledge. Even before the advent of managerialism, the notion of the autonomous professional scientist disengaged from societal influences and external forces was criticised by social scientists theoretically associated with constructivist approaches to scientific knowledge (see McDonnell et al. 2009). This genre of work on the problematisation of scientific knowledge is complex and we will explain its substance a little further on when considering how the knowledge developed by academics is mediated by new managerial ideologies.

Whether professionalism has been defended or criticised, the concept is important since it is brought to bear in discussions of the changing role of academics. In addition, the impact of change on academics who educate all other professions has the potential to alter the occupational socialisation process and shape professional discourses across a range of occupations. First, let us pause for a moment to consider how professionalism has been constructed by key writers in the field. Freidson (2001, p. 17) identifies a couple of 'elementary' though key features of professionalism, namely, the notion that particular work is so specialised that it requires a level of training and experience that makes it inaccessible to those without this, and that is it not amenable to being standardized, rationalised, or commodified. In addition, Freidson argues that, "It involves direct control by specialized workers themselves of the terms, conditions, goals, and content of their particular work" (2001, p. 60).

In Freidson's (2001) *Professionalism: The Third Logic*, he defends the autonomy of professions against vested interests, arguing that strategies such as copyrighting, patenting, and casting knowledge as 'intellectual property' (key features of managerialism) undermine the basis for professionalism as an enterprise that enhances the common good. He postulates that these "… should be vigorously and unremittingly opposed, for it means impoverishing the public domain of knowledge and skill that is freely available for all" (p. 219). Freidson observes that the necessity of professionals to be independent of state control has been gravely undermined, and that "[p]rofessional ethics must claim independence from patron, state, and public that is analogous to what is claimed by a religious congregation" (p. 221).

The kind of issues highlighted by Freidson about professions in general have been taken up by those writing about the changing role of academics, the dominant view being that the professional autonomy of academics has been undermined by the recent changes. Managerialism, critics argue, is associated with a move away from the focus on the individual professional, instead imposing "a range of subjectivities that encourage individuals to behave in the best interests of the organisation" (Kolsaker 2008, p. 514). The primacy of the organisational goals over and above individual intellectual interests (ideally serving the greater good) and the concomitant surveillance and monitoring under entrepreneurial governance structures have come under attack. Olssen (2002) castigates managerialist reforms for the erosion of professional academic autonomy and freedom by turning academics into 'skilled entrepreneurs' who are expected to compete in the 'academic marketplace' by deliberately designing courses that attract students away from those of their colleagues. In the process, he argues, a regard for the intellectual merits of the programme is pitted against the need to dumb down standards and the appeal of the course to the requirements of the market.

The changes have also been framed in terms of the proletarianisation of academics, whose status and freedom is becoming akin to a salaried labourer (see Halsey 1992). Stilwell (2003) laments the manner in which academics are increasingly being commodified, whilst Doring (2002) cautions that academics in their altered role are in danger of becoming 'victims' of change rather than change agents, with detrimental effects on their enthusiasm for engaging with students. In a similar vein, Morley (2003) has focused on how the language of audit that has permeated academic work transforms academics into 'hegemonic tools' (reproducing a dominant ideology) rather than 'counter-hegemonic agents' (challenging dominant ideologies). Writing of the 'audit explosion', Power (1997, p. 2) posits that, "the senseless allocation of scarce resources to surveillance activities" impacts upon creative knowledge production. Controlling academics to engage in the monolingualism of managerialism, and keeping them "busy jumping through artificial hoops", according to Findlow (2008, p. 325), leaves little time for them to challenge policy and values, and ultimately "reduces the role of the knowledge producers in defining public knowledge" (p. 326). The development of such public knowledge is an important aspect of Freidson's (2001, p. 122) notion of the "higher goal [of professions] which may reach beyond that of those they are supposed to serve". Others have equated academic work under the reforms as an "academic assembly line" or "academic production line" (Parker and Jary 1995). Kolsaker (2008) spells out the increasing control over academics' work in Britain that began with the requirement to record course content and define teaching and learning outcomes, and progressed to include the observation of teaching, explicit student feedback, and a research assessment exercise whereupon quantitative indicators are mapped onto research activity. The most recent development is a biennial survey requiring faculty to record their time in half-hour slots (Kolsaker 2008).

An important point made by Musselin (2007) in response to the outcry about the reduction in the professional power of academics is that the increase in control over academics has largely been exercised from within their own ranks. She cites activities such as promotional assessments, editorial board decisions, and research assessment exercises, all of which are academic led. What she argues, however, is that other instruments of regulation have sprouted up alongside peer control, such as institutional surveillance and national requirements that allow others in the public sector to monitor academic work. As Musselin puts it, "[t]here is a great deal of evidence that professional power often supports institutional power … there is a global increase in the level and intensity of controls which are often enacted through the peer review process" (p. 6). Indeed, as we consider further on, whilst some researchers have found resistance to the managerial culture, others have found academics to be positively disposed to it.

4.3 The Impact of Increased Managerialism on the Nature of Teaching and Research

Whilst the application of managerial principles across the higher education sector has implications for academic work practices (as indicated earlier), it also potentially impacts upon teaching innovation and the type and status of knowledge developed within disciplines. Indeed, it has been posited that differences arise in terms of how knowledge is defined between the traditional value system within higher education and that of managerialism. As Findlow (2008, p. 318) notes:

> New managerialism approaches knowledge as a finished product, packaged, positive, objective, externally verifiable and therefore located outside the knower. By contrast, an 'academic exceptionalist' … view of knowledge places it in the minds of knowledgeable individuals, with the holder of the knowledge also the main agent of its transmission … This kind of expert or 'professional knowing', closely related to conventionally acquired 'wisdom' … is produced through an organic process between people in a culture of nurturing new ideas. The process is allowed to take as long as it takes, and knowledge is not seen as a finished product.

An example of how innovation in teaching is affected by managerialist values comes from Findlow (2008) in the case of England. Enhancement of funds for teaching and learning are made available there to address one of the national priority areas outlined by the Higher Education Funding Council for England (HEFCE 2002); however, as Findlow (2008) argues, the 'innovation' being funded is that deemed to be in keeping with institutional priorities that are in effect also state priorities. The language of managerialism ripples through the funding documentation

discourse of managerialism

calls, requiring academics who respond to sell themselves and their proposals in a similar managerialist light. Thus, Findlow argues, 'innovation' is already framed in the lexicon of efficiency and standardisation.

In relation to the impact of managerialism on the status of knowledge developed within disciplines, a key question is whether the application of a managerial model, with its intensification of surveillance, increased output control (Smeenk et al. 2009) and links with industry impacts upon academic freedom to create knowledge uninhibited by vested interests. De Vries and Lemmens' (2006) critical analysis of scientific 'evidence' drew attention to the way in which studies funded by industry were more likely to produce positive results about an intervention (or selectively omit negative findings) compared with those funded independently of vested interests. This problematisation of scientific knowledge—claims that such knowledge is socially mediated rather than epistemologically certain—has emanated from a realm of social science scholarship referred to as the 'Strong Programme' (see Mc-Donnell et al. 2009, p. 174) within constructivist approaches to scientific knowledge. Advanced by theorists such as Bloor (1991) and Latour (1987), the Strong Programme proposes that it is the scientific community that decides which knowledge claims become universal truths based on their own interests, and sets about 'proving' whatever wisdoms they wish to reinforce. They argue that the privileged status of scientific knowledge is culturally derived rather than emanating from some superior method for discovering truth.

It should be noted that the idea of scientific knowledge as essentially a closed system consistent with the dominant knowledge system of the day within the scientific community is not new; as far back as 1935, Fleck ([1935] 1979) identified this, and the problematisation of science was carried forward in the work of Kuhn (1962). Kuhn theorised closed systems as 'paradigms' that offered a particular worldview "in which problems are selected, and those educated and socialised within a scientific community follow a standard repertoire of methodologies and theories and, therefore, particular ways of seeing and interpreting the natural world" (McDonnell 2009, p. 173).

Thus, although the truth claims of science have for decades occupied the work of some social scientists, the renewed categorisation of standards of evidence that often determine success in research bids, privileging randomised-controlled trials in the recent period, raises new issues about the status of types of knowledge that academics are producing under managerialist discourses. Although evaluations of scientific quality have remained steadfastly within the scientific community rather than in the extra-scientific community (Enders et al., in press), external research-funding bodies often prioritise particular areas of research. In effect, this directs what research questions get asked and what knowledge gets created, notwithstanding the fact that, as we go on to consider, academics also find creative ways of following their own research interests. Nonetheless, prioritising particular modes of inquiry marginalises other realms of inquiry that are not deemed to be priorities according to the prevailing political discourses. In addition, the primacy given to some methodological stances over others in bidding for external funding reinforces particular perspectives on what counts as evidence.

The higher education sector has the potential to construct a range of forms of knowledge, including subjugated knowledge; indeed, arguably the creation of subjugated knowledge forms that challenge conventional thinking and that impact on dominant societal discourses has been a key outcome of academic freedom. The proliferation and construction of novel methodological strategies within some disciplines has come about by a critical analysis of conventional approaches to science. Moreover, questions about what counts as sound knowledge or what constitutes 'evidence' have traditionally been both determined and debated in university circles, notwithstanding that the 'outside' activities of some academics in the past, as indicated in an earlier section, served to build socio-technical networks that benefited their own scientific reputation (see Musselin 2007, p. 3).

Overall, the implications of managerialism on the university sector may be more far-reaching than simply regulating the work of what are believed to be work-shy academics; the characteristics and the type of knowledge being created within the sector may well be regulated, monitored and prescribed from outside, with far-reaching consequences for society, transforming scholars into 'knowledge workers' (Musselin 2007, p. 8).

5 Professional Socialisation Versus New Managerial Values: Empirical Studies at the Shop-Floor Level

The emerging picture in the literature thus far points to concerns about changes associated with managerialism, but to what extent are tensions felt between academics' worldviews acquired during occupational socialisation in an earlier period, and work practices and values emanating from the reformed approach to work? If these values are indeed at variance with one another, then the possibility emerges of a loss of organisational commitment. The impact of increased managerialism on the job performance of university staff has been the subject of a number of empirical investigations (e.g. Leišytė 2007; Smeenk et al. 2009; Findlow 2008; Enders et al., in press).

Let us turn now to explore some of this work that provides insights into how the discourse of managerialism is played out in actual academic settings, particularly in relation to job performance and work commitment.

Smeenk et al. (2009, p. 590) set about empirically testing a number of hypotheses on the effectiveness of managerialism, taking into account both its direct effect on performance ('direct effect argumentation') and its indirect effect on the quality of performance mediated by organisational commitment ('indirect effect argumentation'). Using a web survey that spanned six European countries conducted in 2004–2005, the researchers attempted to measure perceived level of managerialism, organisational commitment, and quality of job performances. Their findings challenged the notion of a 'managerial contradiction', that is that managerialism is counter-productive in bringing about the efficiency and effective quality to which it aspires (see Bryson 2004; Findlow 2008). Rather, they reported a modest positive effect of managerialism on the quality of performances. Smeenk et al. put

Survey findings

forward three possible explanations for their findings. The first and most simple of the explanations is that there is no conflict at all—management values are not inherently at variance with academic values. The second interpretation is that universities maintain their own character though adapting, negotiating, and modifying new management principles in line with their ethos. The third explanation of the findings is that universities are in transition, and any possible conflict may boil down to a suspicion of change that will dissipate over the years.

In Kolsaker's (2008) survey of English universities, respondents reported that managerialism augmented both performance and professionalism. In addition, the survey found that managerialism was believed by respondents to supersede trust between academic managers and academics, but not necessarily in a negative sense, as it ensured that academics are valued by society. With regard to professionalism, findings indicated that respondents accepted that external strategies of accountability were necessary to sustain academic professionalism. These findings are broadly at variance with the fears of managerialist pessimists leading Kolsaker to conclude that academics may be "more positive and pragmatic than much of the literature suggests" (p. 522). Kolsaker usefully draws attention to the sensitivities of time lapses in relation to her findings; sceptical commentators whose work proliferated in the 1990s may have been unnerved by the recentness of the shift towards managerialism; however, an acceptance of managerialism across various sectors in society may have signalled a level of acceptance of it amongst academics in the very recent period. Kolsaker (2008) refutes arguments of proletarianisation and demoralisation amongst the ranks of academics, and raises questions about whether managerialism and professionalism are actually incompatible.

The empirical findings of other studies (Findlow 2008; Kolsaker 2008; Leišyte 2007; Enders et al., in press) also suggest that academics carry on with their own affairs and play the game of managerialism at a formal level. Kolsaker (2008, p. 515) argues that although definitionally, managerialism constitutes a recognisable set of values and characteristics that confers privilege over one group (managers) to determine the work of others, in practice—as it is played out at the day-to-day environment—all social actors play their part in "bringing discourses into being ... relations are formed and reformed continually by a complex mix of personal, organisational and political variables" (p. 515). She proposes that managerialism has not spelled the disappearance of collegiality altogether even in the face of university reforms, but rather that new practices combine with older ones in complex ways. That there is some kind of mediation at play between new managerialism and university values as suggested in Kolsaker's (2008) analysis is also close to the possibilities nested in Smeenk et al.'s (2009) second explanation referred to earlier that universities adapt managerialism to their own circumstances. Drawing on empirical data from England, Germany, The Netherlands, and Austria, Enders et al. (in press) similarly indicate that academics adapt managerialism in ways to suit their own agendas. They found that academics were far from passive recipients of institutional change but rather tended to redefine their own ideas in broad terms to conform to research programmes that were likely to get funded. This practice of symbolic compliance was also found amongst academics in Leišyte's (2007) comparative case study of Dutch and English universities.

That recent changes in higher education have been received in a fluid way rather than by wholesale objection or acceptance, is also evidenced in Fanghanel's (2007) discourse analysis of academics' responses to a piece of institutional policy that incorporated both liberal and economic dimensions. How participants (based at a UK university) positioned themselves in relation to the policy was found to be fragmented, with individual participants at times concurring with the tenets of the text, whilst at other points distancing or taking issue with statements. The extent to which 'liberal education' aspects of the text were favoured over 'economic' components (and vice-versa), Fanghanel argues, are filtered through the individual academic's personal and professional experience, his/her views on the nature and purpose of knowledge, and his/her disciplinary socialisation. Thus, the agency of academics was brought to bear in how the document was interpreted.

6   Summary and Conclusion

Thus far, the general picture emerging in the literature is that of a profession in crisis, though moral panic about the situation is tempered by arguments that higher education has always been in transition, and in any case, a good deal of the increased regulation of academics is overseen by those within their own ranks via peer review. Whilst managerialist ideology is increasingly becoming a dominant discourse within universities, the extent to which it has superseded collegiality is debatable. Empirical studies indicate that managerialism has neither been wholeheartedly rejected nor accepted by academics, but rather has been received in a more fluid and haphazard way. It has also been acknowledged that there are variations in how managerialism has rolled out in terms of its timing, pace, and extent, in different social locations (Hood 1995; Pollitt and Bouckaert 2004). Even within the same country, cultural variations may be observed across universities (Shattock 1999), individual departments (Chan 2001), and in the attitudes of individual faculty (Davies 2007; Ylijoki 2003). Smeenk et al. (2009, p. 591) note that 'within variance' may be greater than 'between variance', that is those working in the same country or institution may construct and experience managerialism more differently from one another than do those across countries.

Musselin (2007) points to the lack of empirical data on how scientific knowledge and innovation is affected by the changes, whilst Kolsaker (2008) suggests that future research could expand existing knowledge by focusing on differences in academics' experiences in relation to discipline, degree of seniority, or particular management practices.

References

Bloor, D. (1991). *Knowledge and social imagery* (2nd ed.). Chicago: University of Chicago Press.

Bourdieu, P. (2004). *Science of science and reflexivity* (trans: Nice, R.). Chicago: University of Chicago Press.

Bryson, C. (2004). The consequences for women in the academic profession of the widespread use of fixed term contracts. *Gender, Work, and Organisation, 11*(2), 187–206.

Chan, K. (2001). The difficulties and conflict of constructing a model for teacher evaluation in higher education. *Higher Education Management, 13*(1), 93–111.

Davies, C. (2007). Grounding governance in dialogue? Discourse, practice and the potential for a new public sector organisational form in Britain. *Public Administration, 85*(1), 47–66.

De Vries, R., & Lemmens, T. (2006). The social and cultural shaping of medical evidence: case studies from pharmaceutical research and obstetric science. *Social Science & Medicine, 62*(11), 2694–2706.

Dearlove, J. (2002). A continuing role for academics: the governance of UK universities in the post Dearing era. *Higher Education Quarterly, 56*(3), 257–275.

Doring, A. (2002). Challenges to the academic role of change agent. *Journal of Further and Higher Education, 26*(2), 139–148.

Enders, J., & Musselin, C. (2008). Back to the future? The academic professions in the 21st century. In OECD (Ed.), *Higher education to 2030 volume 1: demography* (pp. 125–150). Paris: OECD.

Enders, J., Kehm, B. M., & Schimank, U. (in press). Turning universities into actors on quasi-markets: how governance affects research.

Fanghanel, J. (2007). Local responses to institutional policy: a discursive approach to positioning. *Studies in Higher Education, 32*(2), 187–205.

Findlow, S. (2008). Accountability and innovation in higher education: a disabling tension? *Studies in Higher Education, 33*(3), 313–329.

Fleck, L. ([1935] 1979). *Genesis and development of a scientific fact* (trans: Bradley, F., Trenn, T. J., & Merton, R. K.). Chicago: University of Chicago Press.

Freidson, E. (2001). *Professionalism: the third logic*. Chicago: University of Chicago Press.

Halsey, A. H. (1992). *The decline of Donnish dominion*. Oxford: Clarendon.

Higher Education Funding Council for England (HEFCE). (2002). *Teaching quality enhancement fund: funding arrangements 2002–2003 to 2004–2005*. Bristol: HEFCE.

Hood, C. (1995). The 'New Public Management' in the 1980s: variations on a theme. *Accounting, Organizations and Society, 20*(2/3), 93–109.

Kolsaker, A. (2008). Academic professionalism in the managerialist era: a study of English universities. *Studies in Higher Education, 33*(5), 513–525.

Kuhn, T. S. (1962). *The structure of scientific revolutions*. Chicago: University of Chicago Press.

Latour, B. (1987). *Science in action: how to follow scientists and engineers through society*. Cambridge: Harvard University Press.

Leišyte, L. (2007). *University governance and academic research: case studies of research units in Dutch and English universities*. Enschede: CHEPS/UT.

Mayo, P. (2009). Competitiveness, diversification and the international higher education cash flow: the EU's higher education discourse amidst the challenges of globalisation. *International Studies in Sociology of Education, 19*(2), 87–103.

McDonnell, O., Lohan, M., Hyde, A., & Porter, S. (2009). *Social theory, health & healthcare*. London: Macmillan.

Mill, J. S. (1965). Principles of political economy. In J. M. Robson (Ed.), *Collected works*. Toronto: Toronto University Presss

Morley, L. (2003). *Quality and power in higher education*. Berkshire: Society for Research into Higher Education (SRHE) and Open University Press.

Musselin, C. (2007). *The transformation of academic work: Facts and analysis* (Research and Occasional Paper Series: CSHE.4.07). Berkeley: Centre for Studies in Higher Education, University of California. http://cshe.berkeley.edu. Accessed 16 Nov 2010.

Neave, G. (1988). On the cultivation of quality, efficiency and enterprise: an overview of recent trends in higher education in Western Europe, 1986–1988. *European Journal of Education, 33*(1/2), 7–23.

Neave, G. (1998). The evaluative state revisited. *European Journal of Education, 33*(3), 265–284.

Olssen, M. (2002). The restructuring of tertiary education in New Zealand: governmentailty, neo-liberalism, democracy. *McGill Journal of Education, 37*(1), 57–88.

Parker, M., & Jary, D. (1995). The McUniversity: organisations, management and academic subjectivity. *Organization, 2*(2), 319–338.

Pollitt C., & Bouckaert, G. (2004). *Public management reform: a comparative analysis*. Oxford: Oxford University Press.

Power, M. (1997). *The audit society: rituals of verification*. Oxford: Oxford University Press.

Scott, J. W. (2002). The critical state of shared governance. *Academe, 88*(4), 41–48.

Shattock, M. (1999). Governance and management in universities: the way we live now. *Journal of Education Policy, 14*(3), 217–282.

Smeenk, S., Teelken, C., Eisinga, R., & Doorewaard, H. (2009). Managerialism, organisational commitment, and quality of job performances among European university employees. *Research in Higher Education, 50*(6), 589–607.

Stilwell, F. (2003). Higher education, commertial criteria and economic incentives. *Journal of Higher Education Policy and Management, 25*(2), 51–61.

Ylijoki, O. H. (2003). Entangled in academic capitalism? A case-study on changing ideals and pratices of university research. *Higher Education, 45*(3), 307–335.

The New Higher Education Professionals

Christian Schneijderberg and Nadine Merkator

1 Introduction

Responsibilities of university leadership and faculty management have increased and so have additional tasks in the areas of teaching and research. The growing complexity of universities results in differentiation and professionalisation of functions, tasks and roles for which specific knowledge, permanently updated information and competences are needed which are no longer available to all actors in the universities. Growing responsibilities and differentiation of functions and tasks increase the acceptance of professional working solutions (Klumpp and Teichler 2008, p. 169). For a special group of professionals who are not primarily active in teaching and research but prepare and support decisions of the management, establish services and actively shape the core functions of research and teaching Klumpp and Teichler (2008) introduced the term "Hochschulprofessionelle" (see also Teichler 2003, 2008; Kehm 2006a, b, c; Kehm et al. 2008a, 2010) which is translated with "higher education professionals" (HEPROs). Inspired by previous research (e.g. Gornitzka and Larsen 2004; Whitchurch 2004), Klumpp and Teichler conducted a quantitative and qualitative survey at two German universities in 2005 in order to evaluate the size and functions of the emerging group of HEPROs. They found a heterogeneous group of HEPROs, mostly highly qualified, satisfying the growing need of university management for systematic knowledge about the university and releasing academic and administrative staff from a variety of functions and tasks (Klumpp and Teichler 2008, pp. 169–171); further characteristics of the group are a high affinity and commitment to the areas of teaching and research, and an on-the-job acquisition of knowledge and skills. The authors summarize that HEPROs are

C. Schneijderberg (✉) · N. Merkator
International Centre for Higher Education Research Kassel (INCHER-Kassel),
University of Kassel, Moenchebergstr. 17, 34109 Kassel, Germany

B. M. Kehm, U. Teichler (eds.), *The Academic Profession in Europe: New Tasks and New Challenges,* The Changing Academy – The Changing Academic Profession in International Comparative Perspective 5, DOI 10.1007/978-94-007-4614-5_5, © Springer Science+Business Media Dordrecht 2013

experts in the field of higher education and have a "high degree of familiarity with the core functions of higher education institutions" (Klumpp and Teichler 2008, p. 170). In Germany, as in Great Britain, Norway or the United States, for instance, typical positions of members of this group are assistant to the Dean or research co-ordinator, typical working areas are internationalisation and international mobility, organisational and staff development, quality assurance or student services (Rosser 2004, p. 319; Klumpp and Teichler 2008; Whitchurch 2008a, p. 377; Krücken et al. 2009, pp. 18–19; Kehm et al. 2010, pp. 32–33; Macfarlane 2011a, p. 61).

It can be argued that Klumpp and Teichler's concept of HEPROs questions the static perception of an administrative academic divide when focusing on functions and tasks instead. A different understanding is presented by the recent concept of "third space professionals" (Whitchurch 2008b, 2010a) which creates an independent sphere for an emerging group of university personnel whose professional identity is neither strictly academic nor strictly administrative. However, this group does not enter the academic space, according to Whitchurch. Whereas the concept of the "para-academic" (Macfarlane 2011a) strictly remains in the academic sphere referring to the "unbundling" of the holistic concept of academic practice and subdivision of academic work by Kinser (2002, p. 13) into "para-academic roles" (Coaldrake 2000, p. 21), Macfarlane argues that the academic all-rounder is disappearing. According to Macfarlane, the rise of the para-academics is a result of the growing numbers and up-skilling of administrative and professional support staff and a parallel de-skilling of the all-round academic (Macfarlane 2011a, pp. 62–63).

Most studies analysing the evolution of administrative university staff situate HEPROs in university administration (Gumport and Pusser 1995; Leslie and Rhoades 1995; Gornitzka et al. 1998; Blümel et al. 2010). Analysing the shift in administration in Norwegian universities Gornitzka et al. (1998, p. 26) identified the emerging group of HEPROs as part of the "silent managerial revolution" in university administration: the replacement of clerks by administrative officers and managers. Omitting the technical terms for the *new* university personnel has created numerous denotations: Rhoades refers to the activists of the silent managerial revolution as administrators or "managerial professionals" (Rhoades 1998), in a publication on student services as "support professionals" (Rhoades 2001, p. 628); in a comparative study on quality management HEPROs in the United States are called "managerial professors" but in Austria "administrators" (Rhoades and Sporn 2002b, p. 381); Rhoades and Sporn (2002a, p. 385) introduce the term "non-academic professionals", and refer to non-academic professionals and academic professionals as "administrators". Also, using the terminology of "managers" for "academic and non-academic managers" or "woman academic managers" alike (Deem 1998) or changing the perception of them towards "new professionals" (Gornall 1999) with an active role between strategy and innovation (Kallenberg 2007) adds several aspects to the overall picture of the HEPROs and their tasks.

Currently, Klumpp and Teichler's "higher education professionals" seems to be the most advanced conception. It is the temporary endpoint of a rich body of research accumulated in the past two decades, mainly from Australia, Great Britain, Norway and the United States. Two, partly separate, partly interwoven trails can be identified: first, a quantitative research trail which grasps the bureaucratisation of universities and growing numbers of academic and administrative positions; second, a qualitative research trail which sheds light on administrative positions in a shifting working environment and challenging relationships between academic and administrative personal and HEPROs. From the rich body of literature qualitative aspects of functions, tasks and roles are extracted and analysed. In the last section, the interface between academic staff and HEPROs will be discussed. Therefore, the overlap of functions, tasks and roles of academic staff is analysed as an outlook for further research. Some evidence can be presented for the shifts in tasks, functions and roles from academic staff to HEPROs.

2   Higher Education and University Personnel at Stake

2.1   A Sketch of the Bigger Picture

The post-industrial environment, namely the "knowledge society" (Drucker 1968; Bell 1973; Stehr 1994) increases the pressures on universities to develop expertise (Brint 1994; Stehr and Grundmann 2010) in order to respond to the rising expectations of relevance, stratification of higher education institutions due to the quality discussion, the substantive changes in curricula, the importance of teaching and learning in a mass higher education system or the importance of lifelong education (Teichler 2007a, pp. 18–19). Recent developments in higher education draw attention to support and service functions of teaching and research, tasks formerly looked at as marginal by academics, now becoming constituent and essential for the success of teaching and research. Gornitzka and Larsen (2004) studied the process of incremental change of the administrative work force for Norwegian universities and found that "in some respects it corresponds to the type of change that results from stable and ordinary responses to environmental change" (Gornitzka and Larsen 2004, p. 468). Organisational change as a response to changing environmental conditions is also an issue for Dill (1982, 1996, 1999); Rhoades (1984); DiMaggio and Powell (1991); Sporn (2001); Gumport and Pusser (1995); Leslie and Rhoades (1995); Finkelstein and Schuster (2001); Harloe and Perry (2005); Teichler (2007a, b). Drivers of this development are:

- The growing autonomy of higher education institutions and new forms of governance in higher education (e.g. Braun and Merrien 1999; Amaral et al. 2003; Kehm and Lanzendorf 2005, 2006, 2007; de Boer et al. 2007);
- Commercialisation of science (e.g. Slaughter and Rhoades 1993; Slaughter and Leslie 1997; Coaldrake 2000; Münch 2006, 2007, 2009);
- Massification of higher education (e.g. Trow 1974, 1999)—although regarded as an overestimated factor by Teichler (1998);
- Globalisation and internationalisation (e.g. Altbach and Teichler 2001; Teichler 2004); and

- The Bologna Process[1] with its policy-driven action lines, e.g. promotion of mobility or of comparable systems of quality assurance (Bologna Declaration 1999; Prag Communiqué 2001; Berlin Communiqué 2003; Neave and Amaral 2008).

Part of the institutional responses to the challenges from outside is the creation of new positions and functions, e.g. for Germany in the areas of quality enhancement, curriculum design, etc. and fostering the growth of already-existing functions, e.g. for Germany: research coordinators, student counselling, internationalisation, etc. of HEPROs. Also, support units for rectors or presidents, vice-rectors or vice-presidents, deans, etc. are being enlarged or newly created.

When analysing the emerging group of HEPROs, one also has to keep in mind that national specificities have a path dependency (Teichler 2007a, p. 16). This becomes evident when dealing with the staff structure of universities, e.g. countries with administrative personnel being employed by the university or being civil servants or both. Staff structure is an issue of power as well. In the United States, non-academic administrators, not only in top management but also in middle-management positions, obtain considerable power (e.g. Becher and Kogan 1992; Rhoades 1998; Middlehurst 2004). A contrary case is Norway, where HEPROs "portray their role as 'low-key' in the interface with academics and especially in relation to elected academic leaders" (Gornitzka and Larsen 2004, p. 464).

2.2 University Personnel in the Arena

The need expressed by Rhoades to "overcome the prevailing simple dichotomy of administrative versus academic staff" (Rhoades 1998, p. 116; also Lewis and Altbach 1995) is still a contemporary need, although "higher education institutions have become multi-professional organisations" (Henkel 2005, p. 163). The organisational change of universities and the accompanying functional differentiation of university personnel have led to a mutation of the dichotomy into a trias, at least. The heuristic approach of professionalisation (e.g. Gornitzka and Larsen 2004; Klumpp and Teichler 2008; Whitchurch 2009) of the trias has gained momentum in the past years as explanatory for the differentiation of university personnel or of management in public domains in general (e.g. Evetts 2003, 2009; Noordegraaf 2007; Blümel et al. 2011). Klumpp and Teichler (2008) added the group of HEPROs to administrative and academic personnel.[2] The term HEPROs has made its way as being used for all professionals working at a university, including professors, in the exploratory concept of "borderless professionals" (Middlehurst 2010). As finding a common terminology has proven to be rather difficult, Whitchurch (2008b)

---

[1] The German sociologist Stichweh (2008) refers to the Bologna Process as the social form of mass higher education.

[2] The *Dearing Report* mentions "higher education personnel professionals" (Dearing 1997, para. 14.15).

suggests the "third space"between the administrative-professional and academic spheres of activity. Whether the identity-based endeavour of a new space will unlock the Gordian knot in overcoming the differences of academic and administrative realms has to remain an open question for the time being.

Nevertheless, it is necessary to discuss and agree on a terminology in order to describe, analyse, and understand the areas of work inside universities and respective positions. In doing so, the three terms academic and administrative personnel and HEPROs are used in the following. The explanation of HEPROs given by Klumpp and Teichler or the concept of a third space by Whitchurch suggest varying hybrid or blended positions and functions between "traditionally" academic and administrative tasks. Therefore, a differentiated analysis of these hybrid or blended positions and functions requires the discussion of the development of positions, functions and activities of academic and administrative personnel. As will be shown below, many researchers approach the issue from the angle of expansion of administrative tasks and bureaucratisation of universities. However, this is just one side of the coin.

The growing demands for organisational development and professionalisation of university governance at central and departmental level have been identified as causes for the evolution and differentiation of functions and tasks in the area between administration, management, research and teaching. Teichler (2005) analyses four basic areas of tasks and functions:

1. Preparation and support of university management: e.g. assistants to the rector/ president, dean, head of a unit in central administration.
2. Services: e.g. librarians, career consultants.
3. New hybrid sphere between management and services: e.g. evaluation officers, academic controlling, head of the international office, coordinators of study programmes, managers of continuing education.
4. Differentiation of research and teaching functions: e.g. full time student counsellors, curriculum design, coordinators of research clusters.

The varying tasks and functions shown in the list stress the need for a multi-dimensional approach to define HEPROs.

Kehm et al. (2008b) show that coordination and organisational development is only one part of the job description and expertise; others are preparation and execution of university management decisions; information generation, processing and distribution, making use of existing knowledge, student learning and student development, and administrative activities. Kehm et al. argue that differentiation of tasks and functions are typical for a professionalisation process: the evolution of university governance breaks down the formerly clear-cut borders of services and management and makes them highly permeable (Kehm et al. 2008b, p. 199). According to them, for Germany, at least four lines of evolution can be identified:

1. For already long-existing tasks and functions in administration, higher qualifications are required, and the job description is altering as well, e.g. clerical staff in charge of student records.

2. Growing requirements in occupations formerly having a rather low level of differentiation make them subject to a process of professionalisation, e.g. student counselling.
3. Tasks and activities, which used to be part of other job descriptions, are becoming full-time positions, e.g. planning and design of study programmes.
4. New tasks and activities are created in universities, e.g. transfer of knowledge and technology or fundraising (Kehm et al. 2008b).

The combination of the analytical frameworks of Teichler and Kehm et al. constitute a complex matrix. The different elements will be visible in the following. Nevertheless, it is evident that the sphere of HEPROs does not yet exist as such. Whitchurch (2008b) has made a valuable first approach in defining the "third space". Unfortunately, many of the research results of the past two decades remain outside the "third space" and its facility for interaction with wider contexts. Moreover, the majority of studies focus on the expansion and differentiation of administrative activities, tasks and functions, while the differentiation of teaching and research functions as described by Teichler (2005) and Kehm et al. (2008b) is missing.

3   From Quantitative to Qualitative Approaches: Bureaucratisation, Identity and Professionalisation

3.1   Quantitative Approaches Towards Academic and Administrative Personnel

The development sketched above has substantial influence on universities. The dichotomy of academic and administrative spheres prevails, as administration and bureaucratisation are regarded as threatening the academic sphere. For the United States, Leslie and Rhoades (1995) conducted a literature analysis. Referring to Bergmann (1991), Leslie and Rhoades interpret the growth of expenditures for presidents, deans, and their assistants compared with teaching budgets in the 1980s as an acceleration of a four-decade pattern. Nationwide, the expenditure for administrative costs[3] per full-time equivalent student in the 1980s was even higher. Referring to Halstead (1991) the share of the so-called education expenditures spent on administration[4] increased by 2.7 % for all public universities, while the instruction share declined by 2 % nationally between 1973/1974 and 1985/1986. With respect to Massy and Warner's (1990, 1991), evaluation of the *Higher Education General Information Survey* (HEGIS)/*Integrated Postsecondary Education Data System* (IPEDS) for the period from 1975 to 1986, Leslie and Rhoades add that administrative costs increased faster than academic costs in all higher education

---

[3] Not including costs for administration of libraries, student services, research, and physical plant.

[4] Including institutional support, student services, and academic support; but excluding libraries.

sectors[5]: per year, in real terms, the median rate of increase for administrative and support expenditures was 4 %, but it was less than 3 % for academic expenditure (Leslie and Rhoades 1995, p. 187). Leslie and Rhoades calculated the changes in the number and salaries of administrators using Equal Employment Opportunity Commission data from 1975 to 1985. Data indicate a 6 % growth in full-time faculty; an 18 % growth of the so-called executive, administrative, and managerial employees; and a 61 % growth for the so-called other professionals, who are degree-holding employees often accounted for in administrative categories. In the following 5 years, from 1985 to 1990, the increase was 9, 14 and 28 %, respectively. Academic personnel did grow at a slower rate than secretarial and clerical staff. A decline was observed among service and maintenance personnel (Leslie and Rhoades 1995, pp. 187–188). Between 1971/1972 and 1984/1985 a general decline of salaries was noted. The average real salaries of faculty and administrators declined by 16 and 13.1 %, respectively. Data provided by Hansen and Guidugli (1990) and Levy (1990) who analysed the disaggregated figures for administrators, reveal increasing salary dispersion among administrators, as well as among academic personnel (Leslie and Rhoades 1995, p. 188).

Further statistical data on the administrative growth in higher education in the United States, more specifically in the State of California, is provided by Gumport and Pusser (1995). They did an analysis of the University of California System for the 25 years period from 1966/1967 to 1991/1992. It was a period of considerable growth: expenditure for the nine campuses, system-wide administration, and auxiliary enterprises taken together was just more than US$ 3.7 billion in 1966–1967 and just more than US$ 9.8 billion in 1991–1992. Altogether this is an increase of 164 % (in constant 1993 dollars). Student full-time equivalents rose from 79,293 (1966/1967) to 156,371 (1991/1992), an increase of just over 97 %. Also, the number of employees grew. The permanently budgeted personnel increased by 104 % from 33,305 (1966/1967) to 68,024 (1991/1992; Gumport and Pusser 1995, pp. 494–495). The growth of expenditure was not the same for all staff categories: the general category administration increased by more than 400 % more rapidly than instruction with 175 %. The total system expenditure shows an increase of 164 % in comparison. The number of positions in administration did grow nearly two and a half times faster than positions in the category instruction. Even during state recession between 1986/1987 and 1991/1992 the number of positions in the category administration increased twice as fast as the number of positions in instruction. For the entire University of California System in 1966/1967, approximately 6 dollars were spent on instruction for each dollar spent on administration compared with approximately 3 dollars spent on instruction for each dollar spent on administration in 1991/1992 (Gumport and Pusser 1995, p. 500).

A third account of the growth of the higher education system in the United States from 1976 to 1995 is presented by Rhoades and Sporn (2002a, see also Rhoades and Sporn 2002b) for full-time and part-time positions. While academic staff in relation to other professional employees represented 69 % in 1976 it decreased to 61 % in

---

[5] This respective increase took place in private colleges, as well.

1995 (Rhoades and Sporn 2002a, pp. 17–18). Rhoades and Sporn further differentiate administrative positions in executive/administrators and support professionals/managerial professionals.

All three accounts from the United States show a considerable growth of the group of administrative personnel for the indicated periods. Gumport and Pusser consider the dramatic increase of administration as "evidence of bureaucratic accretion with respect to expenditures in the University of California" (Gumport and Pusser 1995, pp. 500–501) while Leslie and Rhoades (1995, p. 189) stress that it is crucial to understand the causes for the increase of administrative costs. Unfortunately, data is aggregated at a very high level and tells nothing about the "nature of or the explanations for spiralling administrative costs". The three studies show how the phenomenon of administrative growth was grasped as bureaucratisation, reasons and explanations were sought and a trend towards differentiation of administrative personnel became evident.

Another view on growing numbers of administrative staff was added by Visakorpi (1996). In Finnish universities, due to a perceived rise of the administrative burden of academic staff, the latter asked for and supported the increase of administrative staff—this pattern continues even in times of budget cuts, especially at departmental level (Visakorpi 1996, pp. 38–39). Gornitzka et al. (1998, p. 42) found a similar ambivalence among faculty concerning the striving for less administrative work for themselves and growing numbers of administrative staff in Norwegian universities. Based on official statistics by the Ministry of Education from 1994 Visakorpi shows that, from 1987 to 1992, teaching staff increased by 5.5 %, total non-teaching staff by 20 % and administrative staff by 39 %. The percentage of teaching staff in relation to other personnel altered from 52.7 % in 1987 to 49.3 % in 1993 (Visakorpi 1996, p. 39). Blümel et al. (2010, p. 159), referring to the data of Visakorpi, found a rise of 39 % of the group of non-academic staff: mainly due to a considerable rise of highly qualified administrative personnel and a decline of technical and administrative staff with lower levels of qualifications by 11.8 %. With respect to many new tasks of the modern university Visakorpi assumes: "Non-teaching or non-academic personnel will increasingly be academic; they will need more and more education, including languages, as special skills" (Visakorpi 1996, p. 40).

Gornitzka et al., in the publication *Bureaucratisation of Universities* (1998), analyse the expansion of administrative and academic personnel at four Norwegian universities and specify the trends of administrative differentiation. Data was drawn from the Norwegian civil servants' data register and the research personnel register. In addition, several surveys were conducted: a survey among all staff members with the rank of assistant professor and higher at the universities of Bergen, Oslo, Trondheim, Tromso and 50 interviews with senior administrative and academic staff at the universities of Bergen and Oslo (Gornitzka et al. 1998, pp. 22–23). From 1987 to 1995 the number of total administrative staff, e.g. clerical positions and administrative officers and managers, increased by 58 %. Academic positions increased by 48 % during the same period. The person-years performed by administrative officers and managers more than doubled within less than a decade (from 584 person-years in 1987 to 1,469 person-years in 1995). Also, from 1991 onwards the numbers of professional administrators (administrative officers and managers) outnumbered the clerical positions (Gornitzka et al. 1998, p. 25). Gornitzka et al. also looked at the qualifications and types of positions of administrative officers and managers. In 1993, half of the administrative officers and managers held a university degree, and about 15 % were employed in an academic position (Gornitzka et al. 1998, p. 26). Gornitzka et al. also evaluated the time academic staff spent for administrative activities. In 1991, academic staff spent on average 17 % of the total working day on administration. This percentage remained almost unchanged compared with 1981 and 1970, but shows a slight increase compared with 14 % in 1966 (Gornitzka et al. 1998, p. 27).

The growth of academic and administrative personnel was analysed in more detail in the publication *Towards Professionalisation? Restructuring of Administrative Work Force in Universities* (Gornitzka and Larsen 2004). The data was drawn from the Norwegian civil servants statistics and data from interviews conducted at the University of Oslo. Extending the analysis at the four universities in Norway, Gornitzka and Larsen found that an additional 1,000 person-years (from 1,500 to more than 2,500) in administrative positions were established from 1987 to 1999. The most striking is the growth rate of positions of higher administrative staff with 215 % from 1987 to 1999. In the same period, the number of positions for clerical staff declined by 28 % (Gornitzka and Larsen 2004, p. 458). The number of administrators with a university degree grew as well.

Germany can be described as a latecomer in discussing the evolution of university personnel. Similar to the United States (Gumport and Pusser 1995; Leslie and Rhoades 1995), Finland (Visakorpi 1996), and Norway (Gornitzka et al. 1998; Gornitzka and Larsen 2004), Rhoades and Sporn (2002a), Krücken et al. (2009) and Blümel et al. (2010) found for Germany a general growth of staff at higher education institutions. In Germany, the relative proportion of administrative (63 %) and academic personnel (37 %) is almost three to two (Rhoades and Sporn 2002a, p. 13). No time series data is available that differentiates among administrative positions. Data on administrative positions separate top-level administrators (*im höheren Dienst*; Rhoades and Sporn 2002a) holding a university degree from those lower level positions for persons without a university degree (*nicht im höheren Dienst*). University-trained administrators in central administration, technical positions, library, and other positions represented about 4 % of all administrative positions. Looking only at universities, academic personnel grew by 7.3 % while administrative personnel slightly declined by 0.1 % from 1992 to 1998. Substantive numbers of growth can be shown for Universities of Applied Sciences (*Fachhochschulen*), where positions for academic personnel grew by 24 %, and administrative positions increased by 20 % (Rhoades and Sporn 2002a, p. 14). Rhoades and Sporn concluded that "administrative costs and positions are significant in German higher education" (Rhoades and Sporn 2002a).

Blümel et al. (2010) provide a more elaborated and detailed picture on numbers of academic and administrative personnel for German higher education based on the analysis of data on higher education personnel from 1992 to 2007, provided by the national *HIS ICEland Database*. Overall, numbers of personnel increased in higher education institutions in Germany. Rather surprisingly the increase is due to a growth of academic personnel by 28.3 %, while administrative staff increased by 1.1 %. With respect to the latter, from 1992 to 2007, a shift from lower to higher grades becomes evident, The growth of administrative personnel in the higher grade (*höherer Dienst*) is most striking in administrative function/HEPROs (90.1 %) compared with library services (10 %), technical staff (12.5 %) and other staff (33.8 %; Blümel et al. 2010, pp. 164–165). With regard to 1992–2007 comparison of higher grade staff in the same four areas of work, the ratio provides further details on the shift towards the administrative function of HEPROs. The ratio increased from 55.3 to 67 % while the ratio of library (14.3–10 %), technical (21.6–15.4 %) and other staff (8.9–7.6 %) decreased (Blümel et al. 2010, p. 166). Blümel et al. (2010) did not find any evidence for an expansion of non-academic staff in relation to academic staff. However, they found a shift from lower to higher positions of non-academic personnel, similar to the findings of Gornitzka et al. (1998).

For Germany, the findings above can be complemented by quantitative results from the study *The Role of the New Higher Education Professions for the Redesign of Teaching and Studying (HEPRO)* from 2010 (Kehm et al. 2010; Schneijderberg and Merkator 2011). In a survey at 11 universities[6], a ratio of HEPROs to professors was found which is on average 63–100 (Kehm et al. 2010; Schneijderberg and Merkator 2011). The majority of HEPROs is female (60 %) and 88 % hold a university degree—about one quarter a Ph.D.—while 7 % graduated from a *Fachhochschule*. Only 5 % passed a vocational training and were promoted into a position in the upper grade during their career in university administration (*Praktikeraufstieg*). The disciplinary background of HEPROs varies: 39 % come from the humanities; 30 % from social sciences and 26 % from natural sciences and mathematics. Many have experience in research and teaching; 46 % of the HEPROs hold academic positions; 74 % are employed in a permanent position; 55 % have a permanent contract and 70 % work full-time. More than 500 different names of organisational units were mentioned in the questionnaire. The organisational localisation is rather heterogeneous: 32 % work on department level, about 25 % in central administration and about the same percentage could not be situated at all. The units HEPROs are assigned to were established in 2004, on average. About two-thirds of all respondents reported that the unit, at least partially, takes charge of new activities, functions and tasks (Kehm et al. 2010, pp. 31–32).

The research by Gornitzka et al. (1998) and Gornitzka and Larsen (2004) on Norwegian Universities mark the turning point of the discussion about bureaucratisation of higher education and growth of administrative and academic staff and the results of the study on HEPROs in Germany mark a temporary endpoint of the quantitative research trail. The mixed methods approach of Gornitzka and Larsen (2004) expanded the theoretical basis from organisational theory to the sociology of professions. The mixed-methods approach and theoretical underpinning by the

---

[6] The study included universities of different size, from different parts of Germany, some were research-intensive universities, some more teaching oriented, some technical universities.

sociology of organisation and sociology of professions have substantial influence on the recent enquiry about HEPROs from Germany (Klumpp and Teichler 2008; Blümel et al. 2010; Kehm et al. 2010; Schneijderberg and Merkator 2011).

Qualitative research which sheds light on administrative positions, functions and tasks in a shifting working environment will be explored in the Sect. 3.2. Starting from a basic analysis of administration further aspects and features will be integrated which indicate a shift towards an overlap of administrative and academic tasks and functions.

3.2 Qualitative Approaches Towards Administration and Higher Education Professionals

Administration is characterised by at least three aspects: first as an act or process, second as an activity and third as a definition of a group of people. As an act or process administration is used for the management of a government or large organisation. Administration as an activity of a government or large organisation expresses the exercise of its powers and duties. Administration also stands for a group of people who manage or direct an organisation. All three aspects are important when trying to understand and define the evolution of administrative and academic university staff individually and the relationship between them (Clark 1984; Becher and Kogan 1992; Barnett and Middlehurst 1993; Boyer et al. 1994; Lewis and Altbach 1995; Gumport and Pusser 1995; Leslie and Rhoades 1995; El-Khawas 1996; Lockwood 1996; Gornitzka et al. 1998; McInnis 1992, 1998; Coaldrake 2000; Middlehurst 2000; Rhoades and Sporn 2002a, b; Kogan and Teichler 2007a, b; Teichler 2008; Krücken et al. 2009, Blümel et al. 2010; Kehm et al. 2010; Macfarlane 2011a).

Lockwood (1996), similar to many of the authors named above, starts by situating administrative staff in contrast to academic staff in the institutional context. In the institutional setting of the university, the responsibility is placed mainly on the shoulders of academically qualified individuals in a comparatively non-hierarchical and pluralistic structure of both work and management. Just as institutionalised is the academics focus on peer groups outside the institutions, which tends to be stronger than the inward orientation. The institutionalisation of positions, appraisal and power encountered by administrative staff is more varied as compared with academic staff. Lockwood identifies six characteristics of the administrative model in Great Britain which is rather similar to the situation in Germany (e.g. Bosetzky and Heinrich 1989, pp. 53–54; Naschold and Bogumil 2000), and which is slowly but constantly eroding:

- Administration is recognised as an entity similar to other units in the organisational structure,
- Careers are structured according to the public service,

- A high proportion of administrative staff is permanently employed,[7]
- Staff have high commitment to the employing institution and low external orientation,
- In the case of Great Britain, the majority of personnel in administration are generalists, and
- Although there is an assumption of impartiality of advise and objectivity in information functions of administrative personnel, the administrative activities include decision-making power. (Lockwood 1996, pp. 44–45).

In Germany, a twofold system persists. For routine administrative activities the majority of staff does a vocational training. For administrative activities requiring some decision making and operational independence staff with a higher education degree is employed. The proportion of the latter group in administration is growing (Klumpp and Teichler 2008; Blümel et al. 2010). Lockwood (1996) issues a warning that the on-going erosion of the internal administrative model described above and resulting from shifts in the intra-administrative interface will cause a loss of the expertise of dedicated generalists.

The perception of the development of administration in universities and the growth in numbers of HEPROs are closely connected to the concept of bureaucratisation (Gumport and Pusser 1995; Leslie and Rhoades 1995; Gornitzka et al. 1998; Blümel et al. 2010). Gornitzka et al. (1998) outline the three concepts of administrative bureaucratisation with, first, the classical Weberian type of rational administration, second, the perversion with bureaucracy becoming a purpose in its own right, and, third, bureaucratisation occurring due to the growth of an organisation. In the Weberian view, bureaucratic work is organised and conducted according to formal rules within a set hierarchy, which itself is based on a rational legal authority. Staff is recruited based on formal qualifications and competences to fulfil designated working roles and functions.

For analysing the development of universities, the third concept of bureaucratisation is significant. This is the case when administrative personnel is regarded as part of the organisation that does not carry out the primary functions of research and teaching but is responsible for regulation, supervision and support of the people executing the primary working tasks. Consequently, bureaucratisation in this sense occurs when staff positions for administration increase more than those for teaching and research within the institution (Gornitzka et al. 1998, p. 23). The explanation may apply to strictly administrative work, e.g. secretary or processing work, accounting, etc.; however, it becomes disputable when considering services constituent for research and teaching provided by personnel not primarily in charge of research and teaching. Only when arguing on the basis of the dichotomy of academic and non-academic personnel, the clear-cut conceptualisation persists. When differentiating in positions and roles (also done by Gornitzka et al. 1998, p. 24; Gornitzka and Larsen 2004, pp. 456–457), the bureaucratisation concept gets blurred

---

[7] For Norway, Gornitzka et al. (1998, pp. 38–39) see the aspect of professional ethics connected with the capacity of administration to react to environmental change.

(e.g. services with direct influence on teaching and learning, e.g. HEPROs giving courses on general qualifications, personal presentation skills or how to write a job application). As an example related to research, institutional research (Fincher 1978a, b; Terenzini 1993; Delaney 1997; Teodorescu 2006; Auferkorte-Michaelis 2008) can be pointed out, at least for the case of Germany.

Kogan (2007) argues that changing tasks in higher education have led to changes in internal power relationships among administrative and academic staff (see also Clegg 2007, p. 409), which includes a precipitation of academic hybrid roles (see also Macfarlane 2010, p. 63). Kogan describes the responses of universities to external changes as reshaping of organisational and power structures. Many of the changes have been camouflaged describing them as bureaucratisation. According to Kogan, bureaucratisation is being used in two different ways. On one hand, it means a shift from individual and academic power within the often "mythic collegium" (Kogan 2007, p. 162) to the system or institution of the university. On the other, it means a growth of power, including the growth in numbers of non-academic administration staff. Kogan identifies the first as the major phenomenon and the second as "a possible but not invariant consequence" of this phenomenon (Kogan 2007, p. 162). The question of power shifts might be related to a rise of sheer numbers of administrative staff but it could as well be sought in the assignment and position of administrative personnel (Lockwood 1996), their higher level of qualification and the creation of new areas of work and/or development of areas of work in university management and the organisation of work in central and non-central units (e.g. Leslie and Rhoades 1995; Rhoades and Sporn 2002a, b; Gornitzka and Larsen 2004; Rosser 2004; Klumpp and Teichler 2008).

The questions raised and issues addressed will be discussed when defining administrative personnel, functions, tasks and activities. The definition of administrative personnel is used as a vehicle to extract aspects for further characterising the role of HEPROs. The role of HEPROs, the meaning and implications of administrative activities and the changes in internal power relationships of administrative and academic staff will become apparent in the following part.

3.3   A Collage of Features of Higher Education Professionals

Finding definitions of who belongs to administration was and is like squaring the circle. Scholars dealing with university administration are rather deflating the endeavour with creating publication titles such as *The Deadly Dull Issue of University Administration? Good Governance, Managerialism and Organising Academic Work* (Dearlove 1998) or *Fear and Loathing in University Staffing: The Case of Australian Academic and General Staff* (Dobson and Conway 2003). So, the extensive accounting of staff positions will be complemented by discussing definitions of positions and roles in university administration. Official classifications and schemes give a clue, but fail to give a satisfying picture. However, as Gumport and Pusser point out, for an analysis of administration static accounting misses a substantial part of administration and can only provide a global view of an institutional support category (Gumport and Pusser 1995, pp. 496–497; see also Leslie and Rhoades 1995, p. 189). Arguing from the point of view of expenditures and positions Gumport and Pusser show that an all-encompassing understanding of administrative functions is necessary, not being limited by reporting categories. They encourage research of subcategories, e.g. when operationalising the subcategory academic administration, which "contains expenditures which are identified as administrative support and management functions in the primary missions. It includes expenditures for academic deans, associate and assistant deans and their staffs, travel, supplies, and expenditure" (Gumport and Pusser 1995, p. 497). Practical reasons encourage the use of traditional categories of office and personnel when operationalising administration. Items such as functions and indefinite administrative complexities are difficult to operationalyse based on the available data (Gumport and Pusser 1995).

An alternative approach towards defining administration and administrative positions the exclusive approach was chosen by Gornitzka et al. (1998) for Norwegian universities. Gornitzka et al. (1998) emphasise that the dichotomy of academic and non-academic positions is too simple for an in-depth analysis. They stress that "types of non-academic positions have to be differentiated so as to single out those whose primary task is university administration" (Gornitzka et al. 1998, p. 24). Therefore, positions categorised as "technical auxiliary staff, such as laboratory assistants, engineers and university librarians" (Gornitzka et al. 1998) and maintenance staff, such as cleaning personnel, gardeners and janitors are excluded. University administration in the Norwegian context is constituted by "two basic groups of non-academic positions: clerical staff and higher administrative staff [sometimes Gornitzka et al. use 'officers' instead of staff; note CS], the latter being the core administrators at universities ranging from consultants, middle and senior managers" (Gornitzka et al. 1998). Still, Gornitzka et al. hint to the fact "that in many instances clerical functions in fact verge on being administrative activities" (Gornitzka et al. 1998) which makes it necessary to include them in the university administration category. In a later publication, Gornitzka and Larsen (2004, p. 456) define non-academic staff as technical auxiliary staff, e.g. laboratory assistants, engineers, and maintenance, e.g. gardeners, janitors, cleaning staff. Administrative staff is divided into clerical staff and professional administrative staff/higher administrative staff.

The approach of exclusion was also used by Blümel et al. (2010), when analysing the numbers of administrative and academic staff in German higher education using official statistics. The rather rigid German status system[8] has four categories: lower grade (*einfacher Dienst*), middle grade (*mittlerer Dienst*), upper grade (*gehobener Dienst*) and higher grade (*höherer Dienst*) of civil service[9] according to educational

---

[8] Another wage scheme exists for professors in Germany (Detmer and Preissler 2004, 2006; Pritchard 2006, pp. 106–109).

[9] In Germany, non-academic staff, normally referred to as technical-administrative staff, is like academic staff, part of the public service. This does not mean that all staff is employed as civil servants.

background (Statistisches Bundesamt 2009). Normally, technical administrative personnel with vocational education are employed in the lower grades (e.g. secretaries, clerical staff), while university staff holding at least a master's degree or the pre-Bologna equivalent of *Diplom* or *Magister Artium* get assigned to salary groups in the higher grades. Blümel et al. (2010) refer to the shortcomings of the definitions and statistics of the Federal Statistical Office in categorising non-academic staff. Similar to Gornitzka et al. (1998), they criticise that the dichotomy of academic and non-academic staff is an over-simplification. Surveying non-academic staff only in the functional areas in central and non-central administration of universities or university libraries does not provide a satisfying answer of who are HEPROs and what they are doing. Locked in the four categories of the German status system Blümel et al. (2010, pp. 155–156), similar to Rhoades and Sporn (2002a, pp. 12–15), can only focus on the higher grade or top-level in administration. Consequently, Blümel et al. criticise the missing differentiation in relation to formal roles of technical-administrative staff referring to occupation and organisational units, which results in non-academic staff being rather invisible for the internal and external public.

A performance and power-related definition of roles of administrative staff for Great Britain is presented by Lockwood (1996) who indicates three types of administrative staff having different modes of influence in areas such as academic, financial, social or site management: the clerk, assigned to the recording of an activity, the administrator, being in charge of the organisation of an activity within a realm of decision set by a regularly present authority, and, the manager, who's managing activity takes place within broad policy guidelines. Lockwood argues that the mode of operation depends on the degree of responsibility and the involvement of the administrative staff in a task. For all three types, the main block of work is the performance of a relatively standard set of duties such as the provision of information and advice, implementing decisions, which contains tasks such as producing committee papers, distribution of agendas, taking minutes and the communication and recording of the decision making. The assignments are budgeting, planning, staff or student records. In this set of general duties, the power of decision remains with the decision makers, which are only very marginally influenced by administrative staff. In a second set of work, administrative personnel performs the same set of duties plus decision making and implementation, quasi as a kind of routine management. Assignments are the organisation of archives, audits, businesses, ceremonials or routine maintenance of buildings. A third set of activities is dedicated to more specific working activities, e.g. curricular development, research administration or teaching methods (Lockwood 1996, p. 47).

Rosser (2004) contributes to the discussion on HEPROs by focusing on the aspect of missing recognition. Pointing to a previous study by herself from 2000 she declares "mid-level leaders" to be "the unsung professionals of the academy" (Rosser 2004, p. 317). "Unsung" points to a missing recognition of the contribution of HEPROs, and to the "commitment, training, and adherence to high standards of performance and excellence in their areas of expertise" (Rosser 2004). Rosser identifies mid-level leaders in higher education in the United States as an essential group "whose administrative roles and functions support the goals and mission of the academic enterprise" (Rosser 2004, p. 318). Mid-level leaders coordinate and direct administrative units. They play a key role within the traditional service areas of academic support, business/administrative services, external affairs, and student services (Rosser 2004, p. 319). In her study on the quality of mid-level leaders' work life, satisfaction, morale and their intentions to leave, mid-level leaders were included who are classified as academic or non-academic support staff. Not being faculty, mid-level leaders are referred to as a non-exempt, non-contract group of mid-level administrative staff. They report to a senior-level administrator or dean, and are categorised as administrators, professionals, technicians, or specialists. Normally, these positions are differentiated by functional specialisation, skills, training and experiences (Rosser 2004, p. 324).

The invisibility of the large body of university administrators, and their relationship with academic staff is an issue in Australia (Conway 2000a, b; Dobson and Conway 2003; Graham 2009, 2010). Not depending on official and university statistics and their categorical limitations Dobson and Conway (2003, p. 125) give voice to the administrators' misery of being regarded "as non-persons who do non-work" who "do not want to be defined as a negative or in oppositional terms". Dobson and Conway assume that this invisibility is based on missing reputation of the work done by administrative, technical and other support staff (Dobson and Conway 2003, p. 124). Looking beyond the question of reputation the categories and terminology for administrative, technical and other support staff is stated to be "general staff" by Conway[10] (2000a, b). Administrators are defined as a sub-set of general staff, whose main duty it is to support the "core business activities of teaching, learning and research; those who work in organisational support positions (for example, finance and human resources)" (2000a, b); the term administrators applies for academic managers as well (2000a, b). Consequently, "general staff" is used as a common term in a later publication by Dobson and Conway (2003, p. 126).

Nevertheless, the term general staff is not as institutionalised in Australia as stated by the authors. For example, McInnis (1998, p. 162) uses in his quantitative studies the terminology "administrators" and "professional administrators" (McInnis 1998, p. 168), which according to Dobson and Conway would be "a sub-set of general staff" in the Australian context. In later publications, e.g. on the undergraduate student experience, McInnis switches to "support structures" operated by "a substantial group of highly professional specialists" (McInnis 2002, p. 187). This friction in the use of terminology can be clearly seen as an ambiguity based on academic use and professional associations'[11] efforts to find a suitable terminology (Clegg 2007).

---

[10] Conway had a long career in the management of different higher education institutions and was the President of the Association of Tertiary Education Management (ATEM) from 2001 to 2003 (Conway 2007, pp. VI, 32).

[11] Another account of the difficulty of finding a suitable terminology with reference to the aims of professional associations is the report on professional managers in higher education in Great Britain by Whitchurch (2006b).

The discussion in Australia presented above has provided considerable input to and was critiqued in the research and writings of Whitchurch[12]. In the past years, Whitchurch was one of the most productive authors of literature on HEPROs (Whitchurch 2004, 2006a, b, 2008a, b, 2009, 2010a, b, c; Whitchurch et al. 2009, 2010a; Whitchurch and Gordon 2010; Gordon and Whitchurch 2010). Whitchurch started with an account of changes in university management in Great Britain (Whitchurch 2004) and analysed the "inside out university" (Whitchurch 2006a, pp. 161–163): "Like an amoeba, the 'Inside Out University' has functional elements that may split, coalesce and modify as needs and circumstances evolve" (Whitchurch 2006a). According to her, the emergence of a "twin dynamic" (Whitchurch 2008a, p. 376) comprising a process of increased functional specialisation and a blurring of boundaries between activities across professional spaces has to be respected:

> Three features of changing administrative identities are considered. First, traditional regu-latory and 'civil service'-type roles have been joined by roles requiring specialist expertise and knowledge management, where independent and even political judgements are called for, often involving decisions around levels of risk. Second, new specialisations have been created within functional areas as support services have become more sophisticated (for instance marketing, hitherto an offshoot of student recruitment and/or external relations, has become an activity in its own right). Third, the boundaries between what are increas-ingly termed 'professional service' staff and academic staff, with or without administrative and managerial responsibilities, have become less clear-cut, and their activities interlinked in increasingly complex ways. This has created 'hybrid' forms of staff, with a mix of roles and backgrounds. (Whitchurch 2004, p. 283)

Professionalisation results in the establishment of bodies of knowledge and stan-dards of professional practice. In a literature review done for the *Leadership Foun-dation for Higher Education*, Whitchurch (2006b) considers the term "professional managers" to be the most adequate for HEPROs. She distinguishes "professional managers" from "managers", "administrators", "non-academic staff", "academic related staff", "professional staff" and "support staff", terms used in official clas-sifications of university administration (Whitchurch 2006b, p. 5). She suggests the use of "professional managers " because the professional requirements for the role of this (un)specific group are neither adequately labelled with "administration" nor with "management" (Whitchurch 2006b, pp. 6–7). In later publications on the identity of HEPROs, Whitchurch defines "professional staff" in management on department level or student services as "general managers", in human resources and finances as "specialist professions", and in research and quality management as "'niche' specialist" (Whitchurch 2008b, p. 380) or uses the definition "managerial professionals" introduced by Rhoades (1998) (Whitchurch 2009, p. 407).

Very early, Whitchurch (2004) focused on the issue of identity. Her approach is based on the identity concept of the third space where new identities and roles are being created: the "*third space*, […], is characterised by mixed teams of staff who work on short-term projects such as bids for external funding and quality initiatives, as well as the longer-term projects" (Whitchurch 2008b, p. 386) "moving laterally

---

[12] Whitchurch, before starting her research and teaching career, had a career as a university admin-istrator and manager in four universities in Great Britain.

across functional and organisational boundaries to create new professional spaces, knowledges and relationships" (Whitchurch 2008b, p. 379). The conceptualisation of HEPROs and third space professionals by Whitchurch can be described as a rather similar understanding of the professionalisation of personnel in universities (Whitchurch 2010a; Whitchurch and Gordon 2010). Whitchurch created the four types of "bounded professionals", "cross-boundary professionals", "unbounded professionals", and "blended professionals" (Whitchurch 2008a, b, 2009):

> Individuals who located themselves within the boundaries of a function or organisational location that they had either constructed for themselves, or which had been imposed upon them. These people were characterised by their concern for continuity and the maintenance of processes and standards, and by the performance of roles that were relatively prescribed. They were categorised as bounded professionals.
> Individuals who recognised, and actively used boundaries to build strategic advantage and institutional capacity, capitalising on their knowledge of territories on either side of the boundaries that they encountered. They were likely to display negotiating and political skills, and also likely to interact with the external environment. These were categorised as cross-boundary professionals and, as in the case of bounded professionals, boundaries were a defining mechanism for them.
> Individuals who displayed a disregard for boundaries, focusing on broadly-based projects across the university such as widening participation and student transitions, and on the development of their institutions for the future. These people undertook work that might be described as institutional research and development, drawing on external experience and contacts, and were as likely to see their futures outside higher education as within the sector. They were categorised as unbounded professionals. (Whitchurch 2008b, pp. 382–383)

In a comparative study on Australia, Great Britain and the United States Whitchurch's (2009) fourth type of "blended professionals" got further shape:

> They [blended professionals, note CS] managed areas of work variously described as learning or business partnership, student life, diversity, outreach, institutional research, programme management and community development. They were likely to have been appointed on the basis of external experience obtained in contiguous sectors such as adult or further education, regional development, or the charitable sector, and offered academic credentials in the form of master's degrees and doctorates, although they were not employed on academic terms and conditions. (Whitchurch 2009, p. 408)

The latter two—unbounded and blended professionals—are prime examples of specialists working in the "third space" (Whitchurch 2008b, 2010a) described above. The concept of third space professionals creates an independent sphere for an emerging group of personnel in universities. As an oversimplification it can be claimed that, according to their identity, these professionals are neither academic nor administrative personnel.

3.4   Institutional Research and Higher Education Professionals

Finally, institutional research—a traditional function and task of HEPROs—has for some time been in the focus of researchers (Fincher 1978a, b, 1981, 1982, 2000; Dressel 1981; Rogers and Gentemann 1989; McKinney and Hindera 1992; Terenzini 1993; Delaney 1997; Volkwein 1999; Hossler et al. 2001a, b; Teichler 1996; Neave 2005; Auferkorte-Michaelis 2008). Institutional research, although existing for decades and being well researched, got little to no attention by many authors discussed above. This is rather unfortunate as a rich body of literature provides insight into the working situation and role of institutional researchers, and their contribution to the university. For Fincher (1978a) institutional research is "organizational intelligence", which—based on higher education research—is supposed to guide campus-based planning (Dressel 1981; Farrell 1984; Fincher 1987, 1996) and interventions to enhance institutional development and effectiveness (Rogers and Gentemann 1989; Knight et al. 1997; Hossler et al. 2001a, b). Terenzini (1993) understands the metaphor of organisational intelligence more broadly, not only referring to data gathering about an institution. Institutional intelligence encompasses also analysis and transformation of data into information and reports, and provides insight and informed sense of the organisation. He identifies three kinds of equally important and interdependent organisational intelligence: technical/analytical intelligence (substantive expert knowledge and methodological competences), issues intelligence (understanding of the substantive problems and procedures; Whitchurch 2008b, p. 4), and contextual intelligence (understanding of the culture and customs of higher education, the particular institution and academics; Whitchurch 2008b, p. 5; also Montgomery 1984; Ehrenberg 2005).

Terenzini's insight in the cognitive basis and functions is complemented by a theoretical examination of the role of institutional research. According to Volkwein (1999), institutional researchers have a formative/constitutive internal and a summative external role. They have to satisfy the needs of internal administration and management as well as the requirements of accountability and external stakeholders. A second duality, institutional researchers have to cope with, are the academic and administrative cultures. These cultures are strongly related to the primary functions of research and teaching on the one side and to bureaucracy on the other side. Institutional research operates "in both of these contrasting cultures" and "may be thought of as a halfway house" (Volkwein 1999, p. 10). The third duality derives from the tension between the institutional role of teaching and the professional role of scholarship academics have to deal with. Academics are in charge of teaching, but they are trained and rewarded for their research and scholarship. Volkwein generates a typology of roles for institutional researchers how to deal with these tensions of the three dualities in a productive way. The first role is one of institutional research as information authority, which describes the institution's shape and size, its students and staff, and its activities. The second role is one of institutional research as policy analysis with internal and professional purpose studying and analysing the institution and its policies; both are categorised as internal roles. The third type is institutional research in a spin doctor role, assembling descriptive statistics that "reflect favourably upon the institution" (Volkwein 1999, p. 18), e.g. a role for professionally oriented scholars and researchers, who produce analytical evidence of institutional effectiveness, legal compliance, and goal attainment (Volkwein 1999; see also McKinney and Hindera 1992; Chan 1993). The latter two are externally oriented roles satisfying the need of accountability.

Teodorescu (2006, p. 75) adds the "knowledge brokerage" function of institutional research and refers to institutional researchers as "knowledge managers". He stresses that an institutional research professional "should strive to become a creator and manager of knowledge rather than a provider of data or information" (Teodorescu 2006, p. 78). Teodorescu sees strong parallels to the academic profession: institutional research professionals similar to academics want to have a reputation as knowledgeable persons with valuable expertise who are serving an altruistic cause (Teodorescu 2006, p. 81).

Discussing institutional research and Whitchurchs third space professionals draws the discussion away from administration towards the heartlands of HEPROs. It has become evident, that HEPROs are not administrative personnel in the traditional sense. Also, their functions, tasks and roles are not primarily routine administration. However, the discussion presented above does not seem to produce an easy answer to the question of definition. These difficulties of positioning correspond to the results of the on-going HEPRO survey which found more than 500 different names and functions of units HEPROs are assigned to (Kehm et al. 2010, pp. 31–32). Also taking up, at least partially, new functions and tasks seem to be part of the job description of HEPROs.

4 Academic Personnel

The external influences fostering organisational change have been sketched in Sect. 3.1. However, the evolution of administration, HEPROs, and university as an organisation needs to take into account the steady development of the academic profession as a profession (Parsons and Platt 1968, 1973; Barnett and Middlehurst 1993; Stichweh 1994; El-Khawas 1996; Middlehurst 2000; Oevermann 2005; Schimank 2005; Macfarlane 2010, 2011a). Contrary to the attempt of establishing an identity for third space professionals, the established academic identity and culture is the point of reference for all changes of the academic profession. When studying the literature on the three groups of university staff it seems that it is easiest to agree on terminology and activities of academic staff performing their core functions. Among others (e.g. Clark 1987; Boyer et al. 1994; Altbach 1996; Geurts and Maassen 1996; Enders and Teichler 1997; Welch 1997a, b; Henkel 2002, 2005, 2007; Welch 1997a, b; Rhoades 1998, 2007; Brennan et al. 2007; Kogan and Teichler 2007a; Locke and Teichler 2007; Vabø 2007), Kogan and Teichler (2007b) consider the professoriate as the major point of orientation of academic personnel consisting of external and internal roles in a different mix. "Professors figure in the invisible colleges which are largely informal arrangements through which academic norm-setting is maintained and assessments are made for senior academic posts, fellowships of academies and research grants" (Kogan and Teichler 2007b, p. 12). Quality assurance in teaching and research is maintained by trans-institutional systems. The norms of the invisible colleges "are transmuted into allocative decisions by the management systems" (Kogan and Teichler 2007b). Professors are, in their external roles, supposed to be "acknowledged leaders in their subject field" and "are expected to set the norms for teaching and research in their subject area" (Kogan and Teichler 2007b). In most national systems, professors bear a key role in setting themes and standards for research and scholarship or in curriculum development. Also, the education and mentoring of students and junior academics is part of the job description of professors. On these grounds of expertise and reputation professors take a role in institutional government and academic autonomy, e.g. participate in decisions on promotions, resource allocations, or review the institutional profile. "The operation of the professoriate or, more widely, the academics makes them part of a system" (Kogan and Teichler 2007b). The power of decisions on curriculum or the rules of assessment, examination or evaluation are obvious competences of the professoriate. For the implementation of these formal legislative actions a bureaucracy is required. Another link of professors with the managerial system of the university are functions such as research and teaching and positions such as head of department (Kogan and Teichler 2007b, p. 12).

4.1 Shifts in the Academic Job Descriptions, Para-Academics and Higher Education Professionals

In a nutshell, the basic academic functions comprise of research, teaching and related valorisation activities summarised as the third mission (e.g. Etzkowitz and Leydesdorff 1998, 2000; Etzkowitz et al. 2000; Krücken 2003; Laredo 2007; Musselin 2007; Mora et al. 2010; Schneijderberg and Teichler 2010), with institutional government/management being a focal task. Musselin (2007) has spelled out the three missions as three must dos of today's academics: research (mission one), teaching (mission two) and valorisation (mission three). The three missions not only characterise academic activities, they also represent an explicit augmentation of tasks of academics. The writing of proposals for research grants, negotiation of contracts, or being engaged in knowledge and technology transfers is stipulated and recognised as important aspect of academic work. The diversification of tasks applies to teaching, as well. Teaching activities represent a larger scope of tasks of academic staff. Teaching students and supervising doctoral students are complemented by teaching specialised courses, design of e-learning courses, or finding internships for students (Musselin 2007, p. 177). "As part of the third mission academics work together with regional, national or international bodies and decision makers. Academic staff is supposed to engage with the public at large, e.g. involvement in public debates, public expertise, and offer support to public policy" (Musselin 2007, p. 178). When analysing the functions and tasks of academic staff the distribution of the workload provides further information on the development of the working activities. In a recent study, Tight (2010) found increasing academic workloads and related role overload of professors. Also, shifts within the workload have become evident within the past two decades: less time was spent on teaching, more time on research, and even more time on scientific services/third mission activities (Boyer et al. 1994; Altbach 1996; Enders and Teichler 1995a, b, 1997; Jakob and Teichler 2009, 2011). However, there are variations: In Germany, the teaching load has been passed on from professors to the middle ranks, especially to newly introduced staff positions with an extra-high teaching load (Jakob and Teichler 2009, 2011, pp. 22–33). Knight et al. (2007) found an increase of part-time teachers in universities in Great Britain. Also, more and more academics work on the basis of non-standard contracts in universities in Great Britain (Brown and Gold 2007). Musselin found that in French universities professors "are less and less in contact with concrete scientific work as they raise funds, develop contacts, write project proposals" (Musselin 2007, p. 178). McInnis (2010, p. 158) claims that a systematic preparation of early-career academic staff has become a norm at the national and institutional level in Australia, Great Britain and the United States.

Macfarlane argues that the academic all-rounder is disappearing: "Academic functions are being subcontracted to a growing army of para-academics: individuals who specialise in one element of academic life" (Macfarlane 2011a, p. 60). Consequently, the divergence of functions into either research or teaching or service results in a differentiation of academic identity into different roles either as researcher, or as teacher, or as manager (Macfarlane 2011a, pp. 61–62, 68). Macfarlane situates the development of "para-academics roles" (Coaldrake 2000, p. 21) in the rising numbers and up-skilling of administrative and professional support staff and the parallel process of de-skilling of all-round academics (Macfarlane 2011a, pp. 62–63). Macfarlane is concerned with the process of "hollowing out" (Massy et al. 1994) of academic life and the hollowing out of what it means to be an academic. He does not doubt the professional expertise and efficiency gains due to para-academic services (Macfarlane 2011a, p. 69). However, as "managerial processes have largely supplanted the direct influence of academics with respect to university decision making, even though academics continue to hold positions that formally confer the vestiges of power" (Macfarlane 2011a), pressures on academic personnel are increasing. Already in the last century McInnis noted that "once administrative staffs were considered powerless functionaries" (McInnis 1998, p. 170), but when taking over "high-profile technical and specialist roles that impinge directly on academic autonomy and control over the core activities of teaching and research" they turned into "professional managers" who "often have extensive budgetary control and responsibility for accountability mechanisms" (McInnis 1998). This has led to a decline of self-regulation and work satisfaction among academic staff (McInnis 2010, pp. 154–156) and led to considering professors as being "managed professionals" (Rhoades 1998). The accountability mechanisms establish performance appraisal for research and teaching (Barnett and Middlehurst 1993, pp. 120–121) and have severe impact on academic career paths (Macfarlane 2011a, p. 68)—although, at least for Great Britain, promotion schemes remain stable (Cashmore and Ramsden 2009, pp. 50–53). Also, special reward schemes for teaching have been established in many countries (Macfarlane 2011b; Wilkesmann and Schmid 2011). Musselin interprets the process to single out functions as a process of rising control exercised over academics (Musselin 2007, p. 179). Using a term introduced by Moodie this process can be interpreted as a decline of the "academic rule" (Moodie 1996, p. 131).

The process of differentiation of academic activities analysed by Musselin is being described as a blurring of boundaries as well (e.g. Gornitzka et al. 1998; Gornitzka and Larsen 2004; Leslie and Rhoades 1995; Rhoades 1998). Gornitzka et al. found that there is "no clear boundary between performing primary work, such as teaching and research, and administering it" (Gornitzka et al. 1998, p. 24). Internal university administration comprises "time spent on evaluating applications for positions inside your own university, evaluating students for administration, replying to minor inquiries, etc." (Gornitzka et al. 1998, pp. 24–25). These are tasks of academic personnel, which are "neither teaching nor research but which nevertheless cannot be delegated to administrators. A certain administrative load belongs to academic positions at universities" (Gornitzka et al. 1998, p. 25). For example, curriculum planning and research projects both contain elements of administration and academic activities of research and teaching. Nevertheless, the entanglement of administrative and academic tasks described by Gornitzka et al. is being disentangled. Academic staff shares responsibilities with HEPROs but also lose control over certain academic domains, e.g. curriculum (Barnett and Middlehurst 1993, p. 116; Coaldrake 2000, p. 16). HEPROs are in charge of student counselling, evaluation of applications, curriculum design, teaching schedules, evaluation of teaching, etc. Also, in doing so, HEPROs "are reshaping academic work by virtue of their increasingly pivotal roles in such areas as course management and delivery" (McInnis 1998, p. 168).

As already-indicated examples for a differentiation of research activities and the overlap of academic roles and HEPROs are more difficult to find. Formulating it in a provocative way it seems that academic staff does not let go of the research function as easily as it does with the teaching function. The example of transfer officers as a group of HEPROs shows very well how the extension of tasks and activities open up the research function. These still relatively new positions appear to require a mix of competences and original profiles of academic staff. Often, persons in these positions are university graduates and hold a Ph.D. "but also have management skills" (Musselin 2007, p. 179). To fulfil their tasks, they have to "possess a solid scientific background with strong skills in project management" (Musselin 2007). Musselin concludes that these "new functions at the frontier between academic and management activities are thus created and participate in establishing a new division of academics tasks based on increased specialisation" (Musselin 2007; see also Leslie and Rhoades 1995, pp. 193, 199, 205; Rhoades 2006, pp. 386–388; Krücken 2003; Krücken et al. 2007; Adamczak et al. 2007; Sebalj and Holbrook 2009; Kehm et al. 2010; Kloke and Krücken 2010; Shelley 2010). More examples of relations to the community and business partnerships where HEPROs are involved are: student's employability and employer contacts, research spin-offs, business incubation, enterprise, university-industry relations (Whitchurch 2010b, p. 628).

It has become evident that the working reality of academic staff is becoming more challenging, "as boundaries have become more permeable and transgressive, academics must operate within more open and contested arenas" (Henkel 2005, p. 170). The differentiation of the academic all-rounder into distinctive academic roles can be further analysed when discussing the "academic-turned-manager" (Deem 2006). It is most interesting to see that the academic identity and culture remains important for academic managers. However, it is most interesting to observe the growing demand for professional academic managers, as well.

4.2 The "Academic-Turned-Manager" or the Changing Roles of Academic Managers

Administrative managers find themselves not only acting as independent arbiters, giving impartial advice on the basis of professional expertise, but also becoming involved in political judgements about institutional futures. They increasingly undertake an interpretive function between the various communities of the university and its external partners. As the boundaries of the university have become more permeable administrative and academic management have inter-digitated, and hybrid roles have developed. (Whitchurch 2004, p. 280)

The partly parallel and partly interwoven development of administrative and academic management created "inter-digitated, and hybrid roles"; and it leads to a process of professionalisation as academic managers are claimed to be an "emerging profession" (DeBoer et al. 2010, p. 231). This fits the bigger concern of how to manage "modern universities" (Shattock 2000). In a comparative literature review on academic middle managers in Australia and the Netherlands, Meek et al. (2010b) express the need for "professionalisation of university administration and administrators" as an "important aspect of the new managerialism" (Meek et al. 2010b, p. 41). Nevertheless, they emphasise that the blurring between academic roles and roles of HEPROs did not result in a complete fusion (Meek et al. 2010b). According to authors such as Middlehurst and Elton (1992), this separation can be explained with the academic function providing educational, academic and administrative leadership. Leadership at the institutional level is defined "in terms of institutional strategy, direction and development; the articulation and representation of institutional goals and values; the generation of institutional commitment, confidence and cohesion" (Meek et al. 2010b, p. 258). Management was defined "in terms of policy execution; resource deployment and optimisation; procedural frameworks; and planning, co-ordination and control systems" (Meek et al. 2010b). The two functions can be associated with particular roles, for example, leadership with the role of a rector or president or vice-chancellor and management with roles of HEPROs or senior administrators. Great challenges arise from the call for strong leadership in professional organisations (Middlehurst and Kennie 1995).

A minimalistic definition of the role of managers "is to ensure that the organisation serves its basic purpose" (Lorsch et al. 1978, p. 219 cited by Clegg and McAuley 2005, pp. 20–21). A manager is supposed to "design and maintain the stability of his organisation's operations" and a manager should, "through the process of strategy formulation, ensure that his organisation adapts in a controlled way to its changing environment." A last issue is of importance when analysing the management of a university: A manager should "ensure that the organisation serves those people who control it" (Clegg and McAuley 2005, pp. 20–21). The necessity to react to governmental demands provoked changes in internal management (e.g. Gornitzka 1999; Kogan 2007). Kogan (2007) singled out four basic developments:

1. The growth of managerial and administrative work at both institutional and intra-institutional level.
2. The "changes in the tasks and relative power of academics and administrators within universities" (Kogan 2007, p. 162).
3. The increasing range of tasks for non-academic administrators plus the increase in their numbers.
4. The development of academic administration which Kogan labels "the bureaucratisation of the collegium" (Kogan 2007).

Similar to administering academic activities, the requirements to manage a university as an organisation creates new challenges for professors as temporary or permanent, full-time or part-time manager or "academic-turned-manager" (Deem 2006, p. 208) in the function of a rector or president or vice-chancellor, vice-rector or vice-president or deputy vice-chancellor, dean, deputy dean, etc. (e.g. Dearlove 1998; Amaral et al. 2002, 2003; Reed 2002; Middlehurst 2004, p. 272; Kogan and Teichler 2007b; Ferlie et al. 2008): "The managerial system is headed by a rector, president or vice-chancellor but is serviced by administrators who may be professional managers, or may be recruited from academics" (Ferlie et al. 2008, p. 12). Dill (1982, 1996, 1999) insists, that managing a university requires special skills rooted in the academic culture, which is distinctly different from the culture in other types of organisations:

> To understand the relevance of these skills we must [...] explore three interrelated phenomena: first, the part culture plays in models of management; second, the traits which distinguish universities from other organizations and make the management of culture of particular importance; third, the reasons for the decline of the existing academic culture. (Dill 1982, p. 304)

The two phenomena of the culture of management and the culture of a university as a special organisation open the realm for the discussion of the management-interface of academic personnel and HEPROs. Referring to Clark, Dill names the challenges of managing complex academic organisations with managing "ideologies, or systems of belief," which "permeate academic institutions at least at three different levels: the culture of the enterprise, the culture of the academic profession at large, and the culture of academic discipline" (Dill 1982, p. 309; see also Campbell 2003). Academically educated HEPROs have a notion of this complex difference of cultural work. Therefore, the most challenging enterprise results in finding management pathways (Deem 2006, p. 221) among the multiple levels of cultural logics.[13]

---

[13] It has been known for a long time that facts and fictions of management (Mintzberg 1975) are difficult to separate and have to fit organisationally (Mintzberg 1981). For universities as loosely coupled systems (Weick 1976), the management requires an enormous effort of time and personnel. Rather the "garbage-can model of decision-making" (Cohen et al. 1972) became famous, which was used to explicate the decision making of the organised anarchy in institutions of higher education as highly differentiated social organisations (Dill 1996, p. 51).

Despite different management paradigms (Clarke and Clegg 2000), the way of managing a university is not yet found. Trow (2010 [1993]) classified the conflicting pressures and hybridisation of managerial processes in universities by the distinction between hard and soft management. He defines "soft managerialism" (Trow 2010 [1993], pp. 272–273) as acceptance of a certain extent of inefficiency and ineffectiveness, and changes of any kind as based on an agreement and consent of all those involved. At the other end of the spectrum, "hard managerialism" (Trow 2010 [1993]) is based on management techniques known from hierarchical organisations, e.g. business. It is based on control and not on trust as it involves discourses and techniques of reward and punishment for employees who are considered to be fundamentally untrustworthy and thus incapable of self-reform or change. Examples are the assessment of research (Trow 2010 [1993], pp. 279–281) and teaching (Trow 2010 [1993], pp. 281–287). Trowler criticises the hard managerialism reforms in Great Britain as having "an atomistic and mechanistic understanding of knowledge and learning" (Trowler 1998, pp. 93–94).

The issue of power shifts due to the expansion in status and power of HEPROs has been discussed already in Sect. 3.3. El-Khawas (1995) observed that in universities in the United States, institution-wide committees such as the senate, which are traditionally dominated by academic personnel, have to share the factual decision-making process with administrators/HEPROs. This observation applies to many other countries, as well (cf. Dunn 2003).

Kogan points out that the prime roles of HEPROs are managerial support and service provision: "Academics have to adapt to communication with these professionals who are amateurs in academic matters but professionals in shaping the university, and in aspects of institutional management not normally grasped by academics" (Kogan 2007, pp. 163–164). However, "the cult of the amateur manager-academic" (Deem 2006, p. 222) stays alive, as rectors, vice-chancellors or heads of departments are mainly recruited from the ranks of academics. However, the cult is crumbling: The changing role of academic middle management in many universities across the globe becomes evident with deanship and directorship having "changed from short-term elected positions to appointed positions with clear job specifications to provide strong academic and administrative leadership" (Meek et al. 2010a, p. 2). Academic middle management is differentiated from managers on the top of the organisation on the one hand and from managers at the bottom level, e.g. course coordination, on the other hand. In most national cases, the term refers to "deans of faculty, heads of departments/schools and research directors" (Meek et al. 2010a, p. 3) who are "best placed for implementing institutional policies and strategies" (Meek et al. 2010a, p. 3; also da Motta and Bolan 2008). Management skills are not only required at the top of the universities, but also in middle management positions, which gain increasing responsibilities to "actually manage their faculties" (DeBoer et al. 2010, p. 229). They are expected to combine academic expertise with managerial competence containing explicit responsibility, e.g. contracts and accountability (DeBoer et al. 2010, pp. 229–230; also Clegg and McAuley 2005, p. 21).

It is clear that academic staff and especially professors have a designated role in management as part of the internal government (cf. Kogan and Teichler 2007b). However, some universities in Germany, Great Britain and the United States are already headed by manager type presidents with a short or no academic record. In Australian universities, the career tracks are set for a management career of academic personnel (Macfarlane 2011a, p. 68). There are strong indications, that the professional role of academic-turned-managers will only keep its academic character when the roots and logic remains in the academic culture, being strongly supported by HEPROs.

5   The Overlap Model

The question of who HEPROs are and what they do touches, as was shown above, a broad range of issues in higher education research, professionalisation and organisational research, management theories as well as reports and analyses from the practice. Other areas of research could have been considered as well, such as legal aspects or working conditions. Nevertheless, the picture of HEPROs remains blurred. Drawing on the literature referred to above they may be described best by looking at their roles and functions. An obvious characteristic is the overlap with traditional administrative and academic roles, functions and tasks.

Although a complete picture of the characteristics of HEPROs and of their tasks does not yet exist, we will introduce in the following a bi-polar model, which allows to situate the functions and tasks of HEPROs between the two poles. This model will be completed by an analysis of the differentiation of academic activities—indicated by the Academic Overlap—and the differentiation of administrative activities—indicated by the Administrative Overlap. The overlap model provides a simple clear-cut picture of the three spheres and the overlaps of functions and tasks of academic and administrative personnel and HEPROs; it makes the evolution of categories of university personnel explicit and aligns the elements, functions and roles of administration, management, research and teaching for further research. This could amalgamate into what Middlehurst referred to as the HEPROs of the twenty-first century (Middlehurst 2000, see also 2010).

The following analysis has two starting points: first, the differentiation and emergence of new positions, functions and roles in university administration; second, the "unbundling" (Kinser 2002, p. 13) of the academic all-rounder and the resulting differentiation of research, teaching and university management (Parsons 1968; Parsons and Platt 1968, 1970, 1973; Barnett and Middlehurst 1993; Stichweh 1994; El-Khawas 1996; Oevermann 2005; Schimank 2005; Macfarlane 2011a). The analysis suggests an overlap model based on a bi-polar scheme with administrative personnel at the one end and academic personnel at the other; HEPROs are placed in between. Considering a certain static moment in the model each of the three spheres has a realm of its own. All three personnel spheres interact. Interaction takes

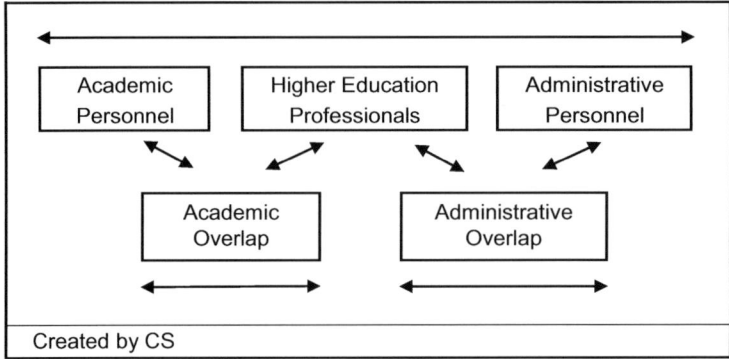

Fig. 5.1 The overlap model

place in a bi-lateral as well as multi-lateral way and is never one-directional. At the fringes of the two poles, the overlaps replace the interfaces (see Fig. 5.1).

Examples of staff located at the *Administrative Overlap* are equal opportunities officers, ombudspersons for students with special needs, persons in charge of knowledge transfer, for research support on a general level, and for institutional research (see Fincher 1978a, b, Terenzini 1993, Volkwein 1999). In more general terms, the core activities of HEPROs are information gathering, processing, and distribution; support, service, and management which are classified primarily as neither strictly academic nor strictly administrative work. These activities require academic training, knowledge and skills. Positions are heads of units in central administration, coordinators at department level, assistants to the Rector/President or Dean, quality assurance officers, etc.

The *Academic Overlap* is constituted by a differentiation of activities which used to be and are in the job description of academic staff. They are characterised by a close relation to the primary academic functions of research and teaching. The approach chosen for analysis is similar to Macfarlane's (2011a) differentiation of academic identities into roles. Understood as a process of differentiation of academic functions and tasks these are not performed solely by academic staff anymore due to various reasons, e.g. big numbers of students, new approaches to teaching and learning, expansion of valorisation activities of universities. Thinking of functions, tasks and positions of HEPROs in the academic overlap teaching seems to be more prominent than research. In German universities at least, HEPROs teach classes for general skills to enhance the employability of graduates; early career academics and professors are supposed to attend didactics training to improve their teaching skills and foster student learning; HEPROs are in charge of curriculum design or the coordination of study programmes; and student counselling, also discipline and subject related, is offered more and more by HEPROs and less and less by academics.

6 Conclusions

The discussion of the evolution of functions in research, teaching and management reveals several shifts of tasks and roles. Indications are strong that new hubs arise in a "shifting arena" (Shelley 2010, p. 439). Also, the academic culture and role of academics can be considered as the point of reference for HEPROs. Dobson and Conway (2003, p. 127) in analysing older publications by Sloper (1975), Plowman (1977), Bacchetti (1978), Silver (1983), and Topley (1990) conclude that HEPROs are requested to base their work on academic values rather than operating in a bureaucratic way. Nevertheless, the relationship of academic personnel and HEPROs seems to be a fundamental question already for some time: "The growing power of non-academic administrators raises the question whether they develop functions and values which are separable from those of the heads of institutions and other academic decision-makers whose work they service" (Becher and Kogan 1992, p. 179). This opens up the field for research on identity and its link to the changing functions and roles of academic staff and HEPROs. Further research could scrutinise the *Academic Overlap* and *Administrative Overlap* and the (possibly) interdependent appearance of HEPROs and para-academics: HEPROs and para-academics could be considered being two of a kind, *quasi* being binovular twins resulting from the evolution of academic and administrative functions. Also, the question could be researched whether HEPROs and para-academic roles merge—fully institutionalising hybrid professional roles in higher education—or whether the line between academic and administrative spheres will be drawn in between them.

Research on functions, tasks and roles of HEPROs and para-academics has just begun. The overlap model could facilitate the analysis. It became clear that today's discussion of HEPROs, their roles, functions and tasks has two channels: one coming from the administrative sphere and the other coming from the academic sphere. The administrative activities of HEPROs are characterised in many cases as augmenting bureaucratisation; and their expansion into the academic sphere as a threat to the academic profession. Dobson and Conway (2003, p. 129) suggest that the development of the area of work of HEPROs is a disturbance to the academic work jurisdiction (Abbot 1988). Shelley (2010) uncovered the "shifting arena" of research managers in universities and the problem of shifting academic and management/administration territories. Macfarlane extends the picture to the academic sphere with introducing para-academic roles. This results from an unbundling of academic functions, continuing specialisation and a change of academic identity (Macfarlane 2011a, pp. 61–62). This development is complemented by the emerging group of HEPROs. In hybrid roles and environments, HEPROs fill in functions and take over tasks that contribute to the work and success of universities.

Understood as an evolution resulting from a stable and ordinary response to environmental change the roles are based on functions and tasks. Borrowing from Harloe and Perry (2005) this manifests as a functional rethinking of professional positions in universities instead of a hollowing out of the (traditional) academic culture of the university. According to Noordegraf (2007), a shift from pure to hybrid forms of professionalism and mixed control become prevalent. The university as an arena can be well grasped with the overlap model. From discussing the *Academic Overlap* and the *Administrative Overlap* it became evident that the bi-polar analysis has to be extended by adding a third dimension. This third dimension unlocks the static positions of academic and administrative personnel. Accordingly, HEPROs are not considered on an in-between position. In the shifting arenas of work, the three groups of academic and administrative personnel and HEPROs do meet. Looked at from above a model consisting of overlapping circles, creating direct overlaps among academic and administrative personnel and HEPROs seems to fit better. Consequently, the overlap would be inhibited according to functions and tasks, no matter whether old or new. Research, teaching and third mission activities are functions and tasks at the *Academic Overlap*. Management and non-routine administration are functions and tasks at the *Administrative Overlap*. This might bridge the gap between the academic profession and HEPROs. Middlehurst (2010) has already challenged the notion of the identity of academic personnel and HEPROs as two worlds apart in an explorative essay introducing the universal higher education professional.

References

Abbot, A. (1988). *The systems of professions. An essay on the division of expert labor*. Chicago: University of Chicago Press.

Adamczak, W., Debusmann, R., Krause, E., & Merkator, N. (2007). *Traumberuf ForschungsreferentIn?* (Werkstattberichte, Vol. 69). Kassel: International Centre for Higher Education Research (INCHER-Kassel).

Altbach, P. (Ed.). (1996). *The international academic profession*. Princeton: Carnegie Foundation for the Advancement of Teaching.

Altbach, P. G., & Teichler, U. (2001). Internationalisation and exchanges in a globalized university. *Journal of Studies in International Education, 5*(1), 5–25.

Amaral, A., Jones, G. A., & Karseth, B. (Eds.). (2002). *Governing higher education. National perspectives on institutional governance*. Dordrecht: Kluwer.

Amaral, A., Meek, L., & Larsen, I. (Eds.). (2003). *The higher education managerial revolution?* Dordrecht: Kluwer.

Auferkorte-Michaelis, N. (2008). Innerinstitutionelle Hochschulforschung—Balanceakt zwischen nutzenorientierter Forschung und reflektierter Praxis. In K. Zimmermann, M. Kamphans, & S. Metz-Göckel (Eds.), *Perspektiven der Hochschulforschung* (pp. 87–96). Wiesbaden: VS-Verlag.

Bacchetti, R. (1978). Forecasting and planning in higher education. *AITEA Newsletter, 3*(3), 5–11.

Barnett, R., & Middlehurs, R. (1993). The lost profession. *Higher Education in Europe, 18*(2), 110–128

Becher, T., & Kogan, M. (1992). *Process and structure in higher education* (2nd ed.). London: Routledge.

Bell, D. (1973). *The coming of post-industrial society: A venture in social forecasting*. New York: Basic Books.

Bergmann, B. R. (1991). Bloated administration: Blighted campuses. *Academe, 77*, 12–16.

Berlin Communiqué. (2003). Realising the European Higher Education Area, Communiqué of the Conference of Ministers responsible for Higher Education in Berlin.

Bologna Declaration. (1999). The Joint Declaration of the European Ministers of Education in Bologna.

Blümel, A., Kloke, K., Krücken, G., & Netz, N. (2010). Restrukturierung statt Expansion. Entwicklung im Bereich des nichtwissenschaftlichen Personals an deutschen Hochschulen. *Die Hochschule, 20*(2), 154–172.

Blümel, A., Kloke, K., & Krücken, G. (2011). Professionalisierungsprozesse im Hochschulmanagement in Deutschland. In A. Langer & A. Schröer (Eds.), *Professionalisierung im Nonprofit Management* (pp. 105–127). Wiesbaden: VS-Verlag.

Boer, H. de, Enders, J., & Schimank, U. (2007). On the way towards new public management? The governance of university systems in England, the Netherlands, Austria, and Germany. In D. Jansen (Ed.), *New forms of governance in research organizations—disciplinary approaches, interfaces and integration* (pp. 37–152). Dordrecht: Springer.

Boer, H. de, Goedegebuure, L., & Meek, V. L. (2010). The changing nature of academic middle management: A framework for analysis. In V. L. Meek, L. Goedegebuure, R. Santiago, & T. Carvalho (Eds.), *The changing dynamics of higher education middle management* (pp. 229–241). London: Springer.

Bosetzky, H., & Heinrich, P. (1989). *Mensch und Organisation. Aspekte bürokratischer Sozialisation* (Schriftenreihe Verwaltung in Praxis und Wissenschaft, 15.) (4th ed.). Köln: Deutscher Gemeindeverlag und Verlag W. Kohlhammer.

Boyer, E., Altbach, P., & Whitelaw, M.-J. (1994). *The academic profession. An international perspective.* Princeton: Carnegie Foundation for the Advancement of Teaching.

Braun, D., & Merrien, F. X. (Eds.). (1999). *Towards a new model of governance for universities? A comparative view.* London: Kingsley.

Brennan, J., Locke, W., & Naidoo, N. (2007). United Kingdom: An increasingly differentiated profession. In W. Locke & U. Teichler (Eds.), *The changing conditions for academic work and careers in selected countries* (Werkstattberichte, Vol. 67, pp. 163–176). Kassel: International Centre for Higher Education Research Kassel (INCHER-Kassel).

Brint, S. (1994). *In an age of experts. The changing role of professionals in politics and public life.* Princeton: Princeton University Press.

Brown, D., & Gold, M. (2007). Academics on non-standard contracts in UK universities: Portfolio work, choice and compulsion. *Higher Education Quarterly, 61*(4), 439–460.

Campbell, D. (2003). Leadership and academic culture in the senate presidency: An interpretive view. *American Behavioral Scientist, 46,* 946–959.

Cashmore, A., & Ramsden, P. (2009). *Reward and recognition in higher education—institutional policies and their implementation.* York: Higher Education Academy.

Chan, S. S. (1993). Changing roles of institutional research in strategic management. *Research in Higher Education, 34*(5), 533–549.

Clark, B. R. (Ed.). (1984). *Perspectives on higher education. Eight disciplinary and comparative views.* Berkeley: University of California Press.

Clark, B. R. (Ed.). (1987). *The academic profession. National, disciplinary and institutional settings.* Berkeley: University of California Press.

Clarke, T., & Clegg, S. (2000). Management paradigms for the new millennium. *International Journal of Management Reviews, 2*(1), 45–64.

Clegg, S. (2007). Forms of knowing and academic development practice. *Studies in Higher Education, 34*(4), 403–416.

Clegg, S., & McAuley, J. (2005). Conceptualising middle management in higher education: A multifaceted discourse. *Journal of Higher Education Policy and Management, 27*(1), 19–34.

Coaldrake, P. (2000). Rethinking academic and university work. *Higher Education Management, 12*(2), 7–30.

Cohen, M. D., March, J. G., & Olsen, J. P. (1972). A garbage can model of organizational choice. *Administrative Science Quarterly, 17*(1), 1–25.

Conway, M. (2000a). What's in a name? Issues for ATEM and administrators. *Journal of Higher Education Policy and Management, 22*(2), 199–201.

Conway, M. (2000b). Defining administrators and new professionals. *Perspectives: Policy and Practice in Higher Education, 4*(1), 14–15.

Conway, M. (2007). *Inherent uncertainty. The association for tertiary education management 1976–2006.* New York: Association for Tertiary Education Management.

Dearing, R. (1997). *Higher education in the learning society. Report of the National Committee of Inquiry into Higher Education.* London: HMSO. http://www.leeds.ac.uk/educol/ncihe/. Accessed Apr 2011.

Dearlove, J. (1998). The deadly dull issue of university administration? Good governance, managerialism and organising academic work. *Higher Education Policy, 11*(1), 59–79.

Deem, R. (1998). 'New Managerialism' and higher education: The management of performances and cultures in universities in the United Kingdom. *International Studies in Sociology of Education, 8*(1), 47–70.

Deem, R. (2006). Changing research perspectives on the management of higher education: Can research permeate the activities of manager-academics? *Higher Education Quarterly, 60*(3), 203–228.

Delaney, A. M. (1997). The role of institutional research in higher education: Enabling researchers to meet new challenges. *Research in Higher Education, 38*(1), 1–16.

Detmer, H., & Preissler, U. (2004). Abenteuer W—Strategien, Risiken und Chancen: Aktuelles zur W-Besoldung. *Forschung und Lehre, 6,* 308–310.

Detmer, H., & Preissler, U. (2006). Die W-Besoldung und ihre Anwendung in den Bundesländern. *Beiträge zur Hochschulforschung, 28*(2), 50–67.

Dill, D. (1982). The management of academic culture: Notes on the management of meaning and social integration. *Higher Education, 11*(3), 303–320.

Dill, D. (1996). Academic planning and organizational design: Lessons from leading American universities. *Higher Education Quarterly, 50*(1), 35–53.

Dill, D. (1999). Academic accountability and university adaptation: The architecture of an academic learning organization. *Higher Education, 38*(2), 127–154.

DiMaggio, P. J., & Powell, W. W. (1991). The iron cage revisited: Institutional isomorphism and collective rationality in organizational fields. In W. W. Powell & P. J. DiMaggio (Eds.), *The new institutionalism in organizational analysis* (pp. 63–82). Chicago: University of Chicago Press.

Dobson, I., & Conway, M. (2003). Fear and loathing in university staffing: The case of Australian academic and general staff. *Higher Education Management and Policy, 15*(3), 123–133.

Dressel, P. (1981). The shaping of institutional research and planning. *Research in Higher Education, 14*(3), 229–258.

Drucker, P. (1968). *The age of discontinuity: Guidelines to our changing society.* New York: Harper & Row.

Dunn, D. D. (2003). Accountability, democratic theory, and higher education. *Educational Policy, 17*(1), 60–79.

Ehrenberg, R. (2005). Why universities need institutional researches and institutional researches need faculty members more than both realize. *Research in Higher Education, 46*(3), 349–363.

El-Khawas, E. (1995). Where is the faculty voice in recent academic decisions? *Tertiary Education and Management, 1*(1), 31–35.

El-Khawas, E. (1996). One professoriate or many? Assessing aspects of differentiation among academics. *Tertiary Education and Management, 2*(2), 146–152.

Enders, J., & Teichler, U. (1995a). *Berufsbild der Lehrenden und Forschenden an Hochschulen. Ergebnisse einer Befragung des wissenschaftlichen Personals an westdeutschen Hochschulen.* Bonn: Bundesministerium für Bildung, Wissenschaft, Forschung und Technologie.

Enders, J., & Teichler, U. (1995b). Das Selbstbild des Hochschullehrerberufs im internationalen Vergleich. *Wirtschaftswissenschaftliches Studium, 24*(9), 489–492.

Enders, J., & Teichler, J. (1997). A victim of its own success? Employment and working conditions of academic staff in comparative perspective. *Higher Education, 34*(2), 347–372.

Etzkowitz, H., & Leydesdorff, L. (1998). The endless transition: A "Triple Helix" of university-industry-government relations. *Minerva, 36,* 203–208.

Etzkowitz, H., & Leydesdorff, L. (2000). The dynamics of innovation: From national systems and "Mode 22" to a triple helix of university-industry-government relations. *Research Policy, 29*(2), 109–123.

Etzkowitz, H., Webster, A., Gebhardt, C., & Terra, B. R. C. (2000). The future of the university and the university of the future: Evolution of ivory tower to entrepreneurial paradigm. *Research Policy, 29*(2), 313–330.

Evetts, J. (2003). Professionalization and professionalism: Explaining professional performance initiatives. In H. Mieg (Ed.), *Professionelle Leistung—Professional Performance. Positionen der Professionssoziologie* (pp. 49–69). Konstanz: UVK-Verlag.

Evetts, J. (2009). New professionalism and new public management: Changes, continuities and consequences. *Comparative Sociology, 8*(2), 247–266.

Farrell, J. (1984). Institutional research and decision making: A bibliographic essay. *Research in Higher Education, 20*(3), 295–308.

Ferlie, E., Musselin, C., & Andresani, G. (2008). The steering of higher education systems: A public management perspective. *Higher Education, 56*(3), 325–348.

Fincher, C. (1978a). On the predictable crisis of institutional research. *Research in Higher Education, 8*(1), 93–96.

Fincher, C. (1978b). Institutional research as organizational intelligence. *Research in Higher Education, 8*(2), 189–192.

Fincher, C. (1981). Is there an institution in institutional research? *Research in Higher Education, 14*(2), 179–182.

Fincher, C. (1982). The missing link in institutional evolution. *Research in Higher Education, 17*(1), 93–96.

Fincher, C. (1987). Improving institutional memory. *Research in Higher Education, 26*(4), 431–435.

Fincher, C. (1996). Institutional change and evolution. *Research in Higher Education, 37*(4), 503–507.

Fincher, C. (2000). Words and numbers. *Research in Higher Education, 41*(4), 527–535.

Finkelstein, M. J., & Schuster, J. H. (2001). Assessing the silent revolution: How changing demographics are reshaping the academic profession. *American Association of Higher Education Bulletin, 54*(2), 3–7.

Geurts, P., & Maassen, P. (1996). Academics and institutional governance: An international comparative analysis of governance issues in Germany, the Netherlands, Sweden and the United Kingdom. In P. Maassen & F. A. Vught van (Eds.), *Inside academia: New challenges for the academic profession*. Utrecht: De Tijdstroom.

Gordon, G., & Whitchurch, C. (Eds.). (2010). *Academic and professional identities in higher education. The challenges of a diversifying workforce*. New York: Routledge.

Gornall, L. (1999). 'New professionals': Change and occupational roles in higher education. *Perspectives: Policy and Practice in Higher Education, 3*(2), 44–49.

Gornitzka, Å. (1999). Governmental policies and organisational change in higher education. *Higher Education, 38*(1), 5–31.

Gornitzka, A., & Larsen, I. (2004). Towards professionalisation? Restructuring of administrative work force in universities. *Higher Education, 47*(4), 455–471.

Gornitzka, Å., Kyvik, S., & Larsen, I. (1998). The bureaucratisation of universities. *Minerva, 36*(1), 21–47.

Graham, C. (2009). Investing in early career general staff. *Journal of Higher Education Policy and Management, 31*(2), 175–183.

Graham, C. (2010). Hearing the voices of general staff: A Delphi Study of the contributions of general staff to student outcomes. *Journal of Higher Education Policy and Management, 32*(3), 1–11.

Gumport, P. J., & Pusser, B. (1995). A case of bureaucratic accretion: Context and consequences. *The Journal of Higher Education, 66*(5), 493–520.

Halstead, K. (1991). *Higher education revenues and expenditures*. Washington: Research Associates of Washington.

Hansen, W. L., & Guidugli, T. F. (1990). Comparing faculty and employment gains for higher education administrators and faculty members. *Journal of Higher Education, 61,* 142–159.

Harloe, M., & Perry, B. (2005). Rethinking or hollowing out the university? External engagement and internal transformation in the knowledge economy. *Higher Education Management and Policy, 17*(2), 29–41.

Henkel, M. (2002). Academic identity in transformation? The case of the United Kingdom. *Higher Education Management and Policy, 14*(3), 137–145.

Henkel, M. (2005). Academic identity and autonomy in a changing policy. *Higher Education, 49*(1–2), 155–176.

Henkel, M. (2007). Shifting boundaries and the academic profession. In M. Kogan & U. Teichler (Eds.), *Key challenges to the academic profession* (Werkstattberichte, Vol. 65, pp. 191–204). Kassel: International Centre for Higher Education Research Kassel (INCHER Kassel) and UNESCO Forum on Higher Education, Research and Knowledge.

Hossler, D., Kuh, G., & Olsen, D. (2001a). Finding fruit on the vines: Using higher education research and institutional research to guide institutional policies and strategies. *Research in Higher Education, 42*(2), 211–221.

Hossler, D., Kuh, G., & Olsen, D. (2001b). Finding (more) fruit on the vines: Using higher education research and institutional research to guide institutional policies and strategies (Part II). *Research in Higher Education, 42*(2), 223–235.

Jakob, A. K., & Teichler, U. (2009). *Employment, work, career: The changing situation of the academic profession in Germany.* Full conference paper. http://www.uni-due.de/personal/PmWiki/uploads/Lehrstuhl/JacobTeichler2009.pdf. Accessed Jun 2012.

Jakob, A. K., & Teichler, U. (2011). *Der Wandel des Hochschullehrerberufs im internationalen Vergleich. Ergebnisse einer Befragung in den Jahren 2007/08.* Bonn: Bundesministerium für Bildung und Forschung.

Kallenberg, A. J. (2007). Strategic innovation in higher education: The roles of academic middle managers. *Tertiary Education and Management, 13*(1), 19–33.

Kehm, B. M. (2006a). Neue Hochschulprofessionen: die 'heimlichen' Manager? In HRK (Ed.), *Von der Qualitätssicherung der Lehre zur Qualitätsentwicklung als Prinzip der Hochschulsteuerung. Projekt Qualitätssicherung* (Beiträge zur Hochschulpolitik, Vol. 2, pp. 258–265). Bonn: HRK.

Kehm, B. M. (2006b). Strengthening quality through qualifying mid-level management. In M. Fremerey & M. Pletsch-Betancourt (Eds.), *Prospects of change in higher education. Towards new qualities and relevance. Festschrift for Matthias Wesseler* (pp. 161–171). Frankfurt a. M.: IKO Verlag für Interkulturelle Kommunikation.

Kehm, B. M. (2006c). Professionalizing management in higher education institutions. In J. L. N. Audy & M. C. Morosini (Eds.), *Inovação e empreendedorismo na Universidade/Innovation and entrepreneurialism in the university* (pp. 231–246). Porto Alegre: EDIPUCRS.

Kehm, B. M., & Lanzendorf, U. (2005). Ein neues Governance-Regime für die Hochschulen—mehr Markt und weniger Selbststeuerung? In U. Teichler & R. Tippelt (Eds.), *Hochschulland-schaft im Wandel* (pp. 41–55). Weinheim: Beltz.

Kehm, B. M., & Lanzendorf, U. (Eds.). (2006). Reforming university governance. Changing conditions for research in four European countries. Bonn: Lemmens.

Kehm, B. M., & Lanzendorf, U. (2007). The impacts of university management on academic work. *Management Revue, 18*(2), 153–173.

Kehm, B. M., Mayer, E., & Teichler, U. (Eds.). (2008a). *Hochschulen in neuer Verantwortung. Strategisch, überlastet, divers?* Bonn: Lemmens.

Kehm, B. M., Mayer, E., & Teichler, U. (2008b). Resümee der Herausgeber. Auf dem Weg zum Ausbau und zur Stabilisierung der Hochschulprofessionen. In B. M. Kehm, E. Mayer, & U. Teichler (Eds.), *Hochschulen in neuer Verantwortung. Strategisch, überlastet, divers?* (pp. 198–200) Bonn: Lemmens.

Kehm, B. M., Merkator, N., & Schneijderberg, C. (2010). Hochschulprofessionelle?! Die unbekannten Wesen. *ZFHE—Zeitschrift für Hochschulentwicklung, 5*(4), 23–39.

Kinser, K. (2002). Faculty at private for-profit universities: The university of phoenix as a new model? *International Higher Education, 28,* 13–14.

Kloke, K., & Krücken, G. (2010). Grenzstellenmanager zwischen Wissenschaft und Wirtschaft? Eine Studie zu MitarbeiterInnen und Mitarbeitern in Einrichtungen des Technologie-Transfers und der wissenschaftlichen Weiterbildung. *Beiträge zur Hochschulforschung, 32*(3), 32–52.

Klumpp, M., & Teichler, U. (2008). Experten für das Hochschulsystem: Hochschulprofessionen zwischen Wissenschaft und Administration. In B. M. Kehm, E. Mayer, & U. Teichler (Eds.), *Hochschulen in neuer Verantwortung. Strategisch, überlastet, divers?* (pp. 169–171). Bonn: Lemmens.

Knight, W., Moore, M., & Coperthwaite, C. (1997). Institutional research: Knowledge, skills, and perceptions of effectiveness. *Research in Higher Education, 38*(4), 419–433.

Knight, P., Baume, D., & Yorke, M. (2007). Enhancing part-time teaching in higher education: A challenge for institutional policy and practice. *Higher Education Quarterly, 61*(4), 420–438.

Kogan, M. (2007). The academic profession and its interface with management. In M. Kogan & U. Teichler (Eds.), *Key challenges to the academic profession* (Werkstattberichte, Vol. 65, pp. 159–174). Kassel: International Centre for Higher Education Research Kassel (INCHER Kassel) and UNESCO Forum on Higher Education, Research and Knowledge.

Kogan, M., & Teichler, U. (Eds.). (2007a). *Key challenges to the academic profession* (Werkstattberichte, Vol. 65). Kassel: International Centre for Higher Education Research Kassel (INCHER Kassel) and UNESCO Forum on Higher Education, Research and Knowledge.

Kogan, M., & Teichler, U. (2007b). Key challenges to the academic profession and its interface with management: Some introductory thoughts. In M. Kogan & U. Teichler (Eds.), *Key challenges to the academic profession* (Werkstattberichte, Vol. 65, pp. 9–16). Kassel: International Centre for Higher Education Research Kassel (INCHER Kassel) and UNESCO Forum on Higher Education, Research and Knowledge.

Krücken, G. (2003). Mission impossible? Institutional barriers to the diffusion of the "third academic mission" at German universities. *International Journal of Technology Management, 25*(1/2), 18–33.

Krücken, G., Meier, F., & Müller, A. (2007). Information, cooperation, and the blurring of boundaries—technology transfer in German and American discourses. *Higher Education, 53*(6), 675–696.

Krücken, G., Blümel, A., & Kloke, K. (2009). *Towards organizational actorhood of universities: Occupational and organizational change within German university administrations*. Speyer: Deutsches Forschungsinstitut für öffentliche Verwaltung (FÖV—Discussion Paper).

Laredo, P. (2007). Revisiting the third mission of universities: Toward a renewed categorization of university activities? *Higher Education Policy, 20*(4), 441–456.

Leslie, L. L., & Rhoades, G. (1995). Rising administrative costs. Seeking explanations. *The Journal of Higher Education, 66*(2), 187–212.

Levy, L. (1990). Long run trends in administrative salaries. *CUPA Journal, 41*(Summer), 11–20.

Lewis, L. S., & Altbach, P. G. (1995). Faculty versus administration. A universal problem. *International Higher Education, 2*, 2–4.

Locke, W., & Teichler, U. (Eds.). (2007). *The changing conditions for academic work and careers in selected countries* (Werkstattberichte, Vol. 67). Kassel: International Centre for Higher Education Research Kassel (INCHER-Kassel).

Lockwood, G. (1996). Continuity and transition in university management: The role of the professional administrative service. *Higher Education Management and Policy, 8*(2), 41–52.

Lorsch J. W., Baughman J. P., Reece J., & Mintzberg H. (1978). Understanding Management. New York: Harper & Row.

Macfarlane, B. (2010). Professors as intellectual leaders: Formation, identity and role. *Studies in Higher Education, 36*(1), 47–73.

Macfarlane, B. (2011a). The morphing of academic practice: Unbundling and the rise of the para-academic. *Higher Education Quarterly, 65*(1), 59–73.

Macfarlane, B. (2011b). Prizes, pedagogic research and teaching professors: Lowering the status of teaching and learning through bifurcation. *Teaching in Higher Education, 16*(1), 127–130.

Massy, W. F., & Warner, T. R. (1990). The lattice and the ratchet. *Policy Perspectives, 2*(4), 1–8, (Pew Higher Education Research Program, The University of Pennsylvania). http://www.the-learningalliance.info/Docs/Jan2004/DOC-2004Jan12-1073931090.pdf. Accessed Jun 2012.

Massy, W. F., & Warner, T. R. (1991). *National symposium on strategic higher education finance and management issues: Proceedings, causes and cures of cost escalation in college and university administrative and support services* (pp. 179–199). Washington: National Association of College and University Business Officers.

Massy, W. F., Wilger, A. K., & Colbeck, C. (1994). Overcoming 'hollowed' collegiality. *Change, 26,* 11–20.

McInnis, C. (1992). Changes in the nature of academic work. *Australian universities' Review, 35*(2), 9–12.

McInnis, C. (1998). Academics and professional administrators in Australian universities: Dissolving boundaries and new tension. *Journal of Higher Education Policy and Management, 20*(2), 161–173.

McInnis, C. (2002). Signs of disengagement? Responding to the changing work and study patterns of full-time undergraduates in Australian universities. In J. Enders & O. Fulton (Eds.), *Higher education in a globalising world. International trends and mutual observations* (pp. 175–190). Dordrecht: Kluwer.

McInnis, C. (2010). Traditions of academic professionalism and shifting academic identities. In G. Gordon & C. Whitchurch (Eds.), *Academic and professional identities in higher education. The challenges of a diversifying workforce* (pp. 147–166). New York: Routledge.

McKinney, B., & Hindera, J. (1992). Science and institutional research. The links. *Research in Higher Education, 33*(1), 19–29.

Meek, V. L., Goedegebuure, L., Santiago, R., & Carvalho, T. (2010a). Introduction. In V. L. Meek, L. Goedegebuure, R. Santiago, & T. Carvalho (Eds.), *The changing dynamics of higher education middle management* (pp. 1–14). London: Springer.

Meek, V. L., Goedegebuure, L., & De Boer, H. (2010b). The changing role of academic leadership in Australia and the Netherlands: Who is the modern dean? In V. L. Meek, L. Goedegebuure, R. Santiago, & T. Carvalho (Eds.), *The changing dynamics of higher education middle management* (pp. 31–54). London: Springer.

Middlehurst, R. (2000). Higher education professionals for the twenty-first century. *Perspectives: Policy and Practice in Higher Education, 4*(4), 100–104.

Middlehurst, R. (2004). Changing internal governance: A discussion of leadership roles and management structures in UK universities. *Higher Education Quarterly, 58*(4), 258–279.

Middlehurst, R. (2010). Developing higher education professionals. Challenges and possibilities. In G. Gordon & C. Whitchurch (Eds.), *Academic and professional identities in higher education. The challenges of a diversifying workforce* (pp. 223–243). New York: Routledge.

Middlehurst, R., & Elton, L. (1992). Leadership and management in higher education. *Studies in Higher Education, 17*(3), 251–264.

Middlehurst, R., & Kennie, T. (1995). Leadership and professionals: Comparative frameworks. *Tertiary Education and Management, 1*(2), 120–130.

Mintzberg, H. (1975). The manager's job—folklore and fact. *Harvard Business Review, 53*(4), 49–61.

Mintzberg, H. (1981). Organization design: Fashion or fit. *Harvard Business Review, 59*(1), 103–116.

Montgomery, J. (1984). Boss sizing as a required skill in institutional research. *Research in Higher Education, 21*(3), 353–356.

Moodie, G. C. (1996). On justifying the different claims to academic freedom. *Minerva, 34*(129), 150.

Mora, J.-G., Detmer, A., & Vieira, M.-J. (Eds.). (2010). *Good practices in university-enterprise partnerships (GOODUEP)*. Valencia: Valencia University of Technology.

Motta, M. V. da, & Bolan, V. (2008). Academic and managerial skills of academic deans: A self-assessment perspective. *Tertiary Education and Management, 14*(4), 303–316.

Münch, R. (2006). Drittmittel und Publikationen. Forschung zwischen Normalwissenschaft und Innovation. *Soziologie, 4,* 440–461.

Münch, R. (2007). *Die akademische Elite.* Frankfurt a. M.: Suhrkamp.

Münch, R. (2009). *Globale Eliten, lokale Autoritäten. Bildung und Wissenschaft unter dem Regime von PISA, McKinsey, & Co.* Frankfurt a. M.: Suhrkamp.

Musselin, C. (2007). Transformation of academic work: Facts and analysis. In M. Kogan & U. Teichler (Eds.), *Key challenges to the academic profession* (Werkstattberichte, Vol. 65, pp. 175–190). Kassel: International Centre for Higher Education Research Kassel (INCHER Kassel) and UNESCO Forum on Higher Education, Research and Knowledge.

Naschold, F., & Bogumil, J. (2000). *Modernisierung des Staates: New Public Management in deutscher und internationaler Perspektive* (2nd ed.). Opladen: Leske & Budrich.

Neave, G. (2005). Euro-Philiacs, Euro-Sceptics and Europhobics. *Higher Education Policy, 11*(2), 113–129.

Neave, G., & Amaral, A. (2008). On process, progress, success and methodology or the unfolding of the Bologna Process as it appears to two reasonably benign observers. *Higher Education Quarterly, 62*(1/2), 40–62.

Noordegraaf, M. (2007). From "Pure" to "Hybrid" professionalism. Present-day professionalism in ambiguous public domains. *Administration and Society, 39*(6), 761–785.

Oevermann, U. (2005). Wissenschaft als Beruf. Die Professionalisierung wissenschaftlichen Handelns und die gegenwärtige Universitätsentwicklung. *Die Hochschule, 1,* 15–51.

Parsons, T. (1968). The academic system: A sociologist's view. *The Public Interest, 13*(Special issue), 173–197.

Parsons, T., & Platt, G. M. (1968). Considerations on the American academic system. *Minerva, 6*(4), 497–523.

Parsons, T., & Platt, G. M. (1970). Age, social structure, and socialization in higher education. *Sociology of Education, 43*(1), 1–37.

Parsons, T., & Platt, G. M. (1973). *The American university.* Cambridge: Harvard University Press.

Plowman, C. (1977). Professionalism in university administration. *AITEA Newsletter, 2*(1), 6–7.

Prag Communiqué. (2001). Towards the European Higher Education Area, Communiqué of the Meeting of European Ministers in Charge of Higher Education in Prague.

Pritchard, R. (2006). Trends in the restructuring of German universities. *Comparative Education Review, 50*(2), 90–112.

Reed, M. I. (2002). New managerialism, professional power and organisational governance in UK universities. In A. Amaral, G. A. Jones, & B. Karseth (Eds.), *Governing higher education. National perspectives on institutional governance* (pp. 163–186). Dordrecht: Kluwer.

Rhoades, G. (1984). Conditioned demand and professional response. *Higher Education, 13*(2), 139–169.

Rhoades, G. (1998). *Managed professionals: Unionized faculty and restructuring academic labor.* Albany: State University Press.

Rhoades, G. (2001). Managing productivity in an academic institution: Rethinking the whom, which, what, and whose of productivity. *Research in Higher Education, 42*(5), 619–632.

Rhoades, G. (2006). The higher education we choose: A question of balance. *The Review of Higher Education, 29*(3), 381–404.

Rhoades, G. (2007). The study of the academic profession. In P. J. Gumport (Ed.), *Sociology of higher education. Contributions and their contexts* (pp. 113–146). Baltimore: Johns Hopkins University Press.

Rhoades, G., & Sporn, B. (2002a). New models of management and shifting modes and costs of production. Europe and the United States. *Tertiary Education and Management, 8,* 3–28.

Rhoades, G., & Sporn, B. (2002b). Quality assurance in Europe and the U. S. professional and political economic framing of higher education policy. *Higher Education, 43*(3), 355–390.

Rogers, B., & Gentemann, K. (1989). The value of institutional research in the assessment of institutional effectiveness. *Research in Higher Education, 30*(3), 345–355.

Rosser, V. J. (2004). A National Study on mid-level leaders in higher education: The unsung professionals in the academy. *Higher Education, 48*(3), 317–337.

Schimank, U. (2005). "New Public Management" and the academic profession: Reflections on the German situation. *Minerva, 43,* 361–376.

Schneijderberg, C., & Merkator, N. (2011). Hochschulprofessionen und Professionalisierung im Bereich der Qualitätsentwicklung. *Qualität in der Wissenschaft, 5*(1), 15–20.

Schneijderberg, C., & Teichler, U. (2010). Partnerschaften von Hochschulen und Unternehmen— Erfahrungen im europäischen Vergleich. *Beiträge zur Hochschulforschung, 32*(3), 8–30.

Sebalj, D., & Holbrook, A. (2009). The profile of university research services staff. *Australian Universities' Review, 51*(1), 30–38.

Shattock, M. (2000). Managing modern universities. in my view. *Perspectives: Policy and Practice in Higher Education, 4*(2), 33–34.

Shelley, L. (2010). Research managers uncovered: Changing roles and 'shifting arenas' in the academy. *Higher Education Quarterly, 64*(1), 41–64.

Silver, P. (1983). *Professionalism in educational administration.* Geelong: Deakin University.

Slaughter, S., & Leslie, L. L. (1997). *Academic capitalism. Politics, policies, and the entrepreneurial university.* Baltimore: Johns Hopkins University Press.

Slaughter, S., & Rhoades, G. (1993). Changes in intellectual property status and policies at a public university: Revising the terms or professional labour. *Higher Education, 26,* 287–312.

Sloper, D. (1975). *University administration as a profession.* Master of Educational Administration thesis, University of New England, Armidale, Australia.

Sporn, B. (2001). Building adaptive universities: Emerging organisational forms based on experiences of European and US universities. *Tertiary Education and Management, 7*(2), 121–134.

Statistisches Bundesamt. (2009). *Personal an Hochschulen, Fachserie 11, Reihe 4.4.* Wiesbaden: Statistisches Bundesamt.

Stehr, N. (1994). *Arbeit, Eigentum und Wissen. Zur Theorie von Wissensgesellschaften.* Frankfurt a. M.: Suhrkamp.

Stehr, N., & Grundmann, R. (2010). *Expertenwissen. Die Kultur und die Macht von Experten, Beratern und Ratgebern.* Weilerswist: Velbrück Wissenschaft.

Stichweh, R. (1994). *Wissenschaft, Universität, Profession. Soziologische Analysen.* Frankfurt a. M.: Suhrkamp.

Stichweh, R. (2008). Universität nach Bologna. Zur sozialen Form der Massenuniversität. Luzerner Universitätsreden (pp. 7–12). www.unilu.ch/files/Luzerner_Unireden_19.pdf. Accessed Jun 2012.

Teichler, U. (1996). The conditions of the academic profession. an international, comparative analysis of the academic profession in Western Europe, Japan and the USA. In Centrum voor Studies van het Hoger Onderwijsbeleid (Ed.), *Inside academia. New challenges for the academic profession*, in cooperation with F. vanVught & P. Massen (pp. 15–65). Utrecht: De Tijdstroom (Management en beleid in het hoger onderwijs, 25).

Teichler, U. (1998). Massification: A challenge for institutions of higher education. *Tertiary Education and Management, 4*(1), 17–27.

Teichler, U. (2003). The future of higher education and the future of higher education research. *Tertiary Education and Management, 9*(3), 171–185.

Teichler, U. (2004). The changing debate on internationalisation of higher education. *Higher Education, 48*(1), 5–26.

Teichler, U. (2005). Quantitative und strukturelle Entwicklung des Hochschulwesens. In U. Teichler & R. Tippelt (Eds.), *Hochschullandschaft im Wandel. Zeitschrift für Pädagogik Oktober 2005 (50. Beiheft)* (pp. 8–24). Weinheim: Beltz.

Teichler, U. (2007a). Germany and beyond: New dynamics for the academic profession. In W. Locke & U. Teichler (Eds.), *The changing conditions for academic work and careers in selected countries* (Werkstattberichte, Vol. 67, pp. 15–38). Kassel: International Centre for Higher Education Research Kassel (INCHER-Kassel).

Teichler, U. (2007b). *Higher education systems. Conceptual frameworks, comparative perspectives, empirical findings.* Rotterdam: Sense.

Teichler, U. (2008). Hochschulforschung international. In K. Zimmermann, M. Kamphans, & S. Metz-Göckel (Eds.), *Perspektiven der Hochschulforschung* (pp. 65–86). Wiesbaden: VS-Verlag.

Teodorescu, D. (2006). Institutional researchers as knowledge managers in universities: Envisioning new roles for the IR profession. *Tertiary Education and Management, 12*(1), 75–88.

Terenzini, P. T. (1993). On the nature of institutional research and the knowledge and skills it requires. *Research in Higher Education, 34*(1), 1–10.

Tight, M. (2010). Are academic workloads increasing? The post-war survey evidence in the UK. *Higher Education Quarterly, 64*(2), 200–215.

Topley, J. (1990). Enhancing the impact of professional administrators. *Journal of Tertiary Education Administration, 12*(2), 339–352.

Trow, M. (1974). Problems in the transition from elite to mass higher education. In OECD (Ed.), *Policies for higher education* (pp. 51–101). Paris: Organisation for Economic Co-Operation and Development.

Trow, M. (1999). From mass higher education to universal access: The American advantage. *Minerva, 37*, 303–328.

Trow, M. (2010). Managerialism and the academic profession: The case of England. In M. Burrage (Ed.), *Martin Trow. Twentieth-century higher education. Elite to mass to universal* (pp. 269–298). Baltimore: Johns Hopkins University Press (first published as: Trow, M. (1993). Managerialism and the academic profession: The case of England. Stockholm: Council for Studies of Higher Education.).

Trowler, P. (1998). What managerialists forget: Higher education credit frameworks and managerialist ideology. *International Studies in Sociology of Education, 8*(1), 91–110.

Vabø, A. (2007). Challenges of internationalization for the academic profession in Norway. In M. Kogan & U. Teichler (Eds.), *Key challenges to the academic profession* (Werkstattberichte, Vol. 65, pp. 99–110). Kassel: International Centre for Higher Education Research Kassel (INCHER Kassel) and UNESCO Forum on Higher Education, Research and Knowledge.

Visakorpi, J. K. (1996). Academic and administrative interface: Application to national circumstances. *Higher Education Management and Policy, 8*(2), 37–41.

Volkwein, F. J. (1999). The four faces of institutional research. In F. J. Volkwein & S. Lanasa (Eds.), *What is institutional research all about? A critical and comprehensive assessment of the profession: New directions for institutional research* (No. 104, pp. 9–19). San Francisco: Jossey-Bass.

Weick, K. E. (1976). Educational organizations as loosely coupled systems. *Administrative Science Quarterly, 21*(1), 1–19.

Welch, A. R. (1997a). All change? The professoriate in uncertain times. *Higher Education, 34*(3), 299–303.

Welch, A. R. (1997b). The peripatetic professor: The internationalisation of the academic profession. *Higher Education, 34*(3), 323–345.

Whitchurch, C. (2004). Administrative managers. a critical link. *Higher Education Quarterly, 58*(4), 280–298.

Whitchurch, C. (2006a). Who do they think they are? The changing identities of professional administrators and managers in UK higher education. *Journal of Higher Education Policy and Management, 28*(2), 159–171.

Whitchurch, C. (2006b). *Professional managers in UK higher education: Preparing for complex futures.* Unpublished paper. *Leadership Foundation for Higher Education.* https://www.lfhe.ac.uk/protected/whitchurchfinal.pdf. Accessed Jun 2012.

Whitchurch, C. (2008a). Beyond administration and management: Reconstructing the identities of professional staff in UK higher education. *Journal of Higher Education Policy and Management, 30*(4), 375–386.

Whitchurch, C. (2008b). Shifting identities and blurring boundaries: The emergence of third space professionals in UK higher education. *Higher Education Quarterly, 62*(4), 377–396.

Whitchurch, C. (2009). The rise of the blended professional in higher education: A comparison between the United Kingdom, Australia and the United States. *Higher Education, 58*(3), 407–418.

Whitchurch, C. (2010a). Optimising the potential of third space professionals in higher education. *Zeitschrift für Hochschulentwicklung, 5*(4), 9–22.

Whitchurch, C. (2010b). Some implications of 'Public/Private Space' for professional identities in higher education. *Higher Education, 60*(6), 627–640.

Whitchurch, C. (2010c). Convergence and divergence in professional identities. In G. Gordon & C. Whitchurch (Eds.), *Academic and professional identities in higher education: The challenges of a diversifying workforce. International Studies in Higher Education* (pp. 167–183). Abingdon: Routledge.

Whitchurch, C., & Gordon, G. (2010). Diversifying academic and professional identities in higher education. some management challenges. *Tertiary Education and Management, 16*(2), 129–144.

Whitchurch, C., Skinner, M., & Lauwerys, J. (2009). Professional staff in UK universities: Recent developments. *Australian Universities' Review, 51*(1), 56–60.

Wilkesmann, U., & Schmidt, C. J. (2011). The impact of new governance on teaching at German universities. Findings from a National Survey in Germany. *Higher Education*, published online 9 Apr 2011. doi:1007/s10734-011-9423-1.

Academic Markets, Academic Careers: Where Do We Stand?

Gaële Goastellec, Elke Park, Gülay Ates and Kevin Toffel

As underlined by a growing number of studies, academic careers are changing. The massification of higher education and the resulting changes in the composition of student bodies and faculty, in the role of diplomas and the content of studies, as well as—more broadly—changes in the role of higher education systems in society have led to a more complex organisation of both academic markets and careers. What do we know about the changing face of academia? How have these changes been analysed so far? What is yet to be explored?

Through a literature review, this paper is an attempt to frame the changes in academic markets and careers in comparative perspective. In order to do so, the first section presents a historical perspective of research on academic markets and the dimensions identified as central in the analysis and understanding of academic markets and careers. The second section addresses the three main stages of academic careers: young academics (Ph.D. candidates and post-doctoral fellows), middle rank and adjunct staff and the professoriate. Finally, the concluding section comprehensively discusses academic career paths.

1 Academic Markets and Recruitment Procedures: A Historical Perspective

The development of research on academic markets is concomitant with the sociology of higher education structuring as a domain. It evolved initially as a sub-stream dedicated to the study of the "academic man", alongside the two main focuses on

G. Goastellec (✉) · E. Park · K. Toffel
Politics and Organizations of Higher Education Research Unit at the Observatory Science, Policy and Society (OSPS), University of Lausanne, Lausanne, Switzerland
e-mail: gaele.goastellec@unil.ch

G.Ates
University of Klagenfurt, Klagenfurt, Austria

University of Vienna, Vienna, Austria

B. M. Kehm, U. Teichler (eds.), *The Academic Profession in Europe: New Tasks and New Challenges,* The Changing Academy – The Changing Academic Profession in International Comparative Perspective 5, DOI 10.1007/978-94-007-4614-5_6,
© Springer Science+Business Media Dordrecht 2013

educational inequalities and higher education effects on students as well as another
sub-stream focusing on governance and organisation.

1.1 From Prestige and Performance to Inbreeding

Building up a historical perspective on the American sociology of higher education,
Burton Clark (2007) identifies the works of Wilson (1943) and Riesman (1956) as
amongst the first to focus on higher education as a profession. Riesman provides
an analysis of a merit-based academic structure, describing prestige rankings of
higher education institutions and the imbrications of local and national disciplinary
interests. Wilson focuses on academic hierarchies and selection problems, academic
status, processes and functions with a special focus on prestige and competition.

The latter has largely influenced the founding work of Caplow and McGee (1958)
who were the precursors in analysing academic careers in relation with labour markets. They provide an in-depth analysis of how vacancies occur and question the
evaluation of performance, departments' strategies regarding salaries, procedures
of recruitment, recruitment processes and governance, etc. Thus, they identify the
main dimensions of academic markets and put recruitment procedures at the core
of the organisation of academic markets. They reveal the governance processes behind academic job vacancies and the decisive dimension of prestige as a measure
of performance. This dimension of prestige is not a new focus: at the beginning of
the twentieth century, Cattel (1906, 1912) already measured the "excellence" of
American universities' departments through the numbers of "big men" they had.

The link between prestige and performance in the academic marketplace is a
continuous topic of concern in the research on academic markets. As underlined by
Caplow and McGee (1958), "disciplinary prestige is a feature of a social system,
not a scientific measurement. It is correlated with professional achievement but not
identical with it" (p. 128). Following McGee, Crane (1970) evaluates the relative
importance attributed to the prestige of doctoral origin and scholarly performance,
showing that greater importance is given to the former in the recruitment process
(in the Anglo-American higher education systems). The relevant research addresses
social mobility and local recruitment, as well as the link between the size of an academic market, the degree of competition and performance.

It is here that a specificity of the academic market compared with other sectors appears: the evaluation by peers (as underlined by Siow 1995). Williams et al.
(1974) also showed that in the UK candidates for junior academic positions had
better chances of being hired when they had first-class honours degrees, were coming from the Oxbridge universities and were applying to the universities where they
graduated. On the scientific activity side, they came to the conclusion that academics that had published at least three books and worked in at least two universities
were more often appointed or promoted. A decade later, a new study on British
Departments of Geography also underlined the importance of academic inbreeding (Johnston and Brack 1983). Recruitment processes and careers remain a highly
sensitive dimension in most higher education systems. A recent study (RIHE 2009)
tends to show that in comparative perspective a certain decline of academic inbreed-

ing can be observed. One hypothesis is that the tendency towards inbreeding is not only linked to national or local rules regarding recruitment or to the increasing internationalisation of higher education system that tend to affirm mobility as a criterion to measure academic excellence. It is also strongly linked to the national dynamics of academic markets—increasing or decreasing in size—and the ratio between the number of applicants and the number of positions: when the pressure at the entrance of the academic market reaches a certain level, academic departments tend to hire their former students more easily. When the number of positions to fulfil is important compared with the number of Ph.D. produced, departments are not under such a pressure to provide an employment opportunity to their former students. Of course, these tendencies also vary depending on the department, on the national and international higher education market and the "value" attributed to its Ph.D.

1.2   The Academic Labour Market

The tension between supply and demand in the academic market has particularly been studied through questioning the possible shortages in faculties: starting in the 1970s, projections of future shortages of faculties in the United States were made which lead to a renewed interest in academic job markets and, more specifically, the adequacy between the number of Ph.D.s produced and the positions to be filled (Cartter 1976). At the end of the 1980s, Bowen and Schuster predicted future academic shortages in sciences and arts. Since then, research increasingly focused on the construction of a supply and demand policy (see for the French case, Zetlaoui 1999; Cytermann 2003; on the Swiss Case, Barras 1994; CUS 1998; Meyer and Nyffeler 2001; Felli et al. 2006; on the United Kingdom, Hursfield and Neathey 2001; HEFCE 2003; Metcalf et al. 2005; on a European comparison, Bonaccorsi et al. 2004). What is mainly discussed here is first, the level of production of Ph.D.s with regard to the academic market and especially the anticipation of baby boomers retirement, the attractiveness of academic careers, especially in some disciplines where the private market strongly competes with academia in terms of remuneration, and the anticipation of the context transformations weighting on faculty needs, such as the students' influx evolution in different institutions and disciplines. These different levels of market opportunities depending on discipline lead to a sharper division across the academic community (Barnett 2004).

The study of the supply and demand dimension also includes the international mobility issue and its corollary, the brain drain/brain gain issue: the brain gain not only concerns internationalised markets such as the United States or Switzerland, Canada and the United Kingdom (see Felli et al. 2007), but also countries such as South Africa which are very attractive to SADC academics. The brain drain issue mainly matters in "developing" countries, losing their best academics not only to financially more attractive countries (see, for example Nunn 2005, or UNESCO 2004 on south-east European countries), but also in countries such as France which produce too many academics in comparison with the size of their markets (Jalowiecki and Gorzelak 2004).

Salaries and other material retributions are part of the supply and demand dimension. This important feature of academic markets, academic wages, was first addressed by economists: in *The Wealth of Nations* (1776) Adam Smith suggested to link professors' incomes to the number of students registered in their class. Two centuries later, Williams et al. (1974) proposed an analysis of factors affecting salaries. Both the evolution of academics salaries in regard to other professions and the flexibility of higher education institutions to define themselves the faculties' individual salaries are important features of academic markets. For example, looking at the United States, Ehrenberg (2002) underlines the decline of academic salaries in public institutions compared with private institutions and the increased dispersion of medium average salaries within the higher education institutions. More recently, in an international study comparing 15 higher education systems, Rumbley et al. (2008) compared academic salaries around the world, pointing out contextual variations (between countries, institutions, disciplines) and statutory variations (rank, tenure, full-time, length of the career, etc.), as well as differences in salaries progression in the course of a career, depending on the national market structure and governance.

Finally, the salary issue is twofold: on the one side, it addresses the heterogeneity of wages depending on status, institution, higher education system and individual characteristics (gender, ethno-racial origin, etc.). On the other side, it examines the classical distortion between the social prestige of the academic profession and its economic power.

1.3   Governance of Academic Careers

To understand the even more complex dynamics at play in academic markets, the latest studies tend to rely on comparative approaches to grasp academic employment rules, governance and career paths (Altbach 2000; Kaulisch and Salerno 2005; Musselin 2005a). They develop a holistic, comprehensive approach of academic market mechanisms, identifying the complex national interplays of labour market salaries, status, recruitment processes, workloads, career patterns, promotion rules, etc. to finally point out the emergence of more regulated internal labour markets as a common evolution of national higher education systems (Musselin 2005b). Regarding the analysis of market governance, she underlines that through the development of individual assessment and incentive devices, higher education institutions play an increased role in issues traditionally managed by the academic profession. This trend is also highlighted by Enders (1999), who notices an increase in institutional-level power regarding faculty management with the simultaneous diversification of the academic profession. Focusing on the United States, some researchers also come to the conclusion that this change in management corresponds to a shift from a collegial model of governance to a management model (Kogan et al. 1994).

With each higher education system being characterised by a specific market legislation and organisation, some authors also point out the societal dimension of academic markets: for example, in "The coconut tree" Altman and Bournois (2004), studying management science academics, outline the main parameters of French academic careers, the social and cultural contexts, through describing recruitment and promotion processes, the role of aggregation for professors etc. Finally, they compare the French academic structure to a coconut tree that is characterised by precise leaf positions based on a combination of grade and time that positions "every actor in a unique, personalised, precise, organic, official and public situation" (Altman and Bournois 2004, p. 323).

Finally, research on academic markets emphasises that the organisation of the academic market is particularly crystallised in the hiring of academic staff, by recruitment or promotion, on internal or external, local, national or international markets. These diverse recruitment processes build up original recruitment criteria and eventually produce direct or indirect discrimination (Musselin and Pigeyre 2008). Their study provides insights of the higher education configurations and more broadly, reveal how they "are interwoven with overall pattern of the higher education system and its external relationships" (Enders 2000, p. 22) and embedded in social norms (Lewis 1975).

2   Stages of Academic Careers

When trying to identify the main stages of academic careers, the researcher is confronted with the diversity of the status composing each national academic market. In order to provide a broad framework for comparison of academic careers, this section identifies three main categories that cover distinct realities depending on national contexts but still, they allow for some comparisons: young academics, including doctoral and post-doctoral students, middle-ranking staff and adjuncts, and the professoriate. This section attempts to picture the trends and the diversity of these three main careers' stages.

2.1   Young Academics and Doctoral Education

The development of doctoral education in Europe is linked to the notion of increasing the national research capacity via doctoral holders. Since 1990, in the United States and Canada, the reform processes "focused on: preparing doctoral students to better balance their research and teaching responsibilities as future faculty members; encouraging students to actively participate as leaders and public intellectuals in the civic arena; and on helping universities to ensure that greater numbers of students who enrol in doctoral programmes complete those programmes (especially underrepresented minorities, who have historically completed at lower rates than majority students)" (Council of Graduate Schools 2006, p. 1). On the European level, the EUA's Doctoral Programmes Project—initiated in 2004—established a particular close intercommunication between the European Higher Education Area and the

European Research Area (EHEA and ERA). The linkage increased awareness to reconsider the role of doctoral education in the knowledge society, to see doctoral candidates as early-stage researchers, and to harmonise the European system of education and research (Council of Graduate Schools 2006; European Commission 2000; European Commission 2004; EUA 2004–2005; Kehm 2006; European Commission 2007; Marginson and Wende 2007). Taking this into account, doctoral education does not only respond to a career inside but also outside academe.

In the last few years, a vast amount of research on Ph.D. candidates and young researchers emerged. Overall qualitative analysis gives insight into the multifaceted factors not only to illustrate and/or explain the heterogeneous doctoral education systems in Europe but also the multifarious situation and perception of (post-)doctoral candidates and holders. In Europe, there is still a diverse landscape, for example, at the dimension of Ph.D. programme duration and/or course design, forms of financing, recruitment, admission procedures, contents of the doctoral thesis agreements and/or status of doctorates (Kehm and Kreckel 2008b).

National reports provide continuous information about the situation, individual perspectives and subjective perceptions of (post-)doctoral candidates and (post-) doctoral graduates (Schlegel 2001; Marsh and Rowe 2002; Gerhardt and Briede 2005; Bundesministerium für Bildung 2006; Pechar and Campbell 2008). The nexus of comparative analyses of doctoral programmes across Europe is that there is still a "diversity not only across different countries in Europe, but also across universities within the same country and across faculties within the same university" (EUA 2004- 2005, p. 6). The comparative analyses of the regulatory framework of doctoral programmes show an ongoing transformation process even beyond Europe (Weiler 2004; Berning and Falk 2005; Kehm 2005, 2006, 2007; Metcalf 2006; Pechar 2008).

2.1.1 Doctorates

All over Europe, the percentage of doctoral holders is increasing (Kehm and Kreckel 2008a). For the years 1998–2006, Auriol (2010) reports a 40 % augmentation in the OECD countries. Referring to Meri (2007), 3 % of the students in the European Union (EU) were in doctoral programmes. In 2004, Europe had twice as many doctoral holders as the United States and six times more than Japan (Meri 2007). Of course, there is a wide variation amongst the disciplines and differences between men and women. In addition, there are differences between postgraduate and post-doctoral levels. Looking at the average age of doctoral holders, in the United Kingdom, 45 % of the doctoral holders are in the 25–29 age group, in Sweden 35 % are in the 30–34 age group, and the German and Swiss majority is between 30 and 34 years old (Burkhardt 2008). Regarding the financial funding of doctorates, candidates of natural and agricultural sciences or engineering state to have financial support through teaching and research-assistant contracts, fellowships or scholarships. Doctorates in the area of medical or social sciences and humanities are reliant on occupations outside of academe, loans, personal or family savings (Auriol

2010). Another pan-European quantitative online survey is the "Eurodoc-survey on the situation of doctoral candidates within Europe". Its main results give information about structures, motivation, working conditions, supervision, assistance, funding, mobility, productivity, obstacles, time-to-degree, employment situation, and desire to stay in academia, self-perception being prepared for job market, and funding (Eurodoc 2011). The distinction between "time-to-degree" ("quality and structure of programme, supervision, funding and additional duties") and "transition to employment" ("generic skills", employability, "career prospects inside and outside academe, and research versus the professional orientation of doctoral studies") remains a heuristic distinction for surveys on doctoral candidates and doctoral graduates (Kehm 2005). As some institutional changes bear new research questions, other research activities are reminiscent of the one of the last 30 years.

At a disciplinary level, the question "What is a doctorate" was asked by Probst and Lepori (2008) and a few years earlier, e.g. by Johnson (2001). Similar questions were asked by Teichler and Sadlak in 2000, although they had a broader focus on a more general dimension. Thus, reshaping the doctoral education sparked a new interest in how to allocate the time between taught courses and/or research training (Marsh and Rowe 2002; Fry and Ketteridge 2003; Kiley and Mullins 2004; Craighead and Craighead 2006; Locke and Teichler 2007; Lovat and Holbrook 2008; Bluett 2010).

According to Scott (Council of Graduate School 2006, p. 5), the question, if the doctorate is seen "as a first step in a research career vs. as an ultimate academic degree (and the related tension between perceptions of doctoral students as employees vs. as trainees)", is still substantial. The understanding of this remains blurry due to the lack of international comparative reliable large-scale quantitative data. Seen from this perspective the nomenclature may give a sense of the status of doctoral candidates. The German term "Nachwuchs", in France the so-called "jeunes chercheurs", in British English "'new blood' lecturer" or "junior staff", and in American English "early career researcher" doctoral education is increasingly seen as a socialisation process towards becoming a researcher and/or future faculty member.

Institutional embeddedness seems to be essential in order to enhance career opportunities for young academics at higher education institutions. While in some disciplines, research-intensive activities start at the bachelor's or master's level (sciences), other fields (the humanities, e.g.) tend to postpone it to the post-doctoral level (Melin and Janson 2006). Various studies showed that the cultural and disciplinary influence has a strong impact on the organisation of the research–lecture interrelation (Abbott 2001; Multrus 2004; Enders 2004). Kreckel's (2008) descriptive analysis presents the influence of historically grown cultures (Francophone, Humboldtian or Anglo-American model) on the relationship between research, training and promoting young talents. Kehm (2005, p. 16) concludes that there are two predominant models of doctoral programmes: "personal relationship" and "contractual relationship". She shows that there is a "distinction between research doctorates and professional doctorates". In Great Britain, for example, a research doctorate leads to an academic career, and professional doctorate to an employment promotion outside academe (Kehm and Kreckel 2008a). Throughout Europe, individual and professional doctorates seem to be increasingly devalued. Referring to Green and Powell (2005, p. 236) "the concept of professionally oriented research, as opposed to academic research, gives a rise to a false dichotomy." Following Fiedler and Hebecker (2006) doctoral graduates are early-stage researchers, who obtained professional training as a key qualification. However, Enders (2004, p. 428) underlines that "it would (…) be a misunderstanding to assume that further diversification will bring about a breakdown of traditional concepts of scholarly work and training. More likely new approaches are emerging that are partly vested within and partly parallel to the prevailing doctoral training context". Nonetheless, according to Kehm and Kreckel (2008b) the research doctorate seems to be the best way to enable an academic career, and this in spite of different doctoral education models in Europe.

In most disciplines, obtaining a doctoral degree is still a necessary step towards an academic career. The social and an institutional embeddedness of doctoral candidates plays a crucial part in the transition process for those who want to remain in university (Jantz and Krüger 2009). In contrast to doctoral candidates in structured programmes, especially candidates in individualised junior–senior relationship and professional doctoral programmes are often not integrated in institutional structures. However, an adjustment towards more structured doctoral programmes emerged and can be seen as a worldwide trend (Reichert and Tauch 2003; Kehm 2009). Candidates in structural doctoral programmes have a curriculum with individual supervision, a pre-assigned time to degree, a provided financial basis and are generally more involved institutionally. These developments have not yet been sufficiently reflected in recent literature, only few investigations distinguish between candidates at individual doctoral study and structured doctoral programmes (Mau and Gottschall 2008; Enders and Kottmann 2009).The formative years of scholars (Teichler 2006) are essential and Kehm and Kreckel (2008a) distinguish between the tenure-track model (GB and USA), the "habilitation" model (G) and a mixture of both models in France. One of the most important findings of Kehm and Kreckel (2008a, p. 284) is:

> Die vielleicht wichtigste Einsicht aus der Perspektive des wissenschaftlichen Nachwuchses ist die, dass gerade das [deutsche, sic!] Karrieresystem, in dem die Funktion der Nachwuchsqualifikation das größte Gewicht hat und das den größten Anteil an Qualifikationsstellen bereitstellt (…) auch gleichzeitig dasjenige ist, das im Vergleich zu den drei anderen [UK, USA, F, sic!] für Promovierende die geringsten Chancen bietet, auf eine selbständige und unbefristete Hochschullehrstelle zu gelangen (…).

The EU report *She Figures 2009* (2009, graph 3.1) demonstrates a gender gap for the EU27, which starts at the Ph.D. level and has an enormous impact on all other levels of the academic career path. At the first two levels of higher education degrees the majority are female students, but at doctoral level male candidates begin to predominate. Furthermore, it is visualised that at the first level of newly qualified doctorates 44 % are female, however, at the next "take-off phase in the academic career" the number decreases to 36 % and the proportion drops to 18 % at the highest career level (European Commission 2009).

2.1.2   Post-doctorate

Looking at the post-doctoral level, Janson et al. (2006) notice a trend towards a longer period of employment insecurity after the receipt of the doctorate for those who would like to remain in academe. For Germany, Böhmer and Hornbostel (2009) show that even for funded post-doctorates this in-between phase before entering into permanent employment extends up to 6 years. Regarding the security of employment at German and Austrian universities this trajectory is a high-risk venture. However, this is less the case in Great Britain and the United States. Generally, German applicants of post-doctoral programmes are a relatively homogenous group with an academic background. The academic pathways of this group were initiated at an early stage.

Qualitative analyses of the situation of post-doctoral students or graduates are more common than systematic representative surveys. The national and disciplinary approaches are mainly concentrating on research/working conditions, autonomy, and the prospects and perspectives to fix-term contracts (Burgess and Band 1998; Gaughan and Robin 2004; Ma and Stephan 2004; Moguérou 2005; Recotillet 2007; Åkerlind 2008; Horta 2009). A similar comparative analysis discusses the training systems, position of young academics and factors affecting the recruitment and retention of young scientists. The paper compares five countries and shows the negative effects of several uncertainties regarding the recruitment and retention of young academics at the Ph.D. level (Huisman and de Weert 2002). One of the main findings is that the uncertainties reduce the attractiveness, status and easy recruitment in the area of research in higher education. For some disciplines, the post-doctoral phase at universities is financially less attractive compared with wages doctorate holders earn in the private sector: a career in academe does not seem to pay off (Recotillet 2007; National Postdoctoral Association 2009).

2.2   *Middle Rank and Adjuncts/Contingent Faculties*

What is the immediate future of young academics? What is the next step before they can access the professoriate? After having presented the doctoral and post-doctoral steps, we focus on the career level located between academic training (Ph.D. and post-doctorate) and the professorship: who is this group and how can it be defined?

According to national and disciplinary specificities, it is not a homogeneous group, neither in age, working conditions, and salary nor job type. However, recent literature defines two main profiles that can help to understand and classify this category of academic workers: middle-ranking[1] staff and adjunct or contingent staff.

---

[1]As we shall see, this designation is somewhat unfortunate. We have chosen it because it is particularly used by Teichler (1996) in an international comparison and we think that it can fairly well account for this population.

This partition is based on two main significant differences: on the one hand, the type of duties and, on the other hand, the type of contracts. Middle-ranking staff is mainly hired as lecturers and researchers with or without tenure track while adjuncts are usually untenured part-timers hired for teaching. It is clear that this categorisation is porous and that the trajectories are more complex than that. Thus, this dichotomous classification has to be considered as an *ideal type* in the very Weberian sense.

In the current context of profound institutional changes related not only to new public management but also to an increasing internationalisation (Brennan 2006; Enders and de Weert 2009), roles and expectations of academics have changed. These structural changes have undoubtedly had an impact on how academic careers are build, i.e. on the successive stages leading to the professorship. If these transformations affect the whole academic world and the entire body of academic staff—from Ph.D. students to professors—they probably have a particularly important impact on the category we are trying to define here.

As a matter of fact, "middle rank" is a poor word because it sets this section of the population in opposition against the juniors (Ph.D. students and post-doctorates) on the one hand, and on the other hand, against the professors. Called "Mittelbau" in Germany, "Maîtres de conferences" in France or "corps intermediaries" in Switzerland, this category is assigned to a middle position, a position of transit. Unlike adjuncts, the middle-ranking stage is an "intermediary position" which is part of the traditional career path.

2.2.1 Being Part of the Middle Rank: A Required Step on the Path of an Academic Career

Although in some cases an academic can go straight from a post-doctoral position to the professoriate, thus skipping the intermediate position, the move via the middle-rank status seems to be almost mandatory in the course of an academic career, although various models coexist. While in France, people will be lecturer (Maître de conférences) and get tenured very early in their career (average around 33 years of age), the "Mittelbau" in Germany cannot hope to obtain tenure before the average age of 42 (Musselin 2005a). German academics have to wait several years after obtaining the doctorate in order to apply for a professorship (Teichler 2008). The same occurs in the Netherlands (Enders et al. 2006). In the United States, it is less clear and it seems that the hierarchy is less obvious (Finkelstein and Frances 2006; Kreckel 2010). As a result, what differs are both the average length of the middle-ranking position in a career, the status associated with the position (tenured/untenured) and the degree of freedom associated with the position.

An important concept to take into account in discussing this stage of an academic career is socialisation (Musselin 2003). Although the professional learning process takes more or less formalised and institutionalised forms according to national contexts, this career stage is often described as a time to learn the academic job. Thus, this intermediate position can be seen as a transition period. However, this definition of middle-ranking staff is deeply linked to the chair system. The chair system being characterised by a relative process of disappearance, including in Germany (Teichler and Bracht 2006), one could expect a change towards a more autonomous status, which is already happening with a certain number of recently created fellowships (Fellow professors in Switzerland, Junior professors in Germany, etc.).

These logics are not trivial. Indeed, as noted by Christine Musselin, whatever the national contexts, there is a "before" and "after" tenure and the routes leading there are extremely contrasted. We can thus consider this period as a pivotal moment of socialisation that begins, as was shown before, during the Ph.D. and seems to continue through the different career stages until the professoriate. This socialisation process can be seen as a period in which the academic staff must prove itself in the academic world (Musselin 2004).

As we already noticed, the specific national contexts vary very strongly. For example, Teichler (1996) pointed out that while 79 % of German academic staff worked under precarious employment conditions (fixed-term contracts in particular), only 9 % of lower ranking Japanese staff were in that case. If most of the professors in European, US and Japanese universities are permanently employed (e.g. more than 90 % in Germany and in the Netherlands), this number decreases considerably when we consider non-professorial staff (Kreckel 2010).

2.2.2 Adjunct Staff: A Dead End?

The "class of adjuncts" refers to very different positions and situations (Musselin 2006)[2]. Generally, adjunct staff is a group of people characterised by particular conditions of precarious employment (i.e. fixed term contract) and little formal commitment to the departments for which they work (i.e. low career perspectives). Contrary to the status of middle-ranking staff, which is usually a specific level on the career path, the position of adjunct does not really provide further career opportunities. As pointed out by Naomi Jeffery Petersen (2005, p. 1) many adjuncts are hired in order to teach but they "are unlikely [to be] part of the infrastructure of programmatic design and administration that core faculty are". Indeed, with teaching as their main responsibility, they do not take part in the decision-making process and are thus not often considered as potential faculties to be hired for the tenured workplace (Ellison 2002; Jeffery Petersen 2005).

Adjuncts must rather be regarded as a supplementary workforce to ensure that the demands of mass-education are met in a context in which the flow of students can vary annually from one discipline to another. Over the last decades, the increase

---

[2] For example, in the nine categories established by Christine Musselin trying to grasp the entirety of the French academics, the name of adjuncts can be associated with two or three different categories…. Moreover, after the name of Teichler (1996) to which I referred above, the class of adjuncts may be associated with that of junior staff. The problem is that, as we shall see, the word "junior" refers implicitly to the young age, which is neither an inherent characteristic of adjuncts nor even a variable that could define all of them….

of adjuncts in universities has been substantial in France (Le Saout and Loirand 1998). In the United States, the percentage of part-timers has doubled between 1968 and 1998 (Wilson as cited in Feldman and Turnley 2001a; Finkelstein and Frances 2006; Monks 2007).

While middle-ranking staff is composed of a relatively young age group, adjuncts are a more diverse population, particularly in terms of age. In their paper, Feldman and Turnley (2001a, b) insist on the influence the career stage has on job satisfaction. One important point they stress is to consider adjunct positions not only in a negative way. Flexibility can sometimes be attractive for academics with young children or for dual-career couples.

Another significant aspect of the adjunct position is that the implications of being an adjunct differ depending on the career stage. For young academics, the position of adjuncts can be perceived as a way to consolidate their knowledge and increase their network; however, many are forced to remain in this position and are unable to find a regular job. The flexibility provided by adjunct positions may be perceived differently, particularly in relation to the time of the career in which it occurs as Feldman and Turnley showed (2001a, b). Although, part of the adjuncts seem to move towards this type of employment because of flexibility, the precariousness of their situation and even more the little prospect of advancement remain apparent in the survey carried out by the two American researchers.

Many articles (Teichler 1996; Enders and Teichler 1997; Feldman and Turnley 2001a, b; Ellison 2002) on both middle-ranking staff and adjuncts address the question of job-satisfaction of this population compared with that of professors (or more generally of academics). They conclude that across Europe satisfaction is generally much lower for junior and middle-ranking staff than for professors (Enders and Teichler 1997). This lack of job-satisfaction is mainly related to two factors: the little and uncertain prospects of advancement and the lack of employment security (Teichler 1996). Apparently the reasons for this dissatisfaction differ only slightly between the two populations although their status and working conditions are different. For both middle-ranking staff and adjuncts, this dissatisfaction is often due to limited career prospects. In addition, the adjunct staff also questions the marginalisation they suffer and how little they are given the possibility to contribute to policy decisions in the department (Le Saout and Loirand 1998; Ellison 2002)[3].

As pointed out by Le Saout and Loirand (1998), salary issues also have to be considered. In France, it seems that the considerably lower salary of adjunct staff could be one of the main motivations for hiring academic personnel on the basis of fixed-term contracts (without tenure-track, see also Monks 2007 for the United States).

American literature is much more prolific on the analysis of the adjunct population than the European. It is obvious that the adjunct category is more strongly represented in American literature because of its more formal and more common

---

[3] It should be noted that this theme comes in both countries for which the statute in question is asked. In Germany because of the relatively hierarchical structure in chair, and the United States because of the fact that the literature cited here deals mainly with the case of community colleges.

representation in higher education institutions but also due to the organisation of adjuncts in associations (e.g. the International Association of Adjunct Practitioners).

We can make the hypothesis that in the HES (Hautes Écoles Spécialisées) in Switzerland, the HBO (Hoger Beroepsonderwijs) in the Netherlands (Enders et al. 2006) or in Community Colleges in the United States (Ellison 2002), which are devoted to teaching and do very little research, adjuncts are certainly over-represented: there is a high probability that adjuncts are mainly used to compensate the massification of education and thus are more represented in the higher education institutions that play this role. Assuming that the capital chiefly recoverable in academia is that of publication—while teaching is considered less important (Teichler 1996; Musselin 2005b, 2008)[4]—it is not surprising that adjuncts are usually recruited for teaching with limited career prospects[5].

It will therefore be interesting to look at the distribution of adjuncts and middle-ranking staff in different institutions and disciplines and to question the subtypes of academics that compose these two broad categories: middle-rank staff can be full- or part-timers, have tenure or not, be characterised by important teaching loads or more research oriented. How are these diverse categories represented in the various national contexts, institutions, and disciplines? What paths exist between these types of working contracts? What are the profiles of the faculties presented in each of these categories? Do we observe gender inequalities? Social inequalities? Ethno-racial inequalities?

This distribution should be further examined and the status occupied by those academics analysed in the light of the types of governance carried out in each country. Is there a relationship to be established between academic careers' structure and status and higher education governance models?

2.3 The Professoriate—Tenure

2.3.1 A Story of Loss

Looking at recent literature on the "professoriate", the overall impression is one of crisis, decline and a loss of prestige and status ("Decline of Donnish dominion" Halsey 1992; "Decline of the Guru" Altbach 2002; *The Professoriate in Crisis* by Finkelstein and Altbach 1997).

There is a sense of good-bye, a literature of regret ("The last professors", "The Shrinking Professoriate"). The traditional "professor" seems to be a dying species

---

[4] Although again, this varies greatly from one discipline to another. As Musselin (2005b) recalls, if disciplines such as biology or physics have few similarities between the work of teaching and of research (teaching theories and methods versus laboratory work) it is quite another story for a discipline such as history where teaching and research activities are more intertwined.

[5] By using the concept of capital in a Bourdieusian sense, we mean here the type of symbolic currency which is efficient into the academic field.

("Gone for good", "The Vanishing Professor") and old ideals of intellectual autonomy, financial security and academic freedom are slowly eroding.

The "Golden Age" for the professoriate "characterised by institutional expansion, autonomy, available research funds and growing prestige and salaries" has come to an end (Altbach 2005, p. 147). Rather, the significant changes in academic work over the last two decades have presented the professoriate with demands for efficiency and accountability and the pressures to adapt to an increasingly competitive environment.

The recent comprehensive analytical accounts on the state of the professoriate (mostly *The Professoriate: Profile of a Profession* by Altbach 2005; Enders and de Weert 2009; Kogan and Teichler 2007) have identified a series of common challenges to the profession, most importantly the issue of performance and accountability/evaluation vs. academic freedom.

Some authors identify an ongoing "proletarianisation" of academic work (Enders and de Weert 2009, p. 256). Professors "are now increasingly treated the same way as ordinary workers" (Enders and de Weert 2009, p. 252). They notice a transition from "professor"—implying high social status, employment security, and the traditional values of autonomy and academic freedom—to "knowledge worker" in less secure forms of employment and responsible to a new corporate style management within universities ("Professor or Knowledge Worker" Gould 2006).

2.3.2 Professorial Tasks: Shifts in the Balance of Teaching and Research

However, the tasks of the professoriate—what professors actually do—have also changed. A "significant reconfiguration of academic work" (Altbach 2005, p. 157) has taken place and brought with it a shift in the balance of teaching and research. Since the early 1990s, various studies identified a significant shift from teaching to research (see also Honan and Teferra 2000). As publications seem to have become a measure of academic quality and prestige, the increasingly competitive nature of academic work has led away from teaching to a stronger emphasis on research in order to succeed in the struggle for academic survival. A recent study on promotion decisions in comprehensive universities showed that along with a factual marked increase in publications in mostly teaching colleges the "pressures for scholarly productivity and research activity increased" (Youn and Price 2009, p. 215). According to a study by Fairweather (2005) on faculty salaries research output was also better rewarded than teaching, and Bauerlein (2009) maintains that the strong focus on scholarship and publications has led to a decline in teaching quality (see also Allen 2009 "The Publishable Perishable Professoriate"). In his influential "Scholarship Reconsidered" (1994), Ernest Boyer already argued that the professoriate should pay more attention to teaching and learning and this position has been upheld widely since (see Court 1999 "Negotiating the Research Imperative"; Braxton 2006). Today, Altbach (2005, p. 157) identifies a "movement to emphasise teaching as central responsibility"; this movement seems to have partly come into effect as some authors already note that—in regard to the award of tenure—"teaching accounts for more than it did a decade ago" (Tierney 2004, p. 229). The relative disregard for teaching during the 1990s and attempts to upgrade and enhance the status of teaching have also been a prominent topic in the German debate, both politically as well as academically (see Schimank 2001; Meier and Schimank 2009; Huber 2004; for an overview of the debate on the alleged de-coupling of teaching and research see de Weert 2009).

Beyond the teaching/research nexus, professorial tasks traditionally include service to the institution, while increasing demands for external income generation present a relatively new phenomenon. Another issue that has recently arisen is the use and role of professors as "managers" or "leaders" within the institutional context, especially with stronger non-academic management structures imposed on most higher education institutions and a certain loss of influence of collegial bodies in the governance of universities. According to a recent UK study, there is currently no clear consensus as to what role professors should play in the operational and strategic steering of universities (Macfarlane 2010; on the role and tasks of professors regarding professional support and leadership see also Tight 2002).

2.3.3 Changes in Work Contract: An Appointment Revolution?

The most important development and prominent "threat" to the "full professor" identified and expressed in various works is, however, the "rise of the part-time profession" (Altbach et al. 2009, p. 90) and the increase in off-track appointments. The American Federation of Teachers concludes: "In recent years, the most notable—and potentially the most destructive—trend in higher education has been a significant shift away from employing tenured and tenure-track faculty members in favour of employing full-time non tenure-track faculty members, part-time/adjunct faculty members and graduate employees" (AFT 2009, p. 3).

Schuster and Finkelstein (2006) provide a comprehensive scope of what they call an "Appointment Revolution". Drawing on data from the Carnegie survey (Boyer et al. 1994) and the National Study of Postsecondary Faculty (NSOPF:04), they show that the number of tenured positions has dramatically declined in favour of non tenure-track fixed contracts: The proportion of full-time faculty who were in fixed contract (non tenure eligible) was barely perceptible in the 1960s, but has risen to over a quarter of the full-time faculty more than the last 30 years, and 58.6 % of new hires in 2003 were non-tenured off track positions (Finkelstein 2007, p. 149). The full-time professoriate is in retreat (see also AFT 1999), and a recent UNESCO report concludes pessimistically: "The professoriate faces significant difficulties everywhere [...and] the decline of a real full-time professoriate is undermining high-quality higher education" (Altbach et al. 2009, p. 89 f.).

Martin Finkelstein further explores this "trend toward hiring off the tenure track" in Kogan and Teichler (2007) and predicts the development of "parallel systems": tenure vs. fixed contract and a growing reliance on contingent faculty rather than full-time tenure-track and tenured faculty (Finkelstein 2007, p. 148).

This trend is supported by the current data from the US Department of Education IPEDS Fall Staff survey. The MLA study, Education in the Balance (2008) also clearly illustrates the decrease in numbers of tenured positions and subsequent increase in fixed term/part-time workers based on the IPEDS data.

Philip Altbach further elaborates on the "new structure of the professoriate" (Altbach 2005, p. 154) by which he means the introduction of a caste system, with few on top in old tenured positions, a new middle class (full-time non-tenure-track faculty), and part-timers as pariah. Whereas in the 1991 encyclopaedia article by Altbach, the term "professoriate" was used interchangeably with "academic profession", today this equation seems no longer valid. The professoriate is rather a very special—potentially endangered—sub-part of the academic profession.

2.3.4 The Erosion of Tenure?

The erosion of tenure as "permanent or continuous employment until retirement" (for a detailed analysis on the definition see Trower 2000a) touches on the heart of academic identity and autonomy. Altbach (2005, p. 155) states: "clearly the era of unfettered professorial autonomy following the award of tenure is coming to a close". With a growing need for institutional flexibility on the part of the universities (firing unproductive staff or faculty "deadwood", counteracting professorial laziness) and diminishing fiscal resources (lower costs by hiring non-tenure-track teachers and part-timers) tenure and professorial job security have been criticised as a hindrance to the economic demands of the "corporate university" and have increasingly come under attack.

In the United States, tenure was introduced in the early to mid-twentieth century as a means to safeguard and protect academic expression from political interference and external pressures and remains a cornerstone of academic identity. The idea of tenure has sparked heated debates during the 1980s and 1990s (see Tierney 2004, p. 228), the so-called "tenure wars" (tenure being "the abortion issue of the academy", Chait 2005, p. 306). There were a number of studies and careful analyses that followed in the framework of the Harvard Project on Faculty Appointments, including Richard P. Chait's comprehensive "Questions of Tenure" (2005) and the volume "Policies on Faculty Appointment" (2000b) edited by Cathy Trower. The latter ultimately consists of a helpful descriptive listing of definitions of tenure and does not provide further analysis. Still, both works minutely dissect the wide range of definitions and ultimately highlight the diverse meaning of tenure in various institutions. Today, the tenure debate has somewhat died down, and no convergent trends across countries emerge (RIHE 2009).

2.3.5 The Chair System: A Pyramidal Hierarchy in Transition

In countries with traditional chair systems ("Ordinarienuniversität"), such as Austria and Germany reforms towards greater institutional flexibility and a loosening of the rigidity of the career structure have been on the agenda for a while now. These reforms or reform-attempts received considerable public attention, however, with few exceptions and not counting the various descriptive accounts of the situation (for an international overview see Kreckel 2008), the implications for academic careers and the professoriate have not yet been fully analysed in secondary literature.

These systems were traditionally characterised by a "built-in gap between professorial staff and all other" and a strongly hierarchical structure as opposed to faculty/tenure-track models (see Enders 2001, p. 4). In Austria, for example, the civil servant status of university professors was abolished and a far-reaching transformation of the university system took place in the early 2000s. Pechar (2005) criticises the introduction of NPM structures in Austrian higher education while at the same time maintaining the strict division between professorial and non-professorial estates and a clear hierarchical split between academic personnel along with "unbearable dependencies" and subordination to professors (also Enders 2001, p. 11).

Recent attempts to introduce a tenure-track career structure ("Laufbahnmodell") in these countries, such as the introduction of assistant or associate professoriates in Austria and Switzerland or the German Junior-Professur have thus far also received relatively little attention in the relevant literature (CH: Kreckel 2008, p. 310; D: Federkeil and Buch 2007).

2.3.6 The Future of the Professoriate

A number of works also explore the changing demographic makeup of the professoriate. The recent ACE Study "Too many rungs on the ladder" (ACE 2008) on faculty demographics and the future leadership of higher education focuses on two main trends, first, the issue of the "graying professoriate" (see also Gilroy 2009; Wheeler 2008) and—again—the rising numbers of part-time and non-tenure-line faculty. In 2005, more than 54 % of full-time faculty in the United States were older than 50 compared with just 22.5 % in 1969 (Schuster and Finkelstein 2006, p. 58). The issue of retirement and new ways to manage retirements is further discussed in Wheeler (2008).

Further, Schuster and Finkelstein (2006) mention a growing "feminisation" of the professoriate and a "clear movement toward diversification among faculty by race and ethnicity" (Schuster and Finkelstein 2006, p. 53). This trend is supported by data from the ISPED Fall Staff survey and various other sources.

Up until today, the Carnegie Study on the Academic Profession (Carnegie Foundation: survey conducted in 1992, publications 1994–1995) remains a cornerstone for research on academic careers and the condition and attitudes of the professoriate. It was the first comprehensive international study on the subject (results for United States published in Altbach 1996; for Germany in Enders and Teichler 1995, see also Teichler 1999) and 18 years later many authors still rely heavily on its results (see Altbach 2005). Recently, the CAP survey on "The Changing Academic Profession" (2005–2007) followed in its footsteps providing broad data and insight in the current state of the professoriate (published results forthcoming).

3 Conclusions: Are Academic Careers Becoming a Political Object?

This chapter has underlined the multi-dimensional aspects of research on the academic marketplace and the increased complexity of this social object they illustrate. Behind the question of academic markets and the different positions they articulate, lies the question of the career paths structure. The increased number of faculties, the multiplication of their roles and status and the complexification of the ins and outs of academic markets have lead to the recent development of both research and policy debates questioning the structure of career paths and their consequence.

3.1 European Market and Policy Debates

On the research policy side, the implementation of a European higher education and research area has increased the sensitivity of the career organisation issue. For example, in 2004, a French report for the minister of education (Bonaccorsi et al. 2004) questioned the impact of the European higher education and research area on the necessity to adapt researchers' status. Beside the status dimension, three dimensions were particularly at shake: mobility, tenure track and salaries.

As well, the European Science Foundation has launched in 2007 a forum, working as an interface between the ESF member organisations, the European Commission, the EUA and the league of European research universities (ESF 2009). The goal of this forum was to develop collaboratively a "roadmap for research career development in Europe" (p. 4), but also to develop tools to promote the different stages of career and improve the coordination between national and European levels. In the end, the purpose was as well to improve the visibility of the ERA by reinforcing the European academic labour market. The report recently published (2009) proposed as an implementation plan the following dimensions:

- Structuring of research careers.
- Improving the attractiveness and competitiveness of European research careers.
- Providing equal playing fields for researchers of all backgrounds.
- Supporting the development of portfolio careers.
- Developing and implementing European policies for research career development.

These reports underline the problematic lying behind the career structure issue on the political side: how to create an attractive European academic market? They also provide with an idea of the various dimensions at stake in the organisation of academic careers, dimensions that are questioned by an increasing number of researchers.

3.2 Characterisation of Careers

If one had to question at the most practical level, the organisation of academic career paths, one probably could start by wondering what makes academic careers different from others. And indeed, some researches do compare academic careers structures' characteristics with those of the private sector. For example, (Baruch and Hall 2004) analyse the evolution of the career systems, showing the shift from an "exclusive, stand alone model" to what other researchers have qualified of "protean" (Hall 1976, 1986), boundaryless (DeFillippi and Arthur 1994), intelligent (Arthur et al. 1995), resilience (Waterman et al. 1994), and post-corporate (Peiperl and Baruch 1997) model. Baruch and Hall also underline an important dimension of the change: "A greater openness of the career information system" (p. 246). In the same private/public career perspectives, Arthur et al. (1995) describe the specificities of academic career models, underlying a relatively flat structure, a high level of empowerment and autonomy, high career mobility, multi-directional career paths, existence of sabbatical, the use of alternative work arrangements, resilience, importance of international and global dimension, etc.

At another level Enders (2001), quoting Neave and Rhoades (1987), recalls the traditional ideal typical differentiation between the chair model—mainly based on the statutory and prestige domination of the professoriate—and the department-college model—characterised by a more collegial-based organisation. Sharing the articulation of three stages, i.e. "contract, regular employee, tenure" and as such highly structured, these model of careers are presented as challenged by the creation of new status that erode the former distinctions.

Other research (Kaulisch and Salerno 2005) evaluate the influence of different career systems on the sequence, timing, and likelihood of major events in academic careers. In a close perspective, Altman and Bournois (2004), focusing on a national case study, attempt to identify a model of career while outlining the main parameters weighting on the academic careers such as the social and cultural context.

A wide range of works focuses on the "formative years of scholars" (Teichler 2006), the stages between receipt of the doctorate and the appointment to professor as the decisive phase in the course of an academic career. (Wissenschaftliche Wege zur Professur oder ins Abseits? Janson et al. 2006; Kreckel 2008; Enders 2001). These mostly descriptive comparative accounts highlight the uncertainty of academic careers due to high selectivity and generally portray embarking on a career in academia as a "high risk endeavour" (also Berberet 2008; Huisman and de Weert 2002). While employment conditions and career patterns for young academics vary substantially by country, short-term employment until about the age of 40 and high levels of selectivity are seen as common characteristics of academic careers in many countries.

On a more analytical level there is growing consensus in recent literature that the traditional structure of academic career paths is currently being challenged fundamentally: "The ground beneath our feet is shifting—in a way it has not perhaps in a century [...] and the traditional academic career characterised by a terminal degree in the discipline and then a career lockstep largely defined by a probationary, pretenure period, and movement through the academic ranks to a full professorship" is becoming a thing of the past (Finkelstein 2007, p. 154).

Meanwhile, some research analyse the impacts of change in higher education governance on academic careers. Harley et al. (2004), for example, underline the necessity to understand power relationships to understand how careers are changing. As well, Enders stipulates that the sensitive dimension regarding the implementation of managerialism and its consequences on academic staff is whether it will improve their support or their control (2001, p. 5).

3.3   Questioning Inequalities in Academic Careers

If a large number of research focusses on the institutional dimension of academic markets and careers, an increasing number of works also question the weight of social inequalities in academic markets. Beside the now classic "gender" dimension to read inequalities of careers, new dimensions of inequalities are now questioned that include both the ethno-racial dimension and the socio-economic one.

For example, Long and Fox (1995) underline the relatively lower attainments of women and minorities in science and discuss the processes through which these differences are produced. In the same vein, Wolfinger et al. (2009), focusing on the becoming of Ph.D. recipients, show that the often-used mode of pipelines to conceptualise academic careers tend not no reveal gender inequalities.

Bonaccorsi et al. (2004) and Kaulisch and Böhmer (2010), interrogating differences in access to tenure position in Germany 8 years after the Ph.D. graduation, reveal differences between disciplines, but surprisingly no gender or socio-economic influence, while international mobility after graduation seems determining. By doing so, they underline the fact that in Germany, inequality patterns occur before the Ph.D. graduation.

In the United States, an increasing number of studies are carried out focusing on the ethno-racial dimension. For example, Diggs et al. (2009) identify the barriers to recruitment and retention of faculty of colour. In the same vein, Trower (2009) compares the tenure-track life of faculties depending on their ethno-racial belonging to show how ethnic belongings influence academic careers.

Finally, in a short but insightful article, Altbach and Musselin (2008), drawing on the recognition that in some countries career structures are dysfunctional, characterise an efficient career structure by the fact that it allows universities to be attractive, stimulating and rewarding to their faculties, and that to achieve these characteristics, career stability, transparency in the career organisations, rigorous and meritocratic procedures, and the guarantee that high academic achievement will lead to career stability and success.

This research on inequalities in academic careers put in light the influence of societal and sectorial changes on the career paths, as well as the impact of these shifts regarding the work of the academic profession. Finally, they share a query on how to make higher education functional through an effective career structure.

References

Abbott, A. (2001). *Chaos of disciplines*. Chicago: University of Chicago Press.

ACE. (2008). *Too many rungs on the ladder? Faculty demographics and the future leadership of higher education* (ACE Issue Brief. September 2008). Washington: American Council on Education.

AFT. (1999). *The vanishing professor*. Washington: American Federation of Teachers.

AFT. (2009). *American academic. The state of the higher education workforce 1997–2007*. Washington: American Federation of Teachers.

Åkerlind, G. (2008). Growing and developing as a university researcher. *Higher Education, 55*, 241–254.

Allen, D. (2009). The publishable perishable professoriate. http://www.academia.org/the-publishable-perishable-professoriate.

Altbach, P. G. (Ed.). (1996). *The international survey of the academic profession. Portraits of fourteen countries*. Princeton: The Carnegie Foundation for the Advancement of Teaching.

Altbach, P. G. (2000). The deterioration of the academic estate: International patterns of academic work. In P. G. Altbach (Ed.), *The changing academic workplace: Comparative perspectives* (pp. 11–33). Chestnut Hill: Center for International Higher Education, Boston College.

Altbach, P. G. (2002). *The decline of the Guru: The academic profession in developing and middle income countries*. New York: Palgrave.

Altbach, P. G. (2005). Academic challenges: The American professoriate in comparative perspective. In A. Welch (Ed.), *The professoriate: Profile of a profession* (pp. 147–165). Dordrecht: Springer.

Altbach, P. G., & Musselin, C. (2008). Academic career structures: Bad ideas. *International Higher Education, 53*, 2–3.

Altbach, P., Reisberg, L., & Rumbley, L. E. (2009). *Trends in global higher education: Tracking an academic revolution*. A report prepared for the UNESCO 2009 World Conference on Higher Education. Paris: UNESCO.

Altman, Y., & Bournois, F. (2004). The "Coconut Tree" model of careers: The case of French academic. *Journal of Vocational Behavior, 64*(2), 320–328.

Arthur, M. B., Claman, P. H., & De Fillipi, R. J. (1995). Intelligent enterprise, intelligent careers. *Academy of Management Executive, 9*, 7–22.

Auriol, L. (2010). *Careers of doctorate holders: Employment and mobility patterns* (STI Working Paper 2010/4). Paris: OECD.

Barnett, R. (2004). The purposes of higher education and the changing face of academia. *London Review of Education, 2*(1), 61–73.

Barras, J. M. (1994). *L'Encouragement de la Relève dans les Hautes Écoles: Quelques Réflexions sous l'Angle de la Planification Universitaire*. Dissertation, Colloque de la CUS et de l'OFES.

Baruch, Y., & Hall, D. T. (2004). The academic career: A model for future careers in other sectors? *Journal of Vocational Behavior, 64*(2), 241–262.

Bauerlein, M. (2009). *Professors on the production line, students on their own* (AEI Future of American Education Project. Working Paper 2009-01). Washington, DC.

Berberet, J. (2008). Perceptions of early career faculty: Managing the transition from graduate school to the professorial career. *TIAA-CREF Institute Research Dialogue, 92*(June). http://www.tiaa-crefinstitute.org/articles/92.html.

Berning, E., & Falk, S. (2005). Das Promotionswesen im Umbruch. *Beiträge zur Hochschulforschung, 27*(1), 48–72.

Bluett, J. (2010). Oh, do not ask 'What is it?' An explication of the PhD through creative practice and its implications for the teaching of English. *English in Education, 44*(1), 45–58.

Böhmer, S., & Hornbostel, S. (2009). *Postdocs in Deutschland: Vergleich von Nachwuchsgruppenleiterprogrammen* (iFQ-Working Paper). Bonn: IFQ Institut für Forschungsinformation und Qualitätssicherung.

Bonaccorsi, F., Goujon, M., Srodogora, S. B., & Lerberghe, P. van. (2004). Les Carrières Scientifiques: Une Approche Fondée sur des Éléments d'Analyse Comparative Européenne. Rapport à Monsieur le Ministre de l'Education Nationale, de l'Enseignement Supérieur et de la Recherche, n°2004-140.

Bowen, H. R., & Schuster, J. H. (1986). *American professors. A national resource imperiled.* Oxford: Oxford University Press.

Boyer, E. L. (1994). *Scholarship reconsidered: Priorities of the professoriate.* Princeton: The Carnegie Foundation for the Advancement of Teaching.

Boyer, E. L., Altbach, P. G., & Whitelaw, M. J. (1994). *The academic profession: An international perspective.* Princeton: The Carnegie Foundation for the Advancement of Teaching.

Braxton, J. M. (Ed.). (2006). *Analyzing faculty work and rewards using Boyer's four domains of scholarship.* San Francisco: Jossey-Bass.

Brennan, J. (2006). The changing academic profession: The driving forces. In RIHE (Ed.), *Reports of changing academic profession project workshop on quality, relevance, and governance in the changing academia: International perspectives* (pp. 37–44). Hiroshima: Research Institute for Higher Education, Hiroshima University.

Bundesministerium für Bildung, Wissenschaft und Kultur. (2006). *Bericht über die Nachwuchsförderung und die Entwicklung der Personalstruktur der Universitäten gem. § 121 (19) UG 2002.* Wien: Bundesministerium für Bildung.

Burgess, R. G., & Band, S. (1998). Developments in postgraduate education and training in the UK. *European Journal of Education, 33*(2), 146–159.

Burkhardt, A. (Ed.). (2008). *Wagnis Wissenschaft. Akademische Karrierewege und das Fördersystem in Deutschland.* Leipzig: Akademische Verlagsanstalt.

Caplow, T., & McGee, R. J. (1958). *The academic marketplace.* New York: Basic Books.

Cartter, A. M. (1976). *PhD's and the academic labor market.* New York: McGraw Hill.

Cattel, J. M. (1906). A statistical study of American men of Science II: The measurement of scientific merit. *Science, 24*(622), 699–707.

Cattell, J. M. (1912). University control. *Science, New Series, 35*(908), 797–808.

Chait, R. P. (Ed.). (2005). *The questions of Tenure.* Cambridge: Harvard University Press.

Clark, B. (2007). Development of the sociology of higher education. In P. J. Gumport (Ed.), *Sociology of higher education, an evolving field.* Baltimore: John Hopkins University Press.

Council of Graduate Schools. (2006). A transatlantic dialogue on doctoral education. *Communicator, 39*(8), 1–2, 5.

Court, S. (1999). Negotiating the research imperative: The views of UK academics on their career opportunities. *Higher Education Quarterly, 53*, 65–87.

Craighead, L. W., & Craighead, W. E. (2006). PhD training in clinical psychology: Fix it before it breaks. *Clinical Psychology: Science and Practice, 13*, 235–241.

Crane, D. (1970). The academic marketplace revisited: A study of faculty mobility using the carter ratings. *The American Journal of Sociology, 75*(6), 953–964.

CUS. (1998). Plan Pluriannuel des Universités et Hautes Écoles Suisses pour la Période 2000–2003, Berne, CUS-CPU, juillet.

Cytermann, J. R. (2003). *Recrutement et Renouvellement des Enseignants-Chercheurs: Disparités entre Établissements et entre Disciplines.* Dissertation, Journée d'étude du RESUP, Paris X Nanterre.

de. Weert, E. (2009). The organised contradictions of teaching and research: Reshaping the academic profession. In J. Enders (Ed.), *The changing face of academic life. Analytical and comparative perspectives* (pp. 134–154). Basingstoke: Macmillan.

DeFillippi, R. J., & Arthur, M. B. (1994). The boundaryless career: A competency-based prospective. *Journal of Organizational Behaviour, 15*(4), 307–324.

Diggs, G. A., Garrisson-Wade, D. F., Estrada, D., & Galindo, R. (2009). Smiling faces and colored spaces: The experiences of faculty of color pursing tenure in the academy. *The Urban Review, 41*(4), 312–333.

Ehrenberg, R. G. (2003). Studying ourselves: The academic labor market. *Journal of Labor Economics, 21*(2), 267–287.

Ellison, A. B. (2002). *The accidental faculty: Adjunct instructors in community colleges.* Unpublished manuscript. ERIC Document Reproduction Service No. ED 466874.

Enders, J. (1999). Crisis? What crisis? The academic professions in the "Knowledge" society. *Higher Education, 38*(1), 71–81.

Enders, J. (2000). A chair system in transition: Appointments, promotions, and gate-keeping in German higher education. In P. G. Altbach (Ed.), *The changing academic workplace: Comparative perspectives* (pp. 36–60). Chestnut Hill: Center for International Higher Education Lynch School of Education, Boston College.

Enders, J. (2001). A chair system in transition: Appointments, promotions, and gate-keeping in German higher education. *Higher Education, 41*(1–2), 3–25.

Enders, J. (2004). Research training and careers in transition: A European perspective on the many faces of Ph.D. *Studies in Continuing Education, 26*(3), 419–429.

Enders, J., & Weert, E. de. (2009). Towards a T-shaped profession: Academic work and career in the knowledge society. In J. Enders & E. Weert de (Eds.), *The changing face of academic life. Analytical and comparative perspectives* (pp. 251–270). Basingstoke: Macmillan.

Enders, J., & Kottmann, A. (2009). *Deutsche Forschungsgemeinschaft. Neue Ausbildungsformen—andere Werdegänge? Ausbildungs- und Berufsverläufe von Absolventinnen und Absolventen der Graduiertenkollegs der DFG.* Weinheim: Wiley.

Enders, J., & Teichler, U. (Eds.). (1995). *Der Hochschullehrerberuf. Aktuelle Studien und ihre hochschulpolitische Diskussion.* Neuwied: Luchterhand.

Enders, J., & Teichler, U. (1997). A victim of their own success? Employment and working conditions of academic staff in comparative perspective. *The Journal of Higher Education, 34*(3), 347–372.

Enders, J., Kaiser, F., & Weert, E. de. (2006). The changing academic profession: The case of the Netherlands. In RIHE (Ed.), *Reports of changing academic profession project workshop on quality, relevance, and governance in the changing academia: International perspectives* (pp. 167–182). Hiroshima: Research Institute for Higher Education, Hiroshima University.

ESF. (2009). *Research careers in Europe. Landscape and horizons. Report by the ESF member organisation forum on research careers.* Strasbourg: European Science Foundation.

EUA. (2004–2005). *Doctoral programmes for the European knowledge society. Report on the EUA doctoral programmes project.* Brussels: European University Association.

Eurodoc. (2011). *The Eurodoc survey on the situation of doctoral candidates 2008/2009. Almost 9000 young researchers gave insights into their situation in the doctoral phase. First findings discussed in experts workshop in Bonn.* Brussels: The European Council of Doctoral Candidates and Junior Researchers (E. pub. release).

European Commission. (2000). Towards a European research area. Communication from the Commission to the Council, the European Parliament, the Economic and Social Committee and the Committee of the Regions. COM 6.

European Commission. (2004). *Europe needs more scientists. Increasing human resources for science and technology in Europe. Report by the High Level Group on Increasing Human Resources for Science and Technology in Europe 2004.* http://europa.eu.int/comm/research/conferences/2004/sciprof/pdf/final_eng.pdf.

European Commission. (2007). *Seventh framework programme (2007–2013): Building the Europe of knowledge.* Luxembourg: Publications Office of the European Union.

European Commission. (2009). *She figures 2009: Statistics and indicators on gender equality in science.* Luxembourg: Publications Office of the European Union.

Fairweather, J. S. (2005). Beyond the rhetoric: Trends in the relative values of teaching and research in faculty salaries. *The Journal of Higher Education, 76*(4), 401–442.

Federkeil, G., & Buch, F. (2007). Fünf Jahre Juniorprofessur—Zweite CHE-Befragung zum Stand der Einführung. CHE Arbeitspapier Nr. 90.

Feldman, D. C., & Turnely, W. H. (2001a). Contingent employment in academic career: Relative deprivation among adjunct faculty. *Journal of Vocational Behavior, 64*(2), 284–307.

Feldman, D. C., & Turnely, W. H. (2001b). A field study of adjunct faculty: The impact of career stage on reactions to non-tenure-track jobs. *Journal of Career Development, 28*(1), 1–16.

Felli, R., Goastellec, G., Baschung, L., & Leresche, J.-P. (2006). Politique Fédérale d'Encouragement de la Relève Académique et Stratégies Institutionnelles des Universités. Les Cahiers de l'Observatoire, Lausanne, OSPS-Unil, N°15.

Felli, R., Goastellec, G., & Leresche, J. P. (2007). Les Marchés du Travail Académique en France et en Suisse: des Imbrications Différenciées. Formation Emploi, 100, 49–64.

Fiedler, W., & Hebecker, E. (2006). Strukturiertes Promovieren in Europa. In W. Fielder & E. Hebecker (Eds.), Promovieren in Europa. Strukturen, Status und Perspektiven im Bologna-Prozess (pp. 11–17). Opladen: Leske und Budrich.

Finkelstein, M. (2007). The new look of academic careers in the United States. In M. Kogan & U. Teichler (Eds.), Key challenges to the academic profession (pp. 145–158, Werkstattberichte, Vol. 65). Kassel: International Centre for Higher Education Research Kassel (INCHER-Kassel) and UNESCO Forum on Higher Education, Research and Knowledge.

Finkelstein, M., & Altbach, P. (Eds.). (1997). The academic profession: The professoriate in crisis. New York: Garland.

Finkelstein, M., & Frances, C. (2006). The American academic profession: Context and characteristics. In RIHE (Ed.), Reports of changing academic profession project workshop on quality, relevance, and governance in the changing academia: International perspectives (pp. 231–254). Hiroshima: Research Institute for Higher Education, Hiroshima University.

Fry, H., & Ketteridge, S. (2003). A handbook for teaching and learning in higher education: Enhancing academic practice. London: Routledge.

Gaughan, M., & Robin, S. (2004). National science training policy and early scientific careers in France and the United States. Research Policy, 33, 569–581.

Gerhardt, A., & Briede, U. (2005). Zur Situation Promovierender in Deutschland. Ergebnisse einer bundesweiten THESIS—Doktorandenfragung. Beiträge zur Hochschulforschung, 1, 74–95.

Gilroy, M. (2009). The graying professoriate. Education Digest, 74, 63–64.

Gould, E. (2006). Professor or knowledge worker? The politics of defining faculty work. Higher Education in Europe, 31(3), 241–249.

Green, H., & Powell, S. (2005). Doctoral study in contemporary higher education. New York: Society for Research into Higher Education, and Open University Press.

Hall, D. T. (1976). Careers in organizations. Glenview: Scott Foresman.

Hall, D. T. (1986). Career development in organizations. San Francisco: Jossey-Bass.

Halsey, A. H. (1992). Decline of donnish dominion. The British academic professions in the twentieth century. Oxford: Oxford University Press.

Harley, S., Muller-Camen, M., & Collin, A. (2004). From academic communities to managed organisations: The implication for academic careers in UK and German universities. Journal of Vocational Behavior, 64(2), 329–345.

HEFCE. (2003). Consultation on "golden hellos". Policy Development Consultation, 13.

Honan, J. P., & Teferra, D. (2000). The American academic profession: Key policy challenges. In P. Altbach (Ed.), The changing academic workplace: Comparative perspectives (pp. 234–258). Boston: Center for International Higher Education.

Horta, H. (2009). Holding a post-doctoral position before becoming a faculty member: Does it bring benefits for the scholarly enterprise? Higher Education, 58(5), 689–721.

Huber, L. (2004). Forschendes Lernen. 10 Thesen zum Verhältnis von Forschung und Lehre aus der Perspektive des Studiums. Die Hochschule, 13(2), 29–49.

Huisman, J., & Weert, E. de. (2002). Academic careers from a European perspective. The Journal of Higher Education, 73(1), 141–160.

Hursfield, J., & Neathey, F. (2001). Recruitment and retention of staff in UK higher education. A survey and case studies. London: IRS Research.

Jalowiecki, B., & Gorzelak, G. J. (2004). La Fuite des Cerveaux, le Gain des Cerveaux et la Mobilité: Théories et Modèles Prospectifs. In UNESCO (Ed.), L'Enseignement Supérieur en Europe (pp. 299–308). Paris: UNESCO.

Janson, K., Schomburg, H., & Teichler, U. (2006). Wissenschaftliche Wege zur Professur oder ins Abseits? Strukturinformationen zu Arbeitsmarkt und Beschäftigung an Hochschulen in

Deutschland und den USA. Studie für das German Academic International Network (GAIN), New York. Kassel: International Centre for Higher Education Research (INCHER-Kassel).

Jantz, J., & Krüger, A. K. (2009). Promovieren in Deutschland. In L. Guzy & A. Mihr (Eds.), *Wohin mit uns? Wissenschaftlerinnen und Wissenschaftler der Zukunft* (pp. 169–180). Frankfurt a. M.: Lang.

Jeffery Petersen, N. (2005). *Adjunct faculty engagement in teaching, scholarship and service: Gaps in role definitions and related stress in schools of education.* Michigan Association of Teacher Educators conference October 28–29, 2005 Saginaw, Michigan.

Johnson, J. C. (2001). Research design for cultural anthropology PhD students. *Anthropology News, 42*(3), 22–22.

Johnston, R. T., & Brack, E. V. (1983). Appointment and promotion in the academic labour market: A preliminary survey of British university departments of geography, 1933–1982. *Transactions of the Institute of British Geographers, 8*(1), 100–111.

Kaulisch, M., & Böhmer, S. (2010). Inequality in academic careers in Germany. Indications from postdoctoral careers. In G. Goastellec (Ed.), *Inequalities in, through and by higher education.* Amsterdam: Sense.

Kaulisch, M., & Salerno, C. (2005). Conceptual framework to study academic career systems. IQ. http://www.forschungsinfo.de/iq/agora/career_systems/career_sytem.html.

Kehm, B. M. (2005). Developing doctoral degrees and qualifications in Europe. Good practice and issues of concern. *Beiträge zur Hochschulforschung, 27*(1), 10–33.

Kehm, B. M. (2006). Doctoral education in Europe and North America: A comparative analysis. In U. Teichler (Ed.), *The formative years of scholars* (pp. 67–78). London: Portland.

Kehm, B. M. (2007). Quo Vadis doctoral education? New European approaches in the context of global changes. *European Journal of Education, 42*(3), 307–319.

Kehm, B. M. (2009). Pressure for change and modernisation. In J. Enders & E. Weert de (Eds.), *The changing face of academic life: Analytical and comparative perspectives* (pp. 155–170). Basingstoke: MacMillan.

Kehm, B. M., & Kreckel, R. (2008a). *Kapitel 6: Internationaler Vergleich. Bundesbericht zur Förderung des wissenschaftlichen Nachwuchses.* Bonn: Bundesministerium für Bildung und Forschung.

Kehm, B., & Kreckel, R. (2008b). Internationaler Vergleich. Wagnis Wissenschaft. Akademische Karrierewege und das Fördersystem in Deutschland. In A. Burkhardt (Ed.), *Wagnis Wissenschaft. Akademische Karrierewege und das Fördersystem in Deutschland* (pp. 535–608). Leipzig: Akademische Verlagsanstalt.

Kiley, M., & Mullins, G. (2004). Examining the examiners: How inexperienced examiners approach the assessment of research theses. *International Journal of Educational Research, 41*(2), 121–135.

Kogan, M., & Teichler, U. (Eds.). (2007). *Key challenges to the academic profession* (Werkstattberichte, Vol. 65). Kassel: International Centre for Higher Education Research Kassel (INCHER-Kassel) and UNESCO Forum on Higher Education, Research and Knowledge.

Kogan, M., Moses, I., & El-Kahwas, E. (1994). *Staffing higher education: Meeting new challenges.* London: Kingsley.

Kreckel, R. (Ed.). (2008). *Zwischen Promotion und Professur. Das wissenschaftliche Personal in Deutschland im Vergleich mit Frankreich, GB, USA, den Niederlanden, Österreich und der Schweiz.* Leipzig: Akademische Verlagsanstalt.

Kreckel, R. (2010). *Quo vadis deutsche Wissenschaft? Wie sieht die Zukunft in der deutschen Hochschullandschaft aus?* Paper presented at the KISSWIN-Nachwuchstagung: "Lust auf wissenschaftliche Karriere in Deutschland", Berlin.

Le Saout, R., & Loirand, G. (1998). Les Charges d'Enseignement Vacataires. Les Paradoxes d'un Statut Perverti. *Genèses, 30*, 146–157.

Lewis, L. S. (1975). *Scaling the ivory tower. Merits and its limits in academic careers.* Baltimore: John Hopkins University Press.

Locke, W., & Teichler, U. (Eds.). (2007). *The changing academic conditions for academic work and careers in select countries* (Werkstattberichte, Vol. 66). Kassel: International Centre for Higher Education Research Kassel (INCHER-Kassel).

Long, J. S., & Fox, M. F. (1995). Scientific careers: Universalism and particularism. *Annual Review of Sociology, 21*, 45–71.

Lovat, T., A., & Holbrook, A. (2008). Ways of knowing in doctoral examination: How well is the doctoral regime? *Educational Research Review, 3*(1), 66–76.

Ma, J., & Stephan, P. E. (2004). *The growing postdoc population at U.S. research universities.* Paper prepared for the IAA-CREF Institute Conference. Recruitment, Retention, and Retirement: The Three R's of Higher Education in the 21st Century. New York: TIAA-CREF Institute and Department of Economics.

Macfarlane, B. (2010). Professors as intellectual leaders: Formation, identity and role. *Studies in Higher Education, 36*(1), 57–73.

Marginson, S., & Wende, M. Van Der. (2007). *Globalisation and higher education* (OECD education working papers series. Working Paper No. 8). Paris: OECD.

Marsh, H. W., & Rowe, K. J. (2002). PhD students' evaluations of research supervision: Issues, complexities, and challenges in a nationwide Australian experiment in benchmarking universities. *The Journal of Higher Education, 73*(3), 313–348.

Mau, S., & Gottschall, K. (2008). Strukturierte Promotionsprogramme in den Sozialwissenschaften. *Soziologie, 37*(1), 41–60.

Meier, F., & Schimank, U. (2009). Matthäus schlägt Humboldt? New Public Management und die Einheit von Forschung und Lehre. *Beiträge zur Hochschulforschung, 31*(1), 42–61.

Melin, G., & Janson, K. (2006). What skills and knowledge should a PhD have? Changing preconditions for PhD education and post doc work. In U. Teichler (Ed.), *The formative years of scholars* (pp. 79–84). London: Portland.

Meri, T. (2007). *Doctorate holders. The beginning of their career. Science and technology—statistics in focus.* Luxembourg: Eurostat.

Metcalf, J. (2006). The changing nature of doctoral programmes. In U. Teichler (Ed.), *The formative years of scholars* (pp. 79–84). London: Portland.

Metcalf, H., Rolfe, H., Stevens, P., & Weale, M. (2005). *Recruitment and retention of academic staff in higher education.* (Research Brief, D. f. E. a. Skills. RB 658. Research Report No. 658). London: National Institute of Economic and Social Research.

Meyer, T., & Nyffeler, B. (2001). L'Encouragement de la Relève Universitaire: Entre la Vocation et la Chaire? Mesures Spéciales de la Confédération pour l'Encouragement de la Relève Universitaire dans les Hautes Écoles. Rapport sur l'Enquête Qualitative 2000. OFES.

Modern Language Association (MLA). (2008). *Education in the balance: A report on the academic workforce in English.* Report of the 2007 ADE Ad Hoc Committee on Staffing. The Modern Language Association of America and the Association of Departments of English. http://www.mla.org/pdf/workforce_rpt03.pdf.

Moguérou, P. (2005). Doctoral and postdoctoral education in science and engineering: Europe in the international competition. *European Journal of Education, 40*(4), 367–392.

Monks, J. (2007). The relative earnings of contingent faculty in higher education. *Journal of Labour Research, 28*(3), 487–501.

Multrus, F. (2004). *Fachkulturen. Begriffsbestimmung, Herleitung und Analysen. Eine empirische Untersuchung über Studierende deutscher Hochschulen.* Dissertation, Universität Konstanz, Konstanz.

Musselin, C. (2003). *Marchés du Travail Scientifique et Mobilités en Europe.* Dissertation, Conseil Scientifique du CNRS.

Musselin, C. (2004). Towards a European academic labour market? Some lessons drawn from empirical studies on academic mobility. *Higher Education, 48*(1), 55–78.

Musselin, C. (2005a). *Le Marché des Universitaires, France, Allemagne, Etats-Unis.* Paris: Sciences-Po.

Musselin, C. (2005b). European academic labor markets in transition. *Higher Education, 49*(1–2), 135–154.

Musselin, C. (2006). The French academic professions. In RIHE (Ed.), *Reports of changing academic profession project workshop on quality, relevance, and governance in the changing academia: International perspectives* (pp. 115–128). Hiroshima: Research Institute for Higher Education, Hiroshima University.

Musselin, C. (2008). *Les Universitaires*. Paris: La Découverte.

Musselin, C., & Pigeyre, F. (2008). Les Effets des Mécanismes de Recrutement Collégial sur la Discrimination: le Cas des Recrutements Universitaires. *Sociologie du travail, 50*(1), 48–70.

National Postdoctoral Association. (2009). Fact Sheet on U.S. Postdoctoral Stipends. http://www.nationalpostdoc.org/atf/cf/%7B89152E81-F2cB-430C-B151-49D071AEB33E%7D/PostdocoralFactSheet.pdf.

Neave, G., & Rhoades, G. (1987). The academic estate in Western Europe. In B. R. Clark (Ed.), *The academic profession: National, disciplinary, and institutional settings* (pp. 211–270). Berkeley: University of California Press.

NSOPF:04. (2005). *2004 National study of postsecondary faculty. Report on faculty and instructional staff in fall 2003*. Washington: US Department of Education. National Center for Education Statistics.

Nunn, A. (2005). *The "Brain Drain". Academic and skilled migration to the UK and its impacts on Africa*. Report to the AUT and NATFHE. Leeds: Leeds Metropolitan University.

Pechar, H. (2005). Hire and Fire? Akademische Karrieren unter den Bedingungen des UG 2002. In H. Welte, M. Auer, & C. Meister-Scheytt (Eds.), *Management an Universitäten zwischen Tradition und (Post-) Moderne* (pp. 317–337). Mering: Rainer Hampp.

Pechar, H. (2008). "Doktorat neu"—ein österreichischer Blick auf eine europäische Reformdebatte. In B. M. Kehm (Ed.), *Hochschule im Wandel. Die Universität als Forschungsgegenstand. Festschrift für Ulrich Teichler* (pp. 319–334). Frankfurt a. M.: Campus.

Pechar, H., & Campbell, D. F. J. (2008). *Internationaler Vergleich und empirische Befragung von WissenschaftlerInnen und DoktorandInnen. Forschungsprojekt im Auftrag des FWF (Fonds zur Förderung der wissenschaftlichen Forschung) und des BMWF (Bundesministerium für Wissenschaft und Forschung)*. Vienna: Institut für Wissenschaftskommunikation und Hochschulforschung.

Peiperl, M., & Baruch, Y. (1997). Back to square zero: The post-corporate career. *Organizational Dynamics, 25*(4), 7–22.

Probst, C., & Lepori, B. (2008). What is a doctorate? Changing meanings and practices in communication sciences in Switzerland. *European Journal of Education, 43*(4), 477–494.

Recotillet, I. (2007). PhD graduates with post-doctoral qualification in the private sector: Does it pay off? *Labour, 21*(3), 473–502.

Reichert, S., & Tauch, C. (2003). *Trends 2003. Progress towards the European higher education area*. Genève: European University Association.

Riesman, D. (1956). *The academic profession. Constraint and variety in American education*. Lincoln: University of Nebraska Press.

RIHE. (2009). *The changing academic profession over 1992–2007: International, comparative and quantitative perspectives* (International Seminar Report, No.°13). Hiroshima: Research Institute for Higher Education, Hiroshima University.

Rumbley, L., Pacheco, I., & Altbach, P. G. (2008). *International comparison of academic salaries: An exploratory study*. Chestnut Hill: Boston College Center for International Higher Education.

Schimank, U. (2001). Jenseits von Humboldt? Muster und Entwicklungspfade des Verhältnisses von Forschung und Lehre in verschiedenen europäischen Hochschulsystemen. *Leviathan Sonderheft, 20*, 295–325.

Schlegel, J. (2001). Prinzipien der Nachwuchsförderung in Deutschland. http://www.nt.tuwien.ac.at/nthft/temp/oefg/text/ws_sicherung/Beitrag_3.pdf.

Schuster, J., & Finkelstein, M. (2006). *The American faculty: The restructuring of academic work and careers*. Baltimore: Johns Hopkins University Press.

Siow, A. (1995). *The organization of the market for professors* (Working Paper UT-ECIPA-SIO-Ws91-01). Toronto.

Teichler, U. (1996). The conditions of the academic profession: An international comparative analysis of the academic profession in Western Europe, Japan and the United States. In P. A. M. Maassen & F. A. Van Vught (Eds.), *Inside academia: New challenges for the academic profession* (pp. 15–65). Utrecht: De Tijdstroom.

Teichler, U. (1999). Der Professor im internationalen Vergleich: Aspekte zu Tätigkeit und Selbstbild. *Forschung und Lehre, 5,* 242–245.

Teichler, U. (Ed.). (2006). *The formative years of scholars.* London: Portland.

Teichler, U. (2008). Academic staff in Germany: Per Aspera ad Astra? The changing academic profession in international comparative and quantitative persepectives. In RIHE (Ed.), *Report of the international conference on the changing academic profession project* (pp. 131–152). Hiroshima: Research Institute for Higher Education, Hiroshima University.

Teichler, U., & Bracht, O. (2006). The academic profession in Germany. In RIHE (Ed.), *Reports of changing academic profession project workshop on quality, relevance, and governance in the changing academia: International perspectives* (pp. 129–150). Hiroshima: Research Institute for Higher Education, Hiroshima University.

Teichler, U., & Sadlak, J. (Eds.). (2000). *Higher education research. Its relationship to policy and practice.* New York: Elsevier.

Tierney, W. G. (2004). Turning the lights out: Tenure in the 21st century. *The Journal of Higher Education, 75*(2), 228–233.

Tight, M. (2002). What does it mean to be a professor? *Higher Education Review, 34*(2), 15–32.

Trower, C. A. (2000a). The ties that bind, the meaning, purpose, and locus of tenure. In C. A. Trower (Ed.), *Policies on faculty appointment: Standard practices and unusual arrangements* (pp. 79–109). Bolton: Anker.

Trower, C. A. (Ed.). (2000b). *Policies on faculty appointment: Standard practices and unusual arrangements.* Bolton: Anker.

Trower, C. A. (2009). Toward a greater understanding of the tenure track for minorities. *Change, 41*(5), 38–45.

UNESCO. (2004). La Fuite des Cerveaux et le Marché du Travail Universitaire et Intellectuel en Europe du Sud-Est. *L'Enseignement Supérieur en Europe, XXIX*(3).

Waterman, R. H., Waterman, J. A., & Collard, B. A. (1994). Toward a career-resilient workforce. *Harvard Business Review, 72*(4), 87–95.

Weiler, H. N. (2004). Hochschulen in den USA—Modell für Deutschland? *Aus Politik und Zeitgeschichte, B 25,* 26–33.

Wheeler, D. (2008). Colleges explore new ways to manage retirements. *The Chronicle of Higher Education.* June 13, 2008. http://chronicle.com/free/v54/i40/40a00101.htm.

Williams, G., Blackstone, T., & Metcalf, D. (1974). *The academic labour market: Economic and social aspects of a profession.* Amsterdam: Elsevier.

Wilson, L. (1943). *The academic man: A study in the sociology of a profession.* New York: Oxford.

Wolfinger, N. H., Mason, M. A., & Goulden, M. (2009). Stay in the game: Gender, family formation and alternative trajectories in the academic life course. *Social Forces, 87*(3), 1591–1621.

Youn, T. I. K., & Price, T. M. (2009). Learning from the experience of others: The evolution of faculty tenure and promotion rules in comprehensive institutions. *The Journal of Higher Education, 80*(2), 204–237.

Zetlaoui, J. (1999). *L'Universitaire et ses Métiers. Contribution à l'Analyse des Espaces de Travail.* Paris: L'Harmattan.

Internationalisation and the Academic Labour Market

Carole Probst and Gaële Goastellec

1 Introduction

While the international dimension has been a constitutive element of the academic environment since the Middle-Ages (Charle and Verger 1994), it has become more of a focus since the 1990s, both on the policy level—in Europe particularly, enhanced through the Bologna process and the aim of building the European Research Area—and as a research subject (Knight and de Wit 1995; Teichler 2004). In their review of research on internationalisation in higher education over the last decade, Kehm and Teichler (2007) identify the following sub-themes as dominating the research landscape (Kehm and Teichler 2007, p. 264):

- Mobility of students and academic staff.
- Mutual influences of higher education systems on each other.
- Internationalisation of the substance of teaching, learning, and research.
- Institutional strategies of internationalisation.
- Knowledge transfer.
- Cooperation and competition.
- National and supranational policies as regarding the international dimension of higher education.

C. Probst (✉)
School of Health Professions,
Zurich University of Applied Sciences,
Winterthur, Switzerland
e-mail: carole.probstschilter@zhaw.ch

G. Goastellec
Politics and Organizations of Higher Education Research Unit
at the Observatory Science, Policy and Society (OSPS),
University of Lausanne,
Lausanne, Switzerland

B. M. Kehm, U. Teichler (eds.), *The Academic Profession in Europe: New Tasks and New Challenges,* The Changing Academy – The Changing Academic Profession in International Comparative Perspective 5, DOI 10.1007/978-94-007-4614-5_7, © Springer Science+Business Media Dordrecht 2013

Internationalisation thus concerns several dimensions of academic life at different levels. In the context of higher education, internationalisation—not to be confounded with globalisation[1]—can be defined as follows:

> Internationalisation of higher education is the process of integrating an international/ intercultural dimension into the teaching, research and service functions of the institution. (Knight 1999, p. 16)

Vabø (2007, referring to Trondal et al. 2001), distinguishes between *old* and *new internationalisation*, where old internationalisation is "typically initiated and managed by academic staff on the individual basis" (Vabø 2007, p. 99) while new internationalisation occurs at the collective, institutional level and is more formal—and recently also more competitive—in its character.

New internationalisation is a transversal dimension of higher education institutions, which develop specific approaches to enhance their internationality, as underlined by Knight (1999): the *activity approach* in which internationalisation is addressed through specific activities or programmes, as for example, student/faculty exchange or curriculum; the *competency approach* in which emphasis is put on the individual and his/her skills, knowledge, attitudes, and values, where the aim of implementing measures is the development of competencies; the *ethos approach* aiming at the promotion of a campus culture supportive for international and intercultural processes; and the *process approach* in which the international dimension is integrated in policies, procedures and programmes, with a strong emphasis on sustainability of the international dimension. Meek (2007, p. 65) proposes to add two more approaches: the *business approach* emphasizing "the maximisation of profit from international student fees" and the *market approach* focusing on "competition, market domination and deregulation". There is no dominant approach, and the different approaches are considered "complementary and certainly not mutually exclusive" (Knight 1999, p. 16).

This text focuses on one particular aspect, namely the internationalisation of the academic labour market, a topic which does not seem to be at the core of most studies on internationalisation of higher education (Kim and Locke 2009), although higher education institutions tend to rank it as the most important dimension of the overall process of internationalisation (Knight 2003).

In fact, as underlined by Marginson and van der Wende (2009), most of the government and higher education actors' discourses assume the positive dimension of academic mobility, to the point that they are "largely diffused and taken for granted in many higher education and research public policies, so that specific measures and devices are developed by many countries in order to promote academic mobility" (Musselin 2004a, p. 56). They question the generally admitted perception that mobility is increasing, showing that although effectively short-term mobility has

---

[1] "Globalisation is the flow of technology, economy, knowledge, people, values, ideas [...] across borders. Globalisation affects each country in a different way due to a nation's individual history, traditions, culture and priorities. Internationalisation of higher education is one of the ways a country responds to the impact of globalisation yet, at the same time respects the individuality of the nation" (Knight 1999, p. 14). See also Altbach (2002) for a similar definition.

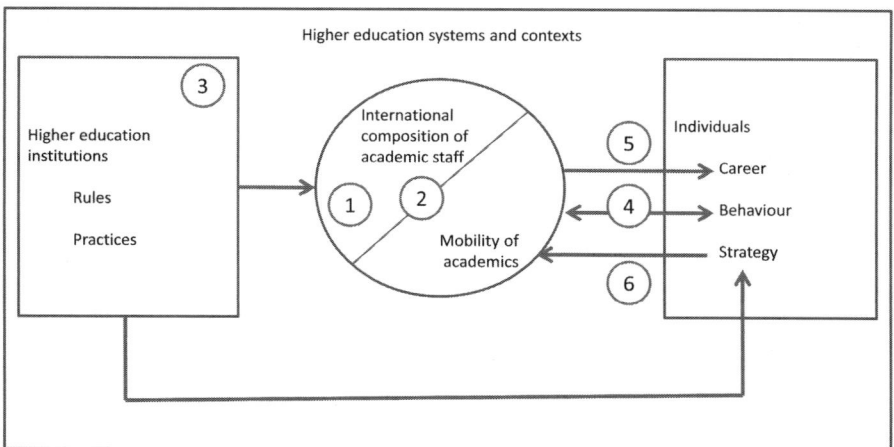

Fig. 7.1 Overview on internationalisation topics

largely augmented, it does not seem to be that much the case of an internationalisation of long-term academic positions, except in a few country such as the United States, or Switzerland (Felli et al. 2007b).

While topics such as the internationalisation of curriculum or of the student body or institutional strategies for internationalisation for sure have an influence on the academic labour market, they are not detailed in the following. As well, conceptual or summarizing papers discussing the implications of internationalisation in the general higher education context (see for example, de Wit 1995; Teichler 1999, 2004; Qiang 2003; Enders 2004; Altbach and Knight 2006; Kehm and Teichler 2007; OECD 2009a) will not be included.

When trying to identify the literature on the academic labour market integration regarding the topic of internationalisation, different types of approaches come to light. Figure 7.1 provides an overview of approaches that will be discussed in the following sections.

This figure is centred on two topics that represent two sides of the same coin: internationalisation of the academic workforce and researchers' mobility. While the former one addresses the topic of academic labour market internationalisation from the point of view of the higher education institutions, systems or societies; the latter addresses the incidence of internationalisation on individual academics. Within these two main research domains, several issues are questioned.

Focusing on the macro or meso level, one can distinguish at least three types of approaches that integrate, to different extents, the internationalisation dimension.

1. A descriptive approach interested in the international composition of academic staff, most often represented in official statistics both at the national and international level.
2. Research questioning flows of academics: the brain drain/brain gain/brain circulation issue between higher education institutions, systems and more widely, societies.

3. An in-depth approach looking at the rules and practices higher education institutions apply when attracting and employing new collaborators (often inspired by sociology of science).

Focusing on the individual level, again at least three approaches to internationalisation can be identified:

4. Quantitative studies looking at the behaviour of individual academics, thus at mobility patterns within academics' careers.
5. Research, often combining qualitative and quantitative instruments, interested in analysing the effects of mobility on individual academics' careers and on individuals' perception of the benefits (and rarely also negative outcomes) of their mobility.
6. A qualitative approach interested in individual academics' strategies regarding mobility, thus their reasons for being mobile.

2   The Macro/Meso Approaches

On the policy level, evidence of the relevance of the topic of international composition of academic staff is easily found: The "adequate flow of competent researchers with high levels of mobility between institutions, disciplines, sectors and countries" is seen as an important element of the European Research Area (Commission of the European communities 2007, p. 1); the "ultimate political goal" of *The European Charter for Researchers and Code of Conduct for the Recruitment of Researchers* is "to contribute to the development of an attractive, open and sustainable European labour market for researchers" (European Commission 2005, p. 4). Instruments for enhancing mobility are provided at the European level, within countries, not only through the funding of international, collaborative research projects or scholarships, but also through the implementation of mobility portals and other information services for academics willing to go abroad.

But does this internationalisation of the mobility sustain an international—or at least European—labour market? The answer to this question is manifold; the characteristics of national labour markets and the way in which internationalisation is perceived at the national and local level differ, and so does the degree of internationalisation of the academic population. In the following, we look at the availability of data on the degree of internationalisation in different countries.

2.1   Describing the International Composition of Academic Staff

It is quite informative that the available OECD data characterising the internationalisation of the academic profession provides information mainly on Ph.D. students (OECD 2004). This denomination of academic staff is probably the sole that all higher education academic markets share; this makes the collection and comparison of quantitative data immediately possible, while it is not the case for the other categories.

Figure 7.2 shows the share of foreign Ph.D. students among different OECD countries in 2006; this share can be taken as an indicator for the internationalisation of both higher education and research (OECD 2004). It comes clear that this share varies a lot among OECD countries; it is high in Switzerland, New Zealand and the United Kingdom, while countries such as Turkey, Greece, Mexico, Chile, and Slovak Republic show rather low shares of foreign Ph.D. students.

A comparison of the data for 1998 and 2006 shows that these numbers evolve rapidly: changes range from −79 % (Slovak Republic) up to +444 % of foreign students (New Zealand). This is also confirmed by country studies: In Norway for example, the share of international doctoral students has increased from 7 to 22 % between 1991 and 2005 (Vabø 2007).

However, the note to the OECD data already reveals a challenge when measuring the internationality of the academic personnel: "International students are defined as non-resident students of reporting countries for all countries except Finland and Switzerland which define them as students with prior education outside the reporting country" (OECD 2009b). When talking about foreign academics, a clear definition of who is to be considered a foreigner is important, in particular, due to national specificities in the length of naturalisation processes which sometimes can take several generations. Similar limitations regarding mobility data were pointed out by the EURODATA study regarding student mobility (Kelo et al. 2006): often, the only available data is information on the nationality of students, but it is not known whether students were living in the "host" country already before taking up their studies or whether they are really genuine mobile students.

As underlined previously, data on the share of foreigners that go beyond the level of the doctorate seem to be more difficult to retrieve. In the *OECD Science, Technology and Industry Scoreboard*, only information about foreign scholars in the United States is available; the Eurostat database on Science and Technology contains many missing values in the dataset on researchers by citizenship. Data from the first Carnegie survey study on the academic profession *(The International Survey of Academic Staff)* reveal considerable differences when looking at whether academics received their highest degree in the country in which they are employed or elsewhere, reflecting differences in national policies and recruitment behaviour (Welch 1997).

More data is available at the level of individual countries. Here, trends towards higher degrees of internationalisation are visible. In Switzerland for example, the overall share of foreign staff at universities has increased from 30.7 % in 1999 to 40 % in 2008 (see Fig. 7.3).

In Switzerland's neighbouring country Germany, the share of non-national academic personnel is considerably lower. Here, in 2008, overall 9.5 % of academics were of foreign nationality. Differences between fields of sciences are visible: While this share is as low as 1.7 % for Sports, it reaches 13.1 % for Mathematics and Sciences (Statistisches Bundesamt 2009). In France, foreigner account for less

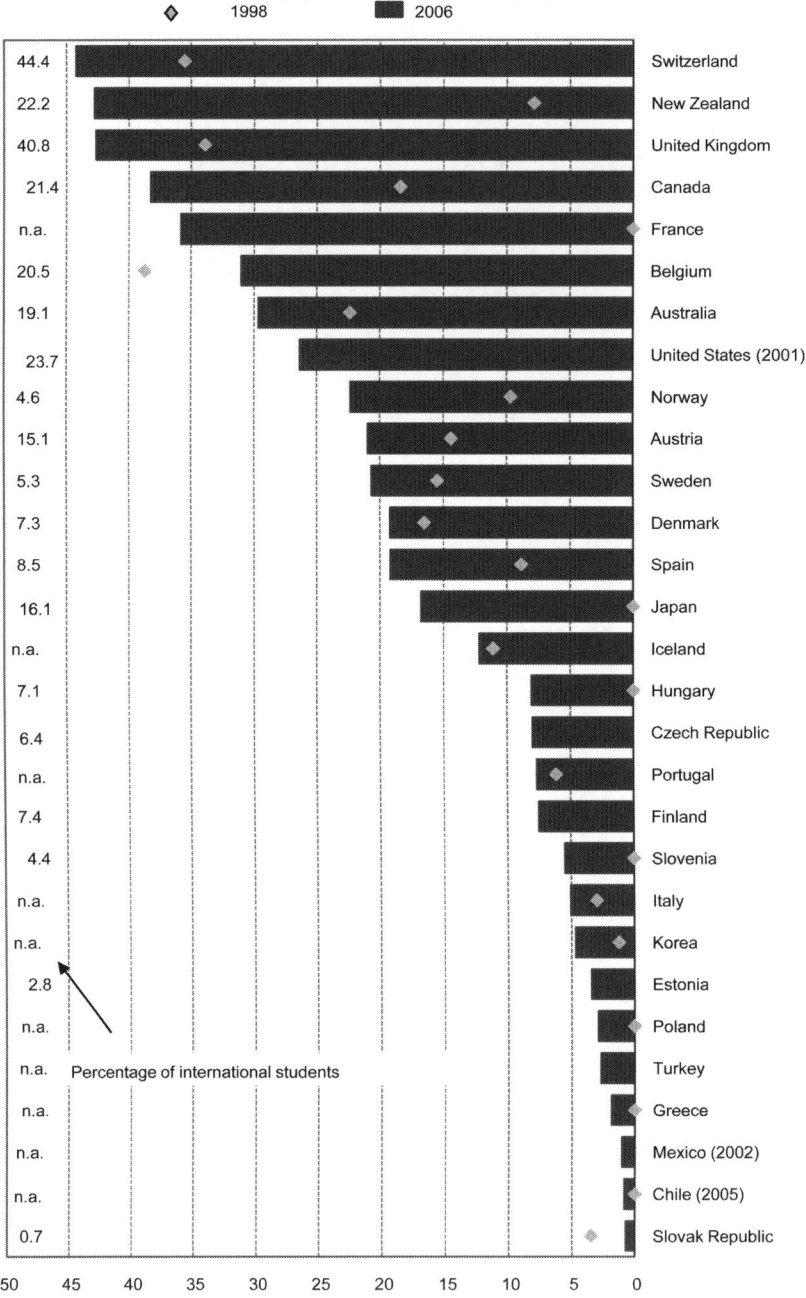

Fig. 7.2 Share of foreign Ph.D. students, 1998 and 2006. (Source: OECD 2009b)

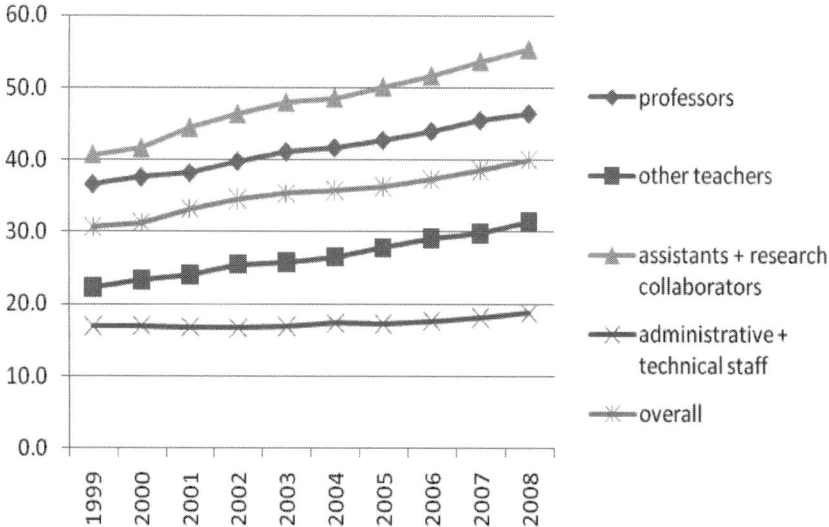

Fig. 7.3 Share of non-national academic personnel at Swiss universities, headcount. (Source: Swiss Statistics, Swiss Federal Statistical Office)

than 10 % of all the French academics, with differences not only between fields but also between institutional types: universities hire 7 % of foreign academics, compared with 12 % in the *Grandes Ecoles* (Bonaccorsi et al. 2004). The degree of internationalisation is thus linked to the level of prestige of one institution (Goastellec and Paradeise 2008).

2.2 Analysing and Questioning the International Flows of Academics

On the basis of the quantitative data produced by international bodies and further analysis of academics' flows between higher education systems of faculties, some researchers analyse one of the most sensitive dimension of the internationalisation of the academic market: the brain drain/brain gain issue. This issue is plural: it questions the attractiveness of the various higher education systems and their societies, and the organisation of the competition for the "best brains", the geographical map of leading research centres in the different disciplines, the knowledge transfer function of mobility, the public authorities' policies implemented in reaction to an identified weakness in the brain drain/brain gain game, etc.

For example, the European Union has several times pointed out the important European outward mobility towards English-speaking countries. As Marginson and van der Wende (1994) recall, many doctoral graduates from Germany, for example, pursue their career in the United States or the United Kingdom, while the attractiveness of the German academic market place for foreigners has decreased. The creation of the excellence initiative in 2005 is aimed at reversing this trend by helping universities to improve their international visibility and competitiveness. The creation of the PRES[2] in France follows the same rationale: bringing together higher education institutions to improve their visibility. It has also been an incentive for the development of European policies to improve the attractiveness of the academic market and the opportunities for academic mobility (for example, the programme ERASMUS Mundus, which is not without similarities with the American Fulbright Program).

However, it has also been acknowledged that mobility of researchers and their knowledge is not a purely linear flow, but a more complex issue. Hence, in the late 1990s the concept of "brain circulation" has been introduced (Fontes 2007).

Based on the United Kingdom Changing Academic Profession Survey, Kim and Locke (2009) identify a typology of flows of academics between and within countries:

- *Study-abroad countries* which graduates tend to leave for the doctorate, but to which they then turn back for their post-doctorate or employment;
- *Magnetic countries* which attract people for work, for study or both; and
- *Self-contained countries* where mobility of academics occurs within the same country or even within the same institution.

Obviously, these categories are not mutually exclusive. Japan for example, is both a *study-abroad* and a *magnetic* country: Many doctoral degree holders go abroad for a post-doctoral period, but a large share of them returns to Japan (a study covering all Japanese doctoral degree holders from the years 2002–2006 shows that 50 % have returned to Japan after 5 years (Misu and Horoiwa 2010)). The knowledge transfer function of mobility becomes evident: Through mobility of post-doctorates, the Japanese system imports knowledge, "catching up with advanced overseas countries" (Huang 2007, p. 97). On the other hand, a raise in the number of courses in English language, adapted to the need of students from North America, Europe and English-speaking countries in general has led to the need to employ more faculty members able to provide courses in English language. This has led to an increase in the number of foreign faculty members in Japan, especially in the private university sector (Huang 2007), and hence probably also has an influence on the internationalisation of curricula, of contents in teaching and in research.

Norway (but also Sweden and Western European and Scandinavian countries in general, Melin 2004) is another example of a *study-abroad* country: Here, academics, particularly doctoral students and post-doctorates, are to some extent expected to go abroad for shorter or longer stays; however, different systemic, academic, social, and practical barriers exist (Vabø 2007).

Examples of *self-contained* countries are China and Italy (Kim and Locke 2009). Also, Spain and France could be added to this list: As Cruz-Castro and Sanz-

---

[2] PRES, Poles Regionaux d'Excellence Scientifique, or regional centers of scientific excellences, have been developed in France during the last years also in reaction to the Shanghai ranking.

Menéndez (2010) have shown, when looking at the access to permanent positions within 3 years after the doctorate, the Spanish labour market does not favour mobility after the doctorate, but rather institutional fidelity. Gaughan and Robin (2004) show similar results for France.

A fourth category, which has not been identified by Kim and Locke, would be countries whose young academics tend to leave and not to come back, thus *brain drain* countries. Some researchers question the consequences for developing countries (UNESCO-CEPES 2004; Nunn 2005). But, this brain drain does not only occur in economically less developed countries outside the Western world. An example from Europe is again Italy, where, according to Coccia and Rolfo (2010), many academics tend to look for positions abroad because of a lack of good career prospects in research within Italian institutions. This brain drain issue is particularly accurate in disciplines in which professional opportunities and working resources strongly differ between countries, such as for example, in life sciences (Musselin 2004b).

Enders and Musselin propose another classification, based on the results from a survey of the academic profession carried out in the early 1990s (Enders and Musselin 2008, referring to Boyer et al. 1994):

- Countries whose scholars wish to be considered as partners at the international level but are often not seen as equal partners. These are often economically less developed countries.
- Countries where the international dimension in communication, cooperation and recognition is seen as of central importance. These are often rather small, but economically developed countries.
- Countries in which both the national and the international orientation are seen as important: not only international visibility is considered of high value, but also the contribution to the local environment is stressed. These are usually larger countries.
- Countries in which internationalisation is mostly visible through the presence of foreign students and researchers, and where international orientation stops at the boarders of the linguistic and cultural region. The United Kingdom and the United States of America are the most striking examples, even though the situation might be changing now.

Overall, there seems to be tension between cooperative internationalisation and competitive globalisation (Enders and de Weert 2004; Enders and Musselin 2008), between two heterogeneous objectives of mobility policies (Marginson and van der Wende 2009): on the one hand, there is the organisation of free academic movement between national higher education systems, where internationalisation is connoted with a positive bias, and a need for international orientation and collaboration is underlined (Musselin 2004a, 2005a; Kehm 2006). On the other hand, there is the reinforcement of national higher education systems academic capacity, thus a focus on national markets can still be observed (Enders and Musselin 2008): As underlined by Enders and de Weert, the higher education institutions "regulatory and funding context was (and still is) national, their contribution to national cultures was (and still is) significant, students tended to be (and still are) trained to become national functionaries and universities played (and still play) a considerable role in the national innovation system" (Enders and de Weert 2004, p. 145).

Such classifications are interesting examples of what can be done when analysing large-scale data on mobility; they become even more relevant when combining the data with an in-depth analysis of the local labour markets, its rules, regulations and practices.

2.3   Analysing National Market Structures and Organisations

Academic systems have been the purpose of various research enterprises, including projects focusing on national market structures and organisations. Differences between national higher education systems and between disciplinary fields have been elaborated thoroughly by different scholars in the field of higher education studies (see for example, Clark 1983; Whitley 1984; Ben-David 1992; Kivinen et al. 1999; Abbott 2001; Becher and Trowler 2001). These differences are visible in many aspects, among them also the structure of academic careers. In Italy, for example, the doctorate is a quite new degree which emerged only in the 1980s (Moscati 2004); before the existence of the doctoral degree, however, Italian graduates had demonstrated their research ability in a Master thesis which had to answer rather high requirements (with a corresponding high drop-out rate).

Nowadays, however, the doctorate seems to bequite a common element in academic careers in most higher education systems—the entry ticket to the academic career, but career structures after the doctorate differ. While the general career structure could be described as composed of the three elements training—consolidation—settlement, these phases are of different duration in different career systems. As there is no unique structure of the academic career which is common to all systems, mobility is challenged: for potentially mobile academics it is difficult to understand whether they fulfil the formal conditions for a position in a foreign system, and for commissions evaluating applications it is difficult to interpret the previous career of foreign applicants.

Musselin (2003, 2004a, 2005a, b) has elaborated such differences in her extensive work on the characteristics of the academic labour market by confronting the US, French, and German situations when it comes to the recruitment of professors. For example, while in Germany, access to a permanent position occurs at the average age of 42 years, after several non-permanent contracts; in France, tenure is accessible rather soon after the doctorate, at the average age of 33 years (Musselin 2004a). These differences are clearly reflected in national academic labour markets: the conditions for admission to permanent positions differ. This strongly enhances on the accessibility of the national labour markets for foreigners: they do not fit the classical career within the country, and therefore committees evaluating candidatures of foreign scholars might not be able to identify the elements corresponding to the local requirements.

Musselin's studies also reveal considerable differences between the ways in which scholars are recruited, from the decision on available posts and their promotion through the recruitment process up to the assignment of the positions. These procedures not only vary between national higher education systems, but also between disciplinary fields. Implicit rules play an important role, and conditions for access are strongly related to the national career systems; for example, in some fields in France, access to professorship is only possible with a specific French diploma. Implicit practices play an important role in the recruitment procedure, which limits chances of foreign applicants: as these practices are not explicitly stated, they are usually unknown to outsiders.

Referring to Musselin's studies and prior studies on the academic career system in Switzerland, Felli et al. (2007a) compare the academic labour market in France and Switzerland. They also show strong differences, including statistical data indicating that the Swiss labour market is more accessible to French scholars than vice versa: while the French academic labour market attracts only a few Swiss academics; however, for highly prestigious positions and at late career stages, the Swiss market attracts many French scholars, starting from the first step in the academic career (the doctorate). A similar situation is found when comparing the situation of Switzerland with another neighbouring country: while in 2008, 772 academics from Switzerland were employed in various positions at German universities (source: Statistisches Bundesamt, Germany), the same number amounts to more than 7,000 for German academics in Switzerland (source: Swiss Statistics, Swiss Federal Statistical Office).

Such national differences are rather pronounced, and both researchers and policy makers conclude that, while in Europe for example, some progress has been made through policy measures as the establishment of programmes enhancing mobility (e.g. the Marie Curie programmes) or the European Charter for Researchers and Code of Conduct for the Recruitment of Researchers, the aim of the European academic labour market is not yet reached (Musselin 2004a; Commission of the European Communities 2007; Enders and Musselin 2008). Labour markets are still rather internal than external (Musselin 2003), and, as has been shown by mobility studies (see below), there are several higher education systems that tend to treat preferentially careers within the same country or even institution.

However, beyond the emergence of policies at the international level, also other tendencies towards a decreasing importance of the nation state as the only denominator of the shape of higher education systems and hence towards international homogenisation at the governance level are observed (Enders 2004; Kehm and Lanzendorf 2006); examples directly concerning the academic career are the German *Juniorprofessuren* and the Swiss SNSF Professorships inspired by the Anglo-Saxon model (Enders and Musselin 2008; Benninghoff et al. 2009).

However, access to the labour market not only occurs at the level of professorship or other (pre-)tenured or permanent positions: it is also strongly promoted at earlier stages of the academic career. Several instruments for promoting stays abroad through scholarships for doctoral students and post-doctorates exist in different countries. Post-doctoral stays are often the only or main mobility experience in an academic's career (Musselin 2004a), and mainly non-permanent mobility at early years in an academic's career seems to be increasing, while long-term mobility does not, with the exception of the United States (Marginson and van der Wende 2009).

For these non-permanent positions, funding often comes from the home country or from a supranational level, and therefore competition for access to these positions occurs in the system where the researcher comes from. Hence, the barrier of implicit rules not known to external is less of an issue in these cases. Compared with the access of foreigners to permanent positions, access to a higher education system through mobility with clear time limits is much less regulated and often occurs within networks of research institutes, thus strengthening already-existing linkages.

3   The Internationalisation of Academic Careers

Studies interested in mobility patterns from the point of view of higher education systems have already been presented above. This section focuses on the individual dimension, the academic career. This point of view is often addressed in studies based on individual data that is available through CVs or questionnaires.

3.1   *Mobility as an Element of Academic Careers*

Quite some work in this direction has been done in Spain, where CV databases or CV collections with quite detailed information are used for management purposes within the higher education sector and accessible for research purposes. The use of CVs as main research device has emerged mainly in the last decade; before, CVs were usually used as additional information source to answer questions not answered by other sources (Dietz et al. 2000). However, since the 1990s, different studies using CVs have been conducted, both for evaluative or developmental purposes (e.g. Morzinski and Schubot 2000; Gaughan and Bozeman 2002) and for understanding the patterns of mobility and collaboration and their impact on academic careers (e.g. Cañibano et al. 2008; Lepori and Probst 2009; Andújar and Cañibano 2010).

Data from CV analyses are often combined with information about publications—either taken from the CVs themselves or through searches in institutional or international publication databases; with these procedures, questions of the impact of mobility on the productivity of a scientist are addressed. Another approach in this direction is the combination of publication data and surveys directed to a clearly defined population.

As these approaches require larger amounts of manual work (especially in the case of CV analyses, where manual coding is still the rule, as standardisation is not at a point to allow for automatic coding, see Dietz et al. 2000; Cañibano et al. 2008; Andújar and Cañibano 2010), the analysed samples are usually much smaller than in the above-mentioned large-scale survey studies. Therefore, and also because they most often focus on mobile academics and do not include their non-mobile colleagues, they do not allow for generalisations on mobility patterns of the whole academic community. However, as these studies are based on quite rich data, beyond describing individual career paths they also allow for analyses of effects of mobility and strategies of individuals when it comes to the question of being mobile or not.

3.2 Effects of Mobility on Academic Careers

While there is "an extensive body of research and literature focusing on the importance of international experience for management careers" (Richardson and McKenna 2003, p. 774), there is less knowledge available about its value in academia and about its impact on academic activities, e.g. the quality of research and teaching, or academic working styles (Richardson and McKenna 2003; Kim and Locke 2009).

Results from the first Carnegie study on the academic profession, conducted in the 1990s, not only show differences between the two groups of mobile and non-mobile academics (Welch 1997, uses the terms of '*peripatetic*' and '*indigenous*'), but also reveal different degrees of internationalisation among countries and disciplines. Among mobile academics, gender disparities are stronger; also, mobile academics tend to be employed with full-time contracts more often than their non-mobile colleagues; and mobile academics favour research over teaching more strongly than their non-mobile colleagues and are more inclined to participate in international activities, including participation to international conferences and collaboration with colleagues from other countries. It seems thus that mobility is positively connected to internationalisation of academic activities, especially when it comes to research and networking.

The group around Carolina Cañibano (Cañibano et al. 2008; Andújar and Cañibano 2010) look not only at the relationship between mobility and productivity of researchers (i.e. publication output), but also between mobility and collaboration with international colleagues. Differences between fields of study emerge, and the connection between mobility and productivity is not answered unambiguously. Even if such a connection can be found, the question of "what was first" remains: does mobility enhance collaboration, or does collaboration enhance mobility? Also, mobility often occurs within an already-established network. For example, senior researchers advise post-doctorates on places to go, and provide their personal contacts (Melin 2004).

Studies based on CVs tend to lack the comparison between mobile and non-mobile researchers: the studies by Cañibano et al. are based on CVs of applicants to a funding programme which puts a prior stay abroad of at least 2 years as a condition. Hence, the analysis only covers differences between researchers that are mobile to different extents, and not between mobile and non-mobile researchers. This topic is approached differently by Cruz-Castro and Sanz-Menéndez (2010), who, based on a survey and publication data of academics receiving a permanent position at a Spanish university or the Spanish research council, thus including mobile and non-mobile researchers, show a modest, but significant positive correlation between mobility and productivity.

However, they also show a negative effect: post-doctoral international mobility does not have a positive effect when looking at those academics who get a permanent position within 3 years after their Ph.D.; strong internal job markets are at play, and institutional loyalty and non-mobility seem to be rewarded higher than publication output and international mobility, leading thus to some degree of inbreeding. Similar conclusions are drawn on the French academic market, where a rather negative impact of mobility on early tenure is found, while in other countries, as the United States or Germany, mobility (however, not necessarily at the international level) at an early stage is encouraged (Gaughan and Robin 2004).

While these studies rely on the analysis of "hard facts" for evaluating the impact of international mobility on an academic career, others analyse the academics' point of view (Richardson and McKenna 2003; Melin 2004, 2005). In these studies, too, an impact on publication is identified: mobility leads to future research collaboration and co-publication, through the contacts established during the period abroad; hence, collaboration between the home and the hosting country is enhanced.

Such analyses most often address positive aspects of mobility, and the topic of negative aspects is usually not included in studies looking at academics' experiences. An exception is the study by Melin (2004) presenting "the dark side" of post-doctoral mobility, based on questionnaire and interview data with a sample from Sweden. A similar issue to what has been shown for the Spanish and French context emerges, even though at a rather low level: 17 % of the respondents in the Swedish survey agreed with the statement that "going on a postdoc stay partly discredited me, for instance because I had not qualified myself at the department", referring particularly to lower salary and time lost for doing publications because of the need of time to start research when going abroad and when coming back home (Melin 2004, p. 233). Generally, this study reveals that systematic negative effects—experienced by 10–20 % of the returnees—refer not to the stay itself, but to the process of coming home, where the transfer of knowledge to the home department and the mentioned feeling that the stay is not valued by the home department are the most critical issues.

The generally positive bias associated with mobility might be a challenge when assessing negative effects through methods involving directly the concerned academics. But, as Melin points out, also the assessment of quantifiable variables is difficult: how can success/failure be defined?

3.3   Reasons for Being Mobile: Mobility as Strategy

Given this general assumptions of positive effects of mobility on academic careers, besides academic interests as the possibility to collaborate with other scholars in one's field, the decision to go abroad for a certain period of time or for the rest of one's academic life can also be a strategic career decision.

For example, doctoral or post-doctoral mobility is often used for enhancing one's career possibility in the home country (Musselin 2004a). The already-mentioned studies from Norway and Japan show this phenomenon; to some extent, these labour markets expect such mobility, they can be defined as *study-abroad countries* (see Sect. 2.2). While in these cases, mobility is often used for enhancing one's career possibilities in the home country, there are other places where career possibilities are strongly limited and therefore mobility is often the only way to find a further position: French doctoral degree holders, for example, go for a post-doctorate programme in abroad most often because they do not find a position in France (Gaughan and Robin 2004); similarly also in Italy, the limited career possibilities lead highly skilled researchers to aim for positions abroad (Coccia and Rolfo 2010).

A study by Richardson and McKenna (2003) asking researchers for their motivations for being mobile underline as most important element "the desire to travel" and to change one's life situation; to a lesser extent, and depending on the host country, also the financial attractiveness of a position abroad is seen as a reason for being mobile, and also reasons related to family topics (e.g. giving the children the chance to grow up in a different environment) are mentioned. Mobility as a factor for future career possibilities in the increasingly international academic labour market is not mentioned as a motivation for going abroad, but an important topic when evaluating the experience abroad, making them more "marketable".

As the study by Melin (2004) has shown, mobility does have effects on further research collaboration and co-publications. This study also shows for the post-doctoral period that typically scholars go to "strong science nations"; the post-doctoral period does not seem to be the moment to explore new environments. This might also be caused by the fact that contacts to the hosting institution are often made through senior colleagues, thus already-existing ties are strengthened through mobility of young researchers.

4   Combining Points of View: Ideas for Topics to Analyse in the EuroAC Project

As it derives clearly from the presented analysis, the international dimension of the academic labour market and of academic careers can be looked at from different points of view; even though comprehensive studies are rare so far, it seems that combinations of different aspects might allow for interesting insights.

The EuroAC study, based both on the CAP questionnaire and further qualitative projects, allows including the international dimension as a transversal topic in different in-depth analyses. When looking at internationalisation in the academic labour market and career, the following topics could be worth of a closer analysis:

- Different types of mobility along the academic career: short-term mobility usually funded through grants, and mobility for permanent positions. At which moment in the career do the different types of mobility occur? This would allow identifying where the international dimension comes into play in different models of the academic career.

- The impact of disciplinary differences vs. national specificities when comparing the forms and times of international mobility within a career in different higher education systems.
- Differences in the careers between different countries: the previous analyses of CAP results leading to classifications of countries could be refined, by checking also for home and hosting country and different definitions of "academic nationality": the nationality at the moment of the first degree, place of the first degree, place of the doctorate.
- A combination of the previous two elements: can we combine different career models with typologies of countries? But also a look at disciplinary differences would be interesting, and therefore the question: do patterns of mobility relate more to national or to disciplinary differences?
- The correlation of internationality with various dimensions looked at in the CAP questionnaire, for example, on the inclusion of international dimensions in teaching and research, on collaboration with international colleagues, etc. A clear definition of an indicator for internationality is a necessary instrument for such analyses.
- The openness of local academic markets to international academics. This analysis can, to some extent, be done through an analysis of the mobility data in the CAP survey. However, it would be interesting to combine it with a more in-depth analysis for some countries in the qualitative study, regarding explicit and implicit organisations of admission. To have an overview on the conditions in different countries and to combine this information with the knowledge about the flow of researchers would lead to interesting informed maps of mobility.

Such analyses would make it possible to find answers to a wide range of questions: On the basis of similar trends potentially observed in the evolution of the academic compositions in the different systems, can we infer an internationalisation of the norms at play in the regulation of academic careers? Does the increased overlapping of national markets favour the diffusion of common expectations regarding the structure of academic careers and the profile of faculties? For example, the goal of parity in access to the professoriate? The shift from internal to external markets, at least in some disciplines? The increased value given to precocity in academic careers?

In addition, the topic of internationalisation of the academic labour market can then be combined with other dimensions of internationalisation: Does mobility have an impact on work organisation and practices, on the inclusion of the international dimension in teaching and research? What about the internationalisation of research and scientific production? The internationalisation of the peer judgement on academic activities? And, as a provocative question: Is internationalisation of a career an indicator of its value?

References

Abbott, A. (2001). *Chaos of disciplines*. Chicago: University of Chicago Press.

Altbach, P. G. (2002). Perspectives on internationalizing higher education. *International Higher Education, 7*(4), 6–8.

Altbach, P. G., & Knight, J. (2006). The internationalization of higher education: Motivations and realities. In National Education Association (Ed.), *The NEA 2006 almanac of higher education* (pp. 27–36). Washington: National Education Association.

Andújar, I., & Cañibano, C. (2010). *Mobility of researchers and transnational networks formation: Indicators for a complex relationship*. Paper presented at the 3rd ENID conference on STI Indicators for policy making and strategic decision, Paris, 3–5 Mar 2010.

Becher, T., & Trowler, P. R. (2001). *Academic tribes and territories. Intellectual enquiry and the culture of disciplines*. Ballmoor: The Society for Research into Higher Education and Open University Press.

Ben-David, J. (1992). *Centers of learning: Britain, France, Germany, United States; with a new introduction by Philip G. Altbach*. New Brunswick: Transaction.

Benninghoff, M., Goastellec, G., & Leresche, J. (2009). L'International Comme Ressource Cognitive et Symbolique: Changements dans l'Instrumentation de la Recherche et de l'Enseignement Supérieur en Suisse. In J. Leresche, P. Larédo, & K. Weber (Eds.), *Recherche et Enseignement Supérieur Face à l'Internationalisation. France, Suisse et Union européenne* (pp. 235–255). Lausanne: PPUR.

Bonaccorsi, F., Goujon, M., Srodogora, S. B., & van Leberghe, P. (2004). *Les Carrières Scientifiques: Une Approche Fondée sur des Éléments d'Analyse Comparative Européenne*. Rapport à Monsieur le Ministre de l'Education Nationale, de l'Enseignement Supérieur et de la Recherche, n°2004-140.

Boyer, E. L., Altbach, P. G., & Whitelaw, M. J. (1994). *The academic profession: An international perspective*. Princeton: Carnegie Foundation for the Advancement of Teaching.

Cañibano, C., Otamendi, F. J., & Andújar, I. (2008). Measuring and assessing researcher mobility from CV analysis: The case of the Ramón y Cajal programme in Spain. *Research Evaluation, 17*(1), 17–31.

Charle, C., & Verger, J. (1994). *Histoire des Universités*. Paris: PUF.

Clark, B. R. (1983). *The higher education system. Academic organization in cross-national perspective*. Berkeley: University of California Press.

Coccia, M., & Rolfo, S. (2010). *Human resource indicators for strategic decisions on Modern Public Research Institutions*. Paper presented at the 3rd ENID conference on STI Indicators for policy making and strategic decision, Paris, 3–5 Mar 2010.

Commission of the European Communities. (2007). *Green paper—The European research area: New perspectives*. Brussels: European Union.

Cruz-Castro, L., & Sanz-Menéndez, L. (2010). Mobility versus job stability: Assessing tenure and productivity outcomes. *Research Policy, 39*, 27–38.

de Wit, H. (1995). *Strategies for the internationalisation of higher education. A comparative study of Australia, Canada, Europe and the United States of America*. Amsterdam: EAIE Secretariat.

Dietz, J. S., Chompalov, I., Bozeman, B., O'Neil Lane, E., & Park, J. (2000). Using the curriculum vita to study the career paths of scientist and engineers: An exploratory assessment. *Scientometrics, 49*(3), 419–442.

Enders, J. (2004). Higher education, internationalisation, and the nation-state: recent developments and challenges to Governance Theory. *Higher Education, 47*, 361–382.

Enders, J., & de Weert, E. (2004). Science, training and career: Changing modes of knowledge production and labour markets. *Higher Education Policy, 17*(2), 129–152.

Enders, J., & Musselin, C. (2008). Back to the future? The academic professions in the 21st century. In OECD (Ed.), *Higher education to 2030—Volume 1: Demography* (pp. 125–150). Paris: OECD.

European Commission. (2005). *The European Charter for researchers. The code of conduct for the recruitment of researchers*. Luxembourg: Office for Official Publications of the European Communities.

Felli, R., Goastellec, G., & Leresche, J. (2007a). Existe-t-il un Marché du Travail Académique Franco-Suisse? *Formation Emploi, 100,* 5–20.

Felli, R., Goastellec, G., & Leresche, J. (2007b). Les Marchés du Travail Académique en France et en Suisse: des Imbrications Différenciées. *Formation Emploi, 100,* 49–64

Fontes, M. (2007). Scientific mobility policies: How Portuguese scientists envisage the return home. *Science and Public Policy, 34*(4), 284–298.

Gaughan, M., & Bozeman, B. (2002). Using curriculum vitae to compare some impacts of NSF research grants with research center funding. *Research Evaluation, 11*(1), 17–26.

Gaughan, M., & Robin, S. (2004). National science training policy and early scientific careers in France and the United States. *Research Policy, 33,* 569–581.

Goastellec, G., & Paradeise, C. (2008). L'Enseignement: une Dimension de plus en plus Internationale. *Cahiers Français. La documentation française, 344,* 12–18.

Huang, F. (2007). Challenges of internationalisation of higher education and changes in the academic profession: A perspective from Japan. In M. Kogan & U. Teichler (Eds.), *Key challenges to the academic profession* (Werkstattberichte, Vol. 65, pp. 81–98). Kassel: International Centre for Higher Education Research Kassel (INCHER-Kassel) and UNESCO Forum on Higher Education, Research and Knowledge.

Kehm, B. (2006). Doctoral education in Europe and North America: A comparative analysis. In U. Teichler (Ed.), *The formative years of scholars. Proceedings from a symposium held at the Haga Forum, Stockholm, 9–11 Nov 2005* (pp. 67–78). London: Portland.

Kehm, B., & Lanzendorf, U. (2006). *Reforming university governance*. Bonn: Lemmens.

Kehm, B. M., & Teichler, U. (2007). Research on internationalisation in higher education. *Journal of Studies in International Education, 11*(3/4), 260–273.

Kelo, M., Teichler, U., & Wächter, B. (2006). *EURODATA—Student mobility in European higher education*. Bonn: Lemmens.

Kim, T., & Locke, W. (2009). *Transnational academic mobility and the academic profession in the UK*. Presentation at the Annual Conference of the Society for Research into Higher Education, Newport, South Wales, 8–10 Dec 2009.

Kivinen, O., Ahola, S., & Kaipainen, P. (1999). *Towards the European model of postgraduate training*. Research report 50. Painosalama Oy, Turku: Research Unit for the Sociology of Education (RUSE), University of Turku.

Knight, J. (1999). Internationalisation of higher education. In OECD (Ed.), *Quality and internationalisation in higher education* (pp. 13–28). Paris: OECD—IMHE Programme on Institutional Management in Higher Education.

Knight, J. (2003). *Internationalization of higher education. Practices and priorities: 2003 IAU survey report*. Paris: International Association of Universities.

Knight, J., & de Wit, H. (1995). Strategies for internationalisation of higher education: Historical and conceptual perspectives. In H. de Wit (Ed.), *Strategies for the internationalisation of higher education. A comparative study of Australia, Canada, Europe and the United States of America* (pp. 5–32). Amsterdam: EAIE Secretariat.

Lepori, B., & Probst, C. (2009). Using curriculum vitae for mapping scientific fields. A small-scale experience for Swiss Communication Sciences. *Research Evaluation, 18*(2), 125–134.

Marginson, S., & van der Wende, M. (2009). Europeanisation, international rankings and faculty mobility. Three cases in higher education globalisation. In OECD (Ed.), *Higher education to 2030—Volume 2: Globalisation* (pp. 109–144). Paris: OECD.

Meek, V. L. (2007). Internationalisation of higher education and the Australian academic profession. In M. Kogan & U. Teichler (Eds.), *Key challenges to the academic profession* (Werkstattberichte, Vol. 65, pp. 65–80). Kassel: International Centre for Higher Education Research Kassel (INCHER-Kassel) and UNESCO Forum on Higher Education, Research and Knowledge.

Melin, G. (2004). Postdoc abroad: Inherited scientific contacts or establishment of new networks? *Research Evaluation, 13*(2), 95–102.

Melin, G. (2005). The dark side of mobility: Negative experiences of doing a postdoc period abroad. *Research Evaluation, 14*(3), 229–237.

Misu, T., & Horoiwa, A. (2010). *Career trends of recent doctoral graduates in Japan. Diversity of career paths and international mobility.* Paper presented at the 3rd ENID conference on STI Indicators for policy making and strategic decision, Paris, 2–5 Mar 2010.

Morzinski, J. A., & Schubot, D. B. (2000). Evaluating faculty development outcomes by using curriculum vitae analysis. *Family Medicine, 32*(3), 185–189.

Moscati, R. (2004). Italy. In J. Sadlak (Ed.), *Doctoral studies and qualifications in Europe and the United States: Status and prospects* (pp. 63–76). Bucharest: UNESCO-CEPES.

Musselin, C. (2003). Internal versus external labour markets. *Higher Education Management and Policy, 15*(3), 9–23.

Musselin, C. (2004a). Towards a European academic labour market? Some lessons drawn from empirical studies on academic mobility. *Higher Education, 48,* 55–78.

Musselin, C. (2004b). The academic workplace: Up to now it is not as bad¼ but … Country Report France. In J. Enders & E. de Weert (Eds.), *The international attractiveness of the academic workplace in Europe* (pp. 141–159). Frankfurt a. M.: Gewerkschaft Erziehung und Wissenschaft.

Musselin, C. (2005a). European academic labour markets in transition. *Higher Education, 49,* 135–154.

Musselin, C. (2005b). *Le Marché des Universitaires. France, Allemagne, Etats-Unis.* Paris: Presses de Sciences Po.

Nunn, A. (2005). *The "Brain Drain". Academic and skilled migration to the UK and its impacts on Africa.* Report to the AUT and NATFHE. Leeds: Leeds Metropolitan University.

Organisation for Economic Co-operation and Development (OECD). (2004). *Science and technology statistical compendium.* Paris: OECD.

Organisation for Economic Co-operation and Development (OECD). (2009a). *Higher education to 2030—Volume 2: Globalisation.* Paris: OECD.

Organisation for Economic Co-operation and Development (OECD). (2009b). *OECD science, technology and industry scoreboard 2009.* Paris: OECD.

Qiang, Z. (2003). Internationalization of higher education: Towards a conceptual framework. *Policy Futures in Education, 1*(2), 248–269.

Richardson, J., & McKenna, S. (2003). International experience and academic careers: What do academics have to say? *Personnel Review, 32*(6), 774–795.

Statistisches Bundesamt. (2009). *Bildung und Kultur. Personal an Hochschulen 2008.* Fachserie 11, Reihe 4.4. Wiesbaden: Statistisches Bundesamt.

Teichler, U. (1999). Internationalisation as a challenge for higher education in Europe. *Tertiary Education and Management, 5,* 5–23.

Teichler, U. (2004). The changing debate on internationalisation of higher education. *Higher Education, 48,* 5–26.

Trondal, J., Stensaker, B., Gornitzka, A., & Maassen, P. (2001). *Internasjonalisering av Høyere Utdanning: Trender og Utfordringer.* Oslo: NIFU STEP.

UNESCO-CEPES. (2004). La Fuite des Cerveaux et le Marché du Travail Universitaire et Intellectuel en Europe du Sud-Est. *L'Enseignement Supérieur en Europe. UNESCO, 29*(3) (unesdoc.unesco.org/images/001390/139060f.pdf).

Vabø, A. (2007). Challenges of internationalization for the academic profession in Norway. In M. Kogan & U. Teichler (Eds.), *Key challenges to the academic profession* (Werkstattberichte, Vol. 65, pp. 99–107). Kassel: International Centre for Higher Education Research Kassel (INCHER-Kassel) and UNESCO Forum on Higher Education, Research and Knowledge.

Welch, A. R. (1997). The peripatetic professor: The internationalisation of the academic profession. *Higher Education, 34*(3), 323–345.

Whitley, R. (1984). *The intellectual and social organization of the sciences.* Oxford: Clarendon.

The Academic Profession: Quality Assurance, Governance, Relevance, and Satisfaction

Luminita Moraru, Mirela Praisler, Simona Alecu Marin
and Cristina Corina Bentea

1 The Academic Profession: Challenges of Its Environment

The academic profession has always been changing. This profession is adaptive and responsive to external changes, and it seeks to interact with its own environment. While reading historical research or looking at academics' reflections on their situation over time (e.g. Wilson 1980; Rice 1986; Altbach 1980, 1996, 1998; Clark 1987), it is striking that, whatever their particular historical moment, these writers all comment that the academic profession is no longer the same. There is clearly no ideal, universal, and stable state of the academic profession. These developments affect the relationships between the academic profession and other parts of society, as well as the position of this particular profession within society. These changes also affect the profession's internal modes of regulation and its autonomy and ability to avoid the intervention of external forces. Finally, the content of academic activities themselves and the norms according to which they are to be achieved are also subject to change (Altbach 2000; Musselin 2007).

Academic careers are influenced by various contexts (Steyrer et al. 2005; Hall 2002). Whereas career research traditionally emphasises personal contexts at the expense of global or societal ones, research on academic careers tends to stress structural factors and conditions influencing careers. Academic careers have been seen as the prototype for "new" careers (Baruch and Hall 2004) and as an opportunity to develop an international academic career (El-Khawas 2002) and to change employment conditions (Enders 2004). There are many international comparative research studies of the academic profession (Altbach 1996, 2000) and of faculty members' working conditions (Enders 2001b; Enders and de Weert 2004). There is literature on academic labour markets that is international in scope (Musselin

L. Moraru (✉) · M. Praisler · S. A. Marin · C. C. Bentea
Dunărea de Jos University,
Galați, Romania
email: luminita.moraru@ugal.ro

B. M. Kehm, U. Teichler (eds.), *The Academic Profession in Europe: New Tasks and New Challenges,* The Changing Academy – The Changing Academic Profession in International Comparative Perspective 5, DOI 10.1007/978-94-007-4614-5_8, © Springer Science+Business Media Dordrecht 2013

2003; Sørensen 1992) and studies concentrate on national higher education system descriptions (Breneman and Youn 1988; Enders 1996; Halsey 1992). A lot of studies have sought to develop typologies of staff structures that support academic careers (Neave and Rhoades 1987 or Enders 2001a).

The public reflection on the academic profession is not characterised by satisfaction and equilibrium. There are opinions that the concept of the traditional academic profession might be history. The professional tensions with which the academic profession has to live nowadays are included by experts in at least four categories: massification, knowledge economy, managerialism, and competition (Teichler and Yagci 2009, p. 107).

In many national systems, the academic profession became more internationalised and more accountable and the academic staff is expected to be more professional in teaching and more productive in research. Also, they are asked to develop new professional skills which are not related to their original disciplines (Henkel 2001). In this context, the definition of academic profession has become ambiguous due to tensions between academic jobs and those of other professionals that are a sort of "satellites" of the academia. As Enders says "The growing importance of scientific knowledge and highly qualified expertise is accompanied by a loss of exclusiveness as far as the role and centrality of higher education and the academic profession as the main source of new scientific knowledge and its dissemination into society are concerned. Higher education seems endangered to lose its monopoly as the main producer of scientific knowledge and technology. In consequence, higher education is facing a growing competition with other research sectors and institutions and their quality of performance is more and more confronted with comparisons to other suppliers of tertiary education or research" (Enders 1999, p. 73). Another challenge to the academic profession is the change of traditional forms of pedagogy. The new Global Information Society imposes virtual pedagogies, electronic forms of learning and communication, and diversification of education and training, much of which is now taking place in settings outside the traditional university. Today, all these changes could raise questions about the attractiveness of an academic career.

Although an academic career seems to remain an attractive choice, there is a challenge to be related to questions about the personal costs of succeeding in academic careers and how to maintain a balance between work and family, personal satisfaction and career requirements. This "cost-benefit-analysis" of academic careers is operating in the general context of abandoning the tenure system and developing a parallel system of fixed-term appointment (Schuster and Finkelstein 2006). As a result, there appears a new dilemma: the academics tend to focus their attention and skills on only one of the three integrated faculty functions (teaching/research/service).

In order to cope with the extreme complexity of the academic tasks, it is necessary to differentiate the roles among academics. Some institutions are in charge of both teaching and research, others focus on teaching or on research. Some academics emphasise the core role of teaching and research, while others understand themselves as academic entrepreneurs (for example—bringing in research grants and contracts to the universities). All academics must develop more teamwork skills, a competence not always developed in academia.

From a management point of view, all academic staff should be engaged in scholarship at a high level which includes staying informed about the latest research in their areas of expertise.

The pressures coming from the international operational environment of the European nation states, concerning, for example, the need to improve national competitiveness and productivity and strengthen social cohesion, are emphasised in the national, international and supra-national higher education policy processes and debates. Advancing the level and relevance of knowledge and improving the functioning of the innovation system have become integral aims in higher education policy in many countries. Two external dynamics affect the development of the higher education system: (1) changes in the importance, production and application of knowledge in European and other societies, and (2) changes in the operational models that aim at strengthening knowledge-based production and social development within higher education policy and of higher education institutions. The external pressures that arise from the operational environment of higher education institutions also essentially affect their internal operations: their organisational structures, leadership, management and financing. The intersection of these internal and external dimensions gives rise to questions concerning the productivity, effectiveness, and efficiency of higher education institutions.

Ford's opinion is that "… one of the defining features of the modern university is its sameness. Because of its twin commitments to job training and to theory, universities everywhere closely resemble one another" (Ford 2002, p. 13). However, each modern university finds itself in a rapidly changing environment and facing challenges that are by now well known: increased competition for scarce resources, massification of education, economic globalisation with the resulting demands from government and society for more and better trained graduates especially in the sciences, the need to establish improved research capabilities for assisting/underpinning national competitiveness. Autonomy is a necessary prerequisite for speedily responding to these challenges. It is well recognised in European universities that university autonomy is bound up with accountability to society, and that accountability brings with it the responsibility to drive the required change and improvement. Thus, universities must use their autonomy and independence for positive strategic development and involvement with society according to its expectations and needs.

Changes in the production of knowledge cause pressures for change in the organisation, leadership, and management of higher education institutions. To succeed in the international and national competition, it is essential for higher education institutions to modify their teaching and research activities towards models that emphasise cross-disciplinarity, use-orientation, and co-operation with other actors in the innovation system. The changes in the production of knowledge and the use-oriented new models require structural changes in the higher education system that strengthen the production and distribution of multi-disciplinary knowledge, and in the generation of which the users of knowledge have participated. The higher education institutions are looking for their competitive edge utilising the tools provided to them by the changes in government steering, such as increases in economic freedom of action, the new salary system and flexibility in working hours, the dialogue in management by results, the creation of quality systems and profiling through their strengths in reacting to regional, national, and global demands. Finding a competitive edge necessitates more professional and strategically oriented leadership and finding a new equilibrium between administrative and academic leadership.

The university "must remain relatively stable in order to continue to fulfil two primary functions: the production of the next generation of researchers and generator of cultural norms" (Meek 2003, p. 24).

2   Quality Assurance in Central and Eastern Europe

The changes in Central and Eastern Europe caused by upheavals at the beginning of the 1990s had great impact on the formation and implementation of educational policies. Virtually, all countries within the South East European region share a major concern: how to improve the quality of education (UNDP 2002). One of the most radical common shifts in the educational policies was in the orientation of universities and of teaching and learning processes to quality assurance. This was an immediate response to the challenges coming from the market-oriented policies. In accordance with a global and, in particular, pan-European trend, this shift was associated with the introduction of characteristic instruments into the examination and assessment procedures. The changes included evaluation of individual study programmes and local, regional and national educational units, as well as of individual and collective achievements, the latter related to classes or age groups (Mitter 2003, p. 75).

In the light of globalisation and reforms in higher education in many countries around the world, the concern for improving the quality of students' learning has come into focus. The traditional assessment system has been scrutinised and the new term "quality assessment" has become the common currency in today's educational arena. Quality assessment is an on-going activity including student participation and necessitates using a variety of assessment techniques, implementing them effectively, providing good feedback to student and using assessment data to improve instruction. Teachers must strive to give students quality work to do if they want students to do quality work for them.

Despite semantic implications that quality will be assured, quality assurance (QA) regimes at all levels (government, institution, department) are typically management processes (inputs) that are independent of performance criteria defined in terms of educational quality (outcomes). Unfortunately, QA regimes tend to reinforce schisms between administration and academic interests in higher education, forcing a focus on administrative processes to the exclusion of quality outcome interests. QA regimes represent the interests of particular stakeholder groups, but whether they contribute to either relevance or quality of educational outcomes is simply part of a broader question of relevance versus quality.

Assurance of quality (i.e. real quality assurance) depends on demonstration of quality against criteria that are understood and accepted by all stakeholders including students, peers, accreditors and various sectors of the community to whom the higher education teaching community is accountable (Nicholls 2001, p. 134).

Assuring quality in higher education, promoting equal access to higher education and empowering learners for informed decision making are key challenges for higher education in a more globalised environment. To respond to this challenge, UNESCO launched a Global Forum on International Quality Assurance, Accreditation and the Recognition of Qualification in Higher Education (2002). It serves to promote international cooperation in higher education by providing a platform for dialogue between different stakeholders and building bridges between intergovernmental organisations. Participants at the forum proposed that "UNESCO's challenge is to provide a structured agenda for new developments and offer an international policy framework for dealing with globalisation and higher education, reconciling the interests of national governments, the traditional public higher education sector, for profit providers and the needs of students and the general public interest" (van Damme 2002, p. 20).

Following the inaugural meeting of the Global Forum in October 2002, an Action Plan for 2004–2005 was developed focusing on UNESCO's standard-setting, capacity building, and clearinghouse functions. The Action Plan aims to provide a framework to assist member states in developing their own policy frameworks. It is based on UN documents and UNESCO's specific mission and functions. Three initiatives are proposed within this category of activities:

- The establishment of a set of guiding principles,
- A review of the Regional Conventions, and
- Research on the concept of public good and the impact of cross border higher education on widening access.

A need for capacity building at the regional and national levels, to promote quality assurance and accreditation mechanisms within a strengthened international framework was recognised. In this regard it was highlighted that national quality assurance frameworks should not discriminate against new providers while at the same time the quality of all educational provisions should be optimal. This initiative will adopt a gradual approach, taking into account activities/projects under way to increase transparency and information.

In its most common use, education quality refers to the extent that an education system is able to achieve the generally accepted goals of education, central to which are cognitive knowledge and skills development (Randall 2001). For the most part, education systems are deemed to be of higher quality when students demonstrate higher levels of learning. While education systems have multiple goals (e.g. the development of relevant employment skills or attitudes that promote civic engagement), most observers still regard the transmission of cognitive knowledge as its principal objective (Chapman et al. 2005). From this perspective, improving quality involves taking actions that increase student achievement.

When discussing the role of specific mechanisms and general approaches to quality assurance in higher education, experts often tend to focus on the differences: while general approaches tend to stress the autonomy of higher education institutions, field-specific approaches accentuate the need for aligning the goals of educational programmes with the expectations of the relevant stakeholders in order to be comparable and ensure their relevance for the labour market.

For higher education institutions faced with demands from various groups of stakeholders to account for the quality of their processes by employing various instruments of internal and external quality assurance, the question with regard to general approaches and specific mechanisms to quality assurance is often not one of "either or" but of how to best combine them in order to limit the burden placed on the organisation and its members. They also emphasize decentralisation of responsibilities; the relationship between academic governance and institutional mission and strategic objectives and to explore alternative models for institutions and actions for individuals and institutions to improve the contributions of the academic profession towards the relevance of higher education in society. In addition, there are other related difficulties: maintaining high academic and research standards; ensuring the quality of faculty appointments; assuring flexibility and rigor in a curriculum; maintaining political and intellectual freedom; balancing a moral obligation to educating the poor and disadvantaged against the costs of financial aid (De Grauwe 2005).

All these quality assurance demands urge the university to organise as soon as possible a systematic, transparent and routine procedure for the evaluation by students of teachers and courses. Feedback to students about the results of these evaluations should be timely and follow-up procedures agreed. It is crucial that this process should be formative and directed at improving the quality of teaching and learning. This can lead to a continuing dialogue between teachers and students, an important element in developing a climate where real improvement can take place. Other procedures affect the quality of performance in a university. These include the appointment of new staff, the quality and number of the incoming students, and the related issue of their formation and motivation. The procedures for appointing professors appear to be quite open and transparent and totally in the hands of the university, i.e. the universities' need to decide their own strategy and to take responsibility for their decisions. It is essential that this important element of autonomy is maintained and that existing procedures are scrupulously applied.

Balancing a staff member's time between research and teaching is a perennial problem in all research universities. At the moment, we encounter high teaching loads in the universities. This is partially due to a large number of study programmes resulting in duplication of courses. However, the increasing weight of modular courses and the shift towards more individual study requirements for students will produce an environment that might contribute to reach the needed balance.

In observing the various sectors of production and service in our modern societies and the various institutions in charge, we note that the higher education and research sector is peculiar in several respects. Higher education can be characterised by a relatively open set of multiple goals; by loose mechanisms of coercion, control and steering from above; by a high degree of fragmentation; and by a strong influence of the principal workers—the academic professionals—on the determination of goals, on the management and administration of institutions, and on the daily routines of work. In addition, if we look at the interrelationships between different sectors of production and services, we might consider the academic profession to be one of the most influential in shaping other sectors as well. This is, for example, underscored by the British social historian Harold Perkin's description of the academic profession as the "key profession… the profession that educates the other professions" (Perkin 1969, p. 13).

2.1   Governance and Quality Assurance

Before we start a sound analysis about 'governance' we need to distinguish between terms such as 'management', 'administration' and 'leadership'. According to Gallagher (2001, p. 1):

> Governance is the structure of relationships that bring about organisational coherence, authorised policies, plans and decisions, and account for their probity, responsiveness and cost-effectiveness. Leadership is seeing opportunities and setting strategic directions (…). Management is achieving intended outcomes through the allocation of responsibilities and resources, and monitoring their efficiency and effectiveness. Administration is the implementation of authorised procedures and the application of systems to achieve agreed results.

The OECD (2006, p. 112) states that:

> Governance is concerned with the determination of values inside universities, their systems of decision-making and resource allocation, their mission and purposes, the patterns of authority and hierarchy, and the relationship of universities as institutions to the different academic worlds within and the worlds of government, business and communities, without.

There is a general consensus regarding leadership as being a process for influencing decisions and guiding people, whereas management involves the implementation and administration of institutional decisions and policies (Taylor and Machado 2006).

The roles of governance and management are essential in the management of transformational change in higher education and, paradoxically, they in turn need to be transformed in order to deliver in this respect.

Institutions generally operate in a complex environment that requires hard choices in strategic priorities. What is required are governance and management that, in structure and process, encourage and facilitate positive, proactive, and continuous institutional transformation together with relationship-building strategies focused on all stakeholders.

At a first glance it might seem as if public universities in many countries are under government control, and the universities as public institutions that are closely linked to the government must accommodate national needs, demands, and expectations. The fact that public universities are largely financed by the government contributes to the idea that universities goals and development agendas must concur with the government's agenda and priorities, as if the universities themselves lack the sense of direction in determining their visions, goals, and priorities. The public universities are deemed accountable to the society and nation in materialising social, economic, political, and technological development goals. The government does influence the direction of public universities in some ways in terms of policies and regulations, but the universities have their own management style, determine the quality of the curriculum, the quality of graduates, also the research priority areas, and identify profitable ventures. Public universities are, by and large, autonomous bodies, even in a centralised education system.

One of the characteristics of the governance in higher education is that it is quite diffused and entails shared responsibilities among a variety of stakeholders. Accordingly, the biggest challenge in governance within the university sector relates to issues of power and responsibilities as dealt with by Senates, the university leadership, academic staff (senior and junior level), students, policy makers and other external stakeholders.

Universities are faced with the dilemma of ensuring an appropriate balance between their academic priorities and the demands placed on them by the expectations of policy makers and other external stakeholders.

Traditional methods of governing educational systems from the national level are being replaced by an approach in which authority to make decisions is delegated, as appropriate, to regional, institutional and individual academic levels. Many countries have developed or are developing a new functional distribution of roles and responsibilities, complemented by appropriate systems of accountability, together with effective systems for evaluating and reporting education outcomes.

New cooperative modes are developing where state and non-state actors participate in mixed networks (Enders 2004, p. 372; Maassen 2006). The new approaches must take into account the essential characteristics of the higher education sector and its professional organisations. While governance arrangements usually emphasise formal structure, bodies and decision-making structures, the governance of higher education institutions is still strongly influenced by informal networks, collegial agreements and more process-oriented decision-making structures (Gornitzka et al. 2005). It must be underlined that governance and the academic culture are linked in a complex texture of interactions and effects. This is the key issue to understand the effectiveness of governance arrangements in higher education. Since teaching, research, and knowledge transfer are dependent on the academic staff, a key issue of governance is to create institutional conditions stimulating the creativity of the professionals (EU 2005). In this perspective, governance is about identifying the institutional structures and processes that create optimal conditions for staff performance.

Providing education of the highest quality is crucial for all countries, no matter the circumstances, to support the social and economic development, to develop the potential of the citizens and to give them satisfaction. Pedagogical reforms are recognised to be an important factor in improving education. It is generally agreed that the mechanisms through which the education is governed can have a very significant effect on its quality and efficiency. Thus, devolving responsibilities to all levels in the academic system can lead to the capitalisation of talents of academic staff and to motivation and job satisfaction. These actions persuade the academic staff to have a personal and professional responsibility to contribute to the achievement of a culture of quality.

In a comparative study by Wielemans and Roth-van-der-Werf (1995, p. 63), decentralisation was found to be the key to the agendas of most European Union (EU) countries as a way to promote quality control and greater efficiency in their education systems. What is seldom visible, however, is that decentralised power, in the name of quality education and with the aim of assuring productivity and customisation, is often accompanied by powerful centralising measures, especially with regard to the core activities of curriculum development and assessment policy. For example, the decentralisation brought about in Flanders by the Basis Decree (the 1991 decree on university education), which accorded to the universities the responsibility of determining the pedagogic project, was accompanied by the introduction of a centralised definition of curriculum outcomes (kerndoelen; Berkhout 2002). Similarly, in South Africa, the decentralisation of power introduced by the South African Schools Act was accompanied by the development of a national outcomes-based curriculum and several standardised forms of assessment such as achievement testing for the foundation phase and common task assignments for the General and Further Education and Training Certificate. In both countries this became a policy that "on one side turns out to be a change in steering systems directed towards a distribution of policy-making from the centre to the periphery,… [and] on the other side…a strengthening of a central steering system" (Lundgren 1990, p. 35).

Changes in governance raise additional issues of regulation. We need to understand the concept of 'regulation', and whether the education institutions have autonomy and flexibility in governing their education services. This implies developing 'self-regulatory' frameworks to assure education quality and academic standards. Most important of all, the power-money dimension is likely to become a source of major tension between the state and non-state sectors, especially when funding sources and education services are diversified. Knill and Lehmkuhl anticipate the development of a new regulatory model: regulated self-regulation. Through this 'regulated self-regulation', "the state plays a central and active role in disposing of powers and resources that are not available to societal actors" (Knill and Lehmkuhl 2002, p. 43). Although the state is responsible for promoting quality education and meeting high expectations in terms of education, it cannot adopt the same interventionist and regulatory framework with regard to non-state actors, especially when education provision and financing is diversified.

A regulated self-regulatory framework could be further developed by re-conceptualising the relationship between the state and professional bodies. It is generally accepted that the overall quality assurance responsibility in education, unlike other goods or services, still lies with the state. But state intervention is also influenced by professional communities. With regard to professional qualifications, for instance, it is not the role of the state to set detailed requirements for approving professional credentials. Instead, professional bodies have a very important role to play in governing professional standards. In order to maintain high standards in education, the state must liaise with the relevant professional organisations, rather than simply making detailed requirements (Mok 2005).

In quality assurance, external intervention has taken various forms. A variety of actions, both supportive and punitive, have been taken by governments, including particularly:

- Attempts to standardise higher education by application of competency standards.
- External peer review protocols.
- Quality assurance audits of educational institutions.
- Conditional funding based on various types of performance criteria.

A further government intervention is pressure for cross-accreditation between states within countries such as the USA, Canada and Australia, and between countries such as in the EU (Cowdroy and Chapman 1999; Sporn 1999; Heitmann 2000). They are also recognised as external responses to perceived failure of the higher education community to adequately demonstrate that it meets a sufficiently broad range of stakeholder expectations (Cowdroy and Chapman 1999; Nicholls 2001; Mok 2005).

No country is immune from the effects of globalisation, and controversy continues to reign about its positive and negative consequences. The globalisation processes are complex and often contradictory, and we need to avoid an overly deterministic view of globalisation. The growing impact of globalisation has caused many modern states to rethink their governance strategies for coping with rapid social and economic changes. So, the education policy and development, just like other public policy domains, is not immune from the impact of these globalisation processes (Burbules and Torres 2000; Pierre and Peters 2000; Mok 2001; Mok and Chan 2002; Mok and Lo 2002; Marginson and van der Wende 2006). For example, all education reform proposals talk about the importance of competition, global competence, diversity, and choice (Mok and Welch 2003; Lee and Gopinathan 2005).

In order to make individual nation-states more competitive, universities across the globe have been under tremendous pressure from governments and the general public to restructure/reinvent education systems. With heavy weight being attached to the principles of 'efficiency and quality' in education, schools, universities and other institutions of learning now encounter far more challenges, and are being subjected to an unprecedented level of external scrutiny. The growing concern for 'value for money' and 'public accountability' has also altered people's value expectations. All providers of education today inhabit a more competitive world where resources are becoming scarcer. At the same time, however, providers have to accommodate increasing demands from the local community, as well as changing expectations of parents and employers. Governments in different parts of the globe are facing increasing financial constraints in their efforts to meet people's pressing demands for higher education. In view of the intensified financial constraints that modern states are facing, it is anticipated that non-state actors, including the market, local communities, the higher education sector and civil society, will assume increasingly important roles in education financing and education provision, while the state will restructure its role in education by becoming more actively involved in becoming a regulator, quality controller, facilitator and coordinator of services.

3   Relevance

Related to quality in higher education, there appears the question: Does relevance in higher education equate with quality? Every programme in higher education attracts the interest of a range of stakeholders with a multiplicity of conflicting concerns about relevance and a multiplicity of conflicting criteria of quality. As Brennan et al. (2007, p. 169) noted "the point about relevance is that it is generally defined by other people" and not by individual academics.

Accreditation, accountability, and quality assurance criteria often seem to be contradictory or even mutually exclusive, and national quality assurance agendas seem to exacerbate the problem for all fields of higher education.

A major challenge in higher education is to demonstrate relevance and educational quality to an increasingly wide range of stakeholders' conflicting expectations in the name of "accountability". In many cases accreditation (particularly by professional registration authorities) is deemed to represent educational quality, however the criteria for accreditation are focused on relevance that satisfies only a very narrow band of stakeholder interests, and do not address many other criteria of quality as discussed further below.

Today, more than ever, a new analysis of the strategic role of higher education and university is needed. We need to observe better their relation with the society, which often leads the universities towards fundamental transformations and new orientations while preserving the balance between scientific aspects and social commitments. The concept of "social relevance" gains prominence. In many cases, societal relevance is something which is required as part of evaluation processes. For example, the UK Quality Assurance Agency has issued a series of "subject benchmarks" which are intended to specify the learning outcomes of different kinds of higher education study programmes. The benchmarks are meant to inform "consumers"—in this case both intending students and the employers of graduates—of the sorts of skills and competencies which are acquired in particular study programmes. Informing "consumers" is essentially about informing the "market" and more generally universities find themselves having to make claims about the individual and social benefits of university to ensure that a steady supply of customers keep knocking at the institutional door. Of course, quality is not to be entirely equated with relevance but it is a significant part of it (Brennan 2007).

Relevance and importance of higher education need to be evaluated according to the extent of balance between societal expectations from various academic institutions and their academic functions. This evaluation must have in view the ethical criteria, political neutrality, the culture of critique, a strengthened link between societal problems and the labour market as well as the adoption of long-term orientations with respect to societal needs and objectives. The main source of concern, however, is achieving education for all as well as goal-oriented specialised education with emphasis on merits and skills, since these two forms of education prepare for living in various situations as well as for changing one's job or profession.

From the point of view of expectations, the quality often depends on perceived relevance to the respective interests of various stakeholder groups (for example, academic teachers who prepare and present the programmes; students who study the programmes; graduates who benefit from the programmes; employers of graduates who benefit from the knowledge and skills of the graduates; accreditation bodies who endorse the programmes on behalf of their respective disciplines; the community that benefits from the contribution of the discipline; education specialists who are concerned with the quality and outcomes of the teaching process).

Each stakeholder group expects all of what it considers relevant to be included in respective educational programmes. What is perceived as relevant by one stakeholder group, however, is often perceived as irrelevant by another, and therefore to be excluded (Cowdroy 2000a, b). This inclusion/exclusion nexus creates conflicts between stakeholder perceptions of relevance and quality and dilemmas for academics and institutions trying to achieve quality education. Consider, for example, accreditation authorities which are stakeholder groups typically preoccupied with ensuring minimum standards (of discipline-based knowledge content). Employers of graduates are other stakeholder groups typically preoccupied with personal attributes such as motivation, initiative, self-direction and cooperation (de Graaff and Ravesteijn 2001).

While all stakeholder groups can agree on some general principles, and many subscribe to "standards" and "excellence" in education, notions of what constitutes standards and excellence were found to vary significantly among stakeholder groups. Pressure on academic departments to maintain accreditation was found to translate into pressure on teachers and students to focus on discipline-based knowledge as the only relevant curriculum and the only legitimate indicator of quality (Cowdroy et al. 2002, p. 170; Eraut 2000).

4 Professionalisation, Satisfaction and Identity in Academic Careers

Developing between the changes in the social, economic and political context, on one hand, and the changes in higher education system, on the other hand, the academic profession has to define a new identity for itself. The "professionalisation" of the academic profession is becoming more important as universities try to respond to issues relating to standards and quality, growing international competition, and generally "doing more with less".

Professionalisation has been much debated since the beginning of the twentieth century. There is a growing debate around the changing nature of academic work and the concept of professionalisation in academia (Avis 1999; Nixon 1996; Nixon et al. 1998; O'Neill and Meek 1994; Taylor 1999; Watts 2000). The literature on professions suggests that the professional status is acquired during a long-lasting education. So, what is a "professional"? There is a wide range of opinions on this topic but some common characteristics emerge. One can say that "professionals" do work that is not routine and well understood. It is work that has a strong intellectual content, frequently leading to unique or novel outcomes. In addition professionals have:

- Specialised knowledge—usually acquired through academic qualifications.
- A high level of practical and intellectual skills.
- A high standard of ethical behaviour—sometimes codified in the form of a formal "code of practice".

Profession is equivalent to having power, prestige, high income, high social status and privileges.

Professionalisation is the social process by which any trade or occupation transforms itself into a profession of the highest integrity and competence. Professionalisation involves establishing norms and criteria of qualification of members of a profession. Also, professionalisation "acknowledges the qualitative diversity of the processes that structure occupational groups and the ways in which they have historically constructed a certain degree not only of autonomy but also of power and security and giving rise to specialisation and the non-substitutability of the competences thus produced, as well as a certain subjective and objective collective existence" (Demailly and de la Broise 2009, p. 3).

Using professionalisation related with the academic role raises some questions. First of all, most of the academics assumed that the conduct and publication of research is, par excellence, for academics. Their professional devotion is given to a specific subject and disciplinary research. The specialising of disciplines has lead to discipline isolation, and the academics therefore first of all construct their professional self-image within the highly specialised "tribes" of their disciplines (Becher 1989; O'Neill and Meek 1994). Accordingly, professionalism is entirely connected to the disciplines, and not to the broader academic function. Moreover, there will be specific division between the areas of professional engagement into research and teaching. In practice, what constitutes professional interests is often identified by what these alliances are against, rather than what they are for (O'Neill and Meek 1994, p. 97).

> "... the academic profession needs training in much the same way as academics consider that other professions need it and indeed provide it for them. This means that the training itself must be professional, that it should normally lead to recognised academic qualifications, that it should be closely allied to practice, and that—above all—it must be associated with relevant research" (Elton 1987, p. 76). Since professionalisation of university academic is an incremental process, it is necessary to provide comprehensive ongoing professional development programmes for academic staff, as part of the overall quality assurance system for higher education.

A factor in driving change in continuing professional development is the advent of new technologies, and their application to the administrative, teaching and research functions within universities. Every aspect of the academic function now requires at least minimal skills in new technologies, and more importantly, an understanding of the pedagogical implications of 'digital delivery'. Hence the academic staff must learn not only the 'how' of operating technical equipment and software, but also how to facilitate a useful and effective information exchange in a digital environment. As a consequence of both the new technologies, and the disaggregation or 'unbundling' of academic work (Coaldrake and Stedman 1999), the lone teacher approach is rapidly disappearing from universities. Collaborative team work becomes the way to build a fruitful academic career.

Most studies of the higher education sector reveal a clear perception that teaching is not valued as much as research (Ramsden et al. 1995). Research has been considered critical in the functioning of modern universities and the quality of major universities has been judged mainly by their research output. Structural change in the funding of the university sector, combined with management decisions on increasing 'flexibility' in staffing appointments, has also resulted in greater separation of "the production of knowledge (research) and its distribution (teaching)" (Rowland et al. 1998, p. 134). This separation is contestable, and is regarded by many academics, such as Rowland et al. and the academics in Dunkin's (1994) survey, as inappropriate. With demands for 'increased productivity' academics will come under pressure for more accountability in relation to their dual role as teacher and researcher. However, many academics perceive that the reward system in universities privileges research over teaching.

In addition, professionalisation is the key issue in establishing the degree in academics commitment and job satisfaction. Organisational commitment is considered as an important variable in understanding employee behaviour and attitudes (Mowday et al. 1982; Meyer and Allen 1984, 1986, 1988; Allen and Meyer 1990). Allen and Meyer's studies confirm that organisational commitment has three components, namely, affective, continuance and normative (Allen and Meyer 1990). Employees with a strong organisational commitment are those with high level of professionalisation and high level of job satisfaction.

Attempts to pursue professionalisation of higher education teaching have had a long history. As O'Neill and Meek (1994, p. 97) note: "... the self-regulation of professions has as much to do with the politics of knowledge as with anything else. This is especially so for the academic profession, with its stake in controlling knowledge production and dissemination". As O'Neill and Meek observe, increasing casualisation in employment in universities also militates against a professional academic role.

Job satisfaction has long been identified as a factor which is related to many aspects of behaviour in organisational construct. Job satisfaction denotes whether employees find their employment sufficiently satisfactory to continue in it, either permanently or until they are prepared for greater responsibilities. Low job satisfaction is associated with low performance, poor quality, grievances and other difficulties.

Locke (1976, p. 130) defined job satisfaction as a "pleasurable or positive emotional state resulting from the appraisal of one's job experiences". In this context, the job satisfaction is a global construct encompassing satisfaction with work, working conditions, pay, benefits, promotion opportunities, team working and organisational practices (Griffin and Bateman 1986).

Job satisfaction is an active factor in professionalisation. Academic job satisfaction influences the job performance in terms of attitudes, perceptions and reactions. Also, job satisfaction influences both the productivity and morale. It is necessary to find the answer to the questions: Is the staff at research-oriented universities more satisfied than the staff at teaching universities? Are the sources of satisfaction or dissatisfaction similar or different? There are two concepts related to the teaching-research nexus in terms of job satisfaction. The first assumes that the two activities are complementary with each other because research enhances teaching (the academics consider teaching as something which follows from research, rather than their main priority). The second concept considers that the two activities are in tension because teaching affects the quality of research. The decrease in number of the academics declaring to give priority to teaching is only one evidence that the notion that academics should do research has become dominant (Balbachevsky and Schwartzman 2008; Arimoto 2008).

The salary level of the academic staff in higher education and research institutions is one of the key issues of job satisfaction. Governments all over the world are trying to cut down costs, increase efficiency, profits and accountability of higher education in the economy (Slaughter and Leslie 1997). "Within developing countries the conditions of work and remuneration of the majority of academics is inadequate ... Academics have to hold more than one job to make ends meet" (Eggins 2008, p. 128). On the other hand, as Teichler and Yagci say (2009, p. 108) "in most economically advanced countries, senior academic staff at universities and public research institutes traditionally had permanent employment contracts, while the situation varied for junior academic staff. In some countries, they had similar contracts as seniors from the very beginning, in others their employment security grew gradually over time, while in others permanent contracts were only awarded with the appointment to senior positions."

This has affected the structure and organisation of the profession, namely, the way academic staff is employed, the academic profession as a career, quality, academic freedom, autonomy, the relationship between teaching and research, etc. Structural change in the funding of the university sector, combined with management decisions on increasing 'flexibility' in staffing appointments, has also resulted in greater separation of "the production of knowledge (research) and its distribution (teaching)" (Rowland et al. 1998, p. 134). This separation is contestable, and is regarded by many academics, such as Rowland et al. and the academics in Dunkin's (1994) survey, as inappropriate. Universally, the status of the profession seems to have declined.

People's lives are multifaceted causing challenging conflicts between professional and personal identities (Day et al. 2006). Identity itself is an unstable concept being related to work-based policy changes and the social and economic environment. Change poses both "threats and opportunities" to academic staff whose "academic identities, including identities as researchers, are forged, rehearsed and remade in local sites of practice" (Lee and Boyd 2003, p. 188). The academic career is influenced by the institutional context, although the individual has the ability to negotiate their roles and responsibilities through the process of prioritising.

The attempt to define the identity is a challenge. First of all, identity is a social construct that develops over time. Churchman (2006) believes that identity is a vehicle for the way one wants "to interact with the rest of the world" (p. 6). Also, academic staff "struggles to define their identity and those of their colleagues" (Churchman 2006, p. 5). As professionals, academics are engaged in solving the dilemmas and challenges that affect their role. In doing so, they "re-story themselves in and against the audit culture" (Stronach et al. 2002, p. 130). Today it is obvious that policy is leading and structuring research, with the result that an academic's research identity is constructed to achieve governmental and managerial aims rather than educational objectives.

Academic identities are disparate and lack homogeneity and compromises in the workplace are becoming more commonplace and inevitable (Churchman 2006). Development of the academic work in a knowledge and performance-based environment involves staff co-operation between and within departments and affects the nature of interaction between hierarchical levels within the institution. In order to produce a positive environment for effective teaching and research, acknowledgement of multiple and disparate academic identities is needed. In order to increase the numbers of financially viable and capable units (Sjolund 2002), state policies in Europe have had a major impact on institutional organisation, affecting not only the way in which institutions now function, but also the role and responsibilities of those who work within them. Today, more institutions have adopted the German model of "integrating research into universities rather than separate institutes" (Grant and Edgar 2003, p. 319). This integration aims at increased coordination of academic research and provides the primary influence for the research agenda. Of course, this changing policy involves new consequences for the roles of academic staff. Also, this policy has influenced the way institutions are funded, creating tensions between supporting research and the demands of teaching and learning. There are changes in perceptions of the academic staff themselves because they must identify how they can adapt to this culture.

5 Conclusion and Research Questions

This study has reviewed the evolution of academic profession in terms of quality assurance, relevance and satisfaction, and university governance change. Also, we tried to depict changes in the professoriate due to international competition that now affect individual faculty and their institutions and we will seek to understand how academic professionals are affected by these shifts as well as how they respond to them.

It is clear that higher education faces new opportunities and new challenges in its role as actor in a more globalised society. Universities are under growing political pressure for reform in face of more acute competition for public resources in tandem with a marked slowdown in the growth of funding. At the same time, the universities are held responsible for quality assurance of the institutions' academic activities.

Quality assurance also serves as a major indicator for the governments to allocate funding and other resources according to the individual institutions' performance in teaching and learning, research, and management. Nevertheless, such a development has been criticised as a means not to improve the quality of education but produce much more pressure to comply with numerous quantifiable and measurable performance indicators that cannot reflect the genuine outcomes of education.

As Currie (2004) said if universities are going to be models of institutions for the society, it is necessary to involve academia in democratic decision-making processes in the face of external pressures and "pure" managerial decision making in universities. What is more important is to maintain scholarly integrity, peer review, and professional autonomy in the face of the growing threat of managerial accountability.

In order to understand how academic professionals are affected by all these shifts as well as how they respond to them, some research questions are proposed:

1. What are the ways to integrate research, teaching, and learning? Today, the academia must face new academic research policies that promote the priority accorded to research universities. In an international dimension, an academic system capable of responding to worldwide competition in academic productivity is needed.
2. What are the optimal approaches to governance to promote quality and improvement in education? Is the approach in which the authority to make decisions is delegated to universities and individual teacher levels the best choice? This shift of decision-making authority involves a greater need for information on the outcomes of education at the various levels.
3. How does academic staff perceive their teaching and research obligations? Are research-oriented academics more satisfied with their work than teaching-oriented academics? What is the place of research academics in the hierarchies within institutions?
4. How relevant is the academic profession to society in the context of the economic crisis during the past 2 years?

References

Allen, N. J., & Meyer, J. P. (1990). The measurement and antecedents of affective, continuance, and normative commitment to the organisation. *Journal of Occupational Psychology, 63*, 1–18.

Altbach, P. G. (1980). The crisis of the professoriate. *Annals of the American Academy of Political and Social Science, 448*, 1–14.

Altbach, P. G. (Ed.). (1996). *The international academic profession. Portraits of fourteen countries.* Princeton: The Carnegie Foundation for the Advancement of Teaching.

Altbach, P. G. (1998). An international crisis? The American professoriate in comparative perspective. In P. G. Altbach (Ed.), *Comparative higher education: Knowledge, the university and development* (pp. 75–91). Greenwich: Ablex Publishing Corporation.

Altbach, P. G. (2000). *The changing academic workplace: Comparative perspective.* Boston: Center for International Higher Education.

Arimoto, A. (2008). International implications of the changing academic profession in Japan. In RIHE (Ed.), *The Changing academic profession in international comparative and quantitative perspectives* (Report of the International Conference on the Changing Academic Profession Project No. 12) (pp. 1–33). Hiroshima: Research Institute for Higher Education, Hiroshima University.

Avis, J. (1999). Shifting identity: New conditions and the transformation of practice—Teaching within post-compulsory education. *Journal of Vocational Education and Training, 51*(2), 245–264.

Balbachevsky, E., & Schwartzman, S. (2008). Brazilian academic profession: Some recent trends. In RIHE (Ed.), *The changing academic profession in international comparative and quantitative perspectives* (Report of the International Conference on the Changing Academic Profession Project No. 12) (pp. 327–345). Hiroshima: Research Institute for Higher Education, Hiroshima University.

Baruch, Y., & Hall, D. T. (2004). The academic career: A model for future careers in other sectors? *Journal of Vocational Behavior, 64*(2), 241–262.

Becher, T. (1989). *Academic tribes and territories.* Milton Keynes: Open University Press.

Berkhout, S. J. (2002). *Conceptual and contextual diversity: Comparing the centralisation/decentralisation dynamics in Belgium and South Africa.* Paper presented at the International Conference on Education and Decentralisation: African Experiences and Analyses, 10–14 June, Johannesburg.

Breneman, D. W., & Youn, T. I. K. (Eds.). (1988). *Academic labor markets and careers.* New York: Falmer.

Brennan, J. (2007). The academic profession and increasing expectations of relevance. In M. Kogan & U. Teichler (Eds.), *Key challenges to the academic profession* (Werkstattberichte, Vol. 65, pp. 19–28). Kassel: International Centre for Higher Education Research Kassel (INCHER Kassel) and UNESCO Forum on Higher Education, Research and Knowledge.

Brennan, J., Locke, W., & Naidoo, R. (2007). United Kingdom: An increasingly differentiated profession. In W. Locke & U. Teichler (Eds.), *The changing conditions for academic work and careers in selected countries* (Werkstattberichte, Vol. 66, pp. 163–176). Kassel: International Centre for Higher Education Research Kassel (INCHER-Kassel).

Burbules, N. C., & Torres, C. A. (Eds.). (2000). *Globalization and education: Critical perspectives.* New York: Routledge.

Chapman, D. W., Weidman, J. C., Cohen, M., & Mercer, M. (2005). The search for quality: A five country study of national strategies to improve educational quality in Central Asia. *International Journal of Educational Development, 25*(5), 514–530.

Churchman, D. (2006). Institutional commitments, individual compromises: Identity-related responses to compromise in an Australian University. *Journal of Higher Education, 28*(1), 3–15.

Clark, B. R. (1987). *Academic life, small worlds, different worlds.* Princeton: Princeton University Press.

Coaldrake, P., & Stedman, L. (1999). *Academic work in the 21st century: Changing roles and practices.* Occasional Papers Series, 99-H. Canberra: DETYA.

Cowdroy, R. (2000a). *At the boundaries the rules must change.* Les Cahiers de l'Enseignement de l'Architecture (Vol. 6). Louvaine-La Neuve: European Association for Architectural Education.

Cowdroy, R. (2000b). *Contract assessment: Self-evaluation and empowerment for excellence.* Les Cahiers de l'Enseignement de l'Architecture (Vol. 6). Louvaine-La Neuve: European Association for Architectural Education.

Cowdroy, R., & Chapman, M. (1999). *Architectural competencies.* Report to the Architects Accreditation Council of Australia, Canberra.

Cowdroy, R., Williams, A., Graaff, E., de, & Mauffette, Y. (2002). *Resolving relevance quality and quality assurance: A transitional criteria approach. Quality conversations.* Proceedings of the 25th HERDSA Annual Conference 7–10 July 2002. Perth: Higher Education Research and Development Society of Australasia, Inc.

Currie, J. (2004). The neo-liberal paradigm and higher education: A critique. In F. K. Odin & P. T. Manicas (Eds.), *Globalization and higher education* (pp. 42–62). Honolulu: University of Hawaii Press.

Day, C., Kington, A., Stobart, G., & Sammons, P. (2006). The personal and professional selves of teachers: Stable and unstable identities. *British Educational Research Journal, 32*(4), 601–616.

de. Graaff, E., & Ravesteijn, W. (2001). Training complete engineers: Global enterprise and engineering education. *European Journal of Engineering Education, 26*(4), 419–427.

De Grauwe, A. (2005). Improving the quality of education through school-based management: Learning from international experiences. *Review of Education, 51,* 269–287.

Demailly L., & de la Broise, P. (2009). The implications of deprofessionalisation: Case studies and possible avenues for future research *Socio-logos. Revue de l'association française de sociologie, 4.* http://socio-logos.revues.org/2305.

Dunkin, R. (1994). Award winning university teachers' beliefs about teaching vs. research. *HERD, 13*(1), 85–91.

Eggins, H. (2008). The changing academic profession: Implications for the Asia-Pacific region. In R. M. Salazar-Clemeña & L. V. Meek (Eds.), *Competition, collaboration and change in the academic profession: Shaping higher education's contribution to knowledge and research* (pp. 122–133). Quezon City: Libro Amigo.

El-Khawas, E. (2002). Developing an academic career in a globalising world. In J. Enders & O. Fulton (Eds.), *Higher education in a globalising world. International trends and mutual observations. A Festschrift in Honour of Ulrich Teichler* (pp. 241–254). Dordrecht: Kluwer.

Elton, L. (1987). *Teaching in higher education: Appraisal and training.* London: Kogan Page.

Enders, J. (1996). *Die wissenschaftlichen Mitarbeiter. Ausbildung, Beschäftigung und Karriere der Nachwuchswissenschaftler und Mittelbauangehörigen an den Universitäten.* Frankfurt a. M.: Campus.

Enders, J. (1999). Crisis? What crisis? The academic professions in the 'Knowledge' society. *Higher Education, 38,* 71–81.

Enders, J. (2001a). Between state control and academic capitalism: A comparative perspective on academic staff in Europe. In J. Enders (Ed.), *Academic staff in Europe, changing contexts and conditions* (pp. 1–23). Westport: Greenwood.

Enders, J. (Ed.). (2001b). *Academic staff in Europe, changing contexts and conditions.* Westport: Greenwood.

Enders, J. (2004). Higher education, internationalization, and the nation-state: Recent developments and challenges to governance theory. *Higher Education, 47*(3), 361–382.

Enders, J., & de Weert, E.,(Eds.). (2004). *The international attractiveness of the academic workplace in Europe.* Frankfurt a. M.: Gewerkschaft Erziehung und Wissenschaft.

Eraut, M. (2000). Non-formal learning and tacit knowledge in professional work. *British Journal of Educational Psychology, 70*(1), 113–136.

Ford, M. P. (2002). *Beyond the modern university: Toward a constructive Postmodern University.* Westport: Praeger.

Gallagher, M. (2001). *Modern university governance: A national perspective.* Paper presented at "The Idea of a University: Enterprise or Academy?" Conference organised by the Australia Institute and Manning Clark House. Canberra: The Australian National University.

Gornitzka, Å., Kogan, M., & Amaral, A. (2005). *Reform and change in higher education. Analysing policy implementation.* Dordrecht: Springer.

Grant, K., & Edgar, D. (2003). Using the theory of policy networks and communities to explore who determines the Scottish higher education research policy: Issue for educational managers. *The International Journal of Educational Management, 17*(7), 318–329.

Griffin, R. W., & Bateman, T. S. (1986). Job satisfaction and organizational commitment. In C. L. Cooper & I. T. Robertson (Eds.), *International review of industrial and organizational psychology* (pp. 157–188). New York: Wiley.

Hall, D. T. (2002). *Careers in and out of organizations.* Thousand Oaks: Sage.

Halsey, A. H. (1992). *Decline of donnish dominion. The British academic professions in the twentieth century.* Oxford: Clarendon.

Heitmann, G. (2000). Quality assurance in German engineering education against the background of European developments. *International Journal of Engineering Education, 16*(Special Issue; 2), 117–126.

Henkel, M. (2001). *Academic identities and policy change in higher education.* London: Kingsley.

Knill C., & Lehmkuhl, D. (2002). Private actors and the state: Internationalization and changing patterns of governance. *Governance, 15*(1), 41–63.

Lee, A., & Boyd, D. (2003). Writing groups, change and academic identity: Research development as local practice. *Studies in Higher Education, 28*(2), 187–200.

Lee, M. H., & Gopinathan, S. (2005). Reforming university education in Hong Kong and Singapore. In K. Mok & R. James (Eds.), *Globalization and higher education in East Asia: Contemporary issues in education series* (pp. 56–98). Singapore: Marshall Cavendish Academic.

Locke, E. A. (1976). The nature and causes of job satisfaction. In M. D. Dunnette (Ed.), *Handbook of industrial and organizational psychology* (pp. 129–134). Chicago: McNally.

Lundgren, U. P. (1990). Educational policymaking, decentralisation and evaluation. In M. Granheim, M. Kogan, & U. Lundgren (Eds.), *Evaluation as policymaking: Introducing evaluation into a national decentralised educational system* (pp. 42–65). London: Kingsley.

Maassen, P. A. M. (2006). *The modernisation of European higher education. A multi-level analysis.* Paper presented to the Directors General Meeting for Higher Education, 19–20 October, Helsinki.

Marginson, S., & Van Der Wende, M., (2006). *Globalisation and higher education.* Paper prepared for OECD. http://www.cshe.unimelb.edu.au.

Meek, V. L. (2003). *Market coordination, research management and the future of higher education in the post-industrial era, UNESCO Forum Occasional Paper Series.* Paper produced for the UNESCO Forum Regional Scientific Committee for Asia and the Pacific Paris, September 2003.

Meyer, J. P., & Allen, N. J. (1984). Testing the "Side-bet Theory" of organizational commitment: Some methodological considerations. *Journal of Applied Psychology, 69,* 372–378.

Meyer, J. P., & Allen, N. J. (1986). *Development and consequences of three components of commitment.* Paper presented at the annual meeting of the Administrative Sciences Association of Canada, Whistler, BC, Canada.

Meyer, J. P., & Allen, N. J. (1988). Links between work experiences and organisational commitment during the first year of employment. A longitudinal analysis. *Journal of Occupational Psychology, 61,* 195–209.

Mitter, W. (2003). A decade of transformation: Educational policies in Central and Eastern Europe. *International Review of Education, 49,* 1–2.

Mok, K.-H. (2001). *Globalization, marketization and higher education: Trends and developments in East Asia.* Paper presented at the International Conference on Marketization and Higher Education in East Asia, 7–8 April. Shanghai: CEPRU.

Mok, K.-H. (2005). Globalisation and governance: Educational policy instruments and regulatory arrangements. *Review of Education, 51,* 289–311.

Mok, K.-H., & Chan, D. (Eds.). (2002). *Globalization and education: The quest for quality education in Hong Kong.* Hong Kong: Hong Kong University Press.

Mok, K.-H., & Lo, H. C. (2002). Marketization and the changing governance in higher education: A comparative study. *Higher Education Management and Policy, 14*(1), 51–82.

Mok, K.-H., & Welch, A. (Eds.). (2003). *Globalization and educational restructuring in the Asia Pacific region.* Basingstoke: Macmillan.

Mowday, R. T., Porter, L. W., & Steers, R. M. (1982). *Employee-organizational linkages: The psychology of commitment, absenteeism, and turnover.* San Diego: Academic.

Musselin, C. (2003). Internal versus external labour markets. *Higher Education Management and Policy, 15*(3), 9–23.

Musselin, C. (2007). The transformation of academic work: Facts and analysis. Berkeley: University of California, Centre de Sociologie des Organisations. Research & Occasional Paper Series: CSHE.4.07. http://cshe.berkeley.edu/. Accessed Feb 2007.

Neave, G., & Rhoades, G. (1987). The academic estate in Western Europe. In B. R. Clark (Ed.), *The academic profession. National, disciplinary, and institutional settings* (pp. 211–270). Berkeley: University of California Press.

Nicholls, G. (2001). *Professional development in higher education.* London: Kogan Page.

Nixon, J. (1996). Professional identity and the restructuring of higher education. *Studies in Higher Education, 21*(1), 5–16.

Nixon, J., Beattie, M., Challis, M., & Walker, M. (1998). What does it mean to be an academic? A colloquium. *Teaching in Higher Education, 3*(3), 272–298.

OECD. (2006). *Reviews of national policies for education—Tertiary education in Portugal.* Lisbon: Organisation for Economic Co-operation and Development.

O'Neill, A., & Meek, V. L. (1994). Academic professionalism and the self-regulations of performance. *Journal of Tertiary Education Administration, 16*(1), 93–107.

Perkin, H. J. (1969). *Key profession: The history of the association of university teachers.* London: Routledge & Kegan Paul.

Pierre, J., & Peters, G. (2000). *Governance, politics and state.* Basingstoke: Macmillan.

Ramsden, P., Margetson, D., Martin, E., & Clarke, S. (1995). *Recognising and rewarding good teaching in Australian higher education (final report).* Canberra, Australian Government Publishing Office Canberra: Project commissioned by the Committee for the Advancement of University Teaching. Griffith Institute of Higher Education, Griffith University. http://www.autc.gov.au/caut/rrgt/titlepag.html.

Randall, J. (2001). Academic review in the United Kingdom. In D. Dunkerley & W. Wong (Eds.), *Global perspectives on quality in higher education* (pp. 57–69). Aldershot: Ashgate.

Rice, R. E. (1986). The academic profession in transition: Toward a new social fiction. *Teaching Sociology, 14*(1), 12–23.

Rowland, S., Byron, C., Furedi, F., Padfield, N., & Smyth, T. (1998). Turning academics into teachers? *Teaching in Higher Education, 3*(2), 133–141.

Schuster, J., & Finkelstein, M. (2006). *The restructuring of academic work and careers: The American faculty.* Baltimore: Johns Hopkins University Press.

Sjolund, M. (2002). Politics versus evaluation: The establishment of three new universities in Sweden. *Quality in Higher Education, 8*(2), 173–181.

Slaughter, S., & Leslie L., (1997). *Academic capitalism: Politics, policies and the entrepreneurial university.* Baltimore: John Hopkins University Press.

Sørensen, A. B. (1992). Wissenschaftliche Werdegänge und akademische Arbeitsmärkte. In K. U. Mayer (Ed.), *Generationsdynamik in der Forschung* (pp. 83–109). Frankfurt a. M.: Campus.

Sporn, B. (1999). Current issues and future priorities for European higher education systems. In P. G. Altbach & P. McGill Peterson (Eds.), *Higher education in the 21st century: Global challenge and national response.* Annapolis Junction: Institute of International Education.

Steyrer, J., Mayrhofer, W., & Meyer, M. (2005). Karrieren. Eine Einführung. In W. Mayrhofer, M. Meyer, & J. Steyrer (Eds.), *Macht? Erfolg? Reich? Glücklich? Einflussfaktoren auf Karrieren* (pp. 12–24). Wien: Linde.

Stronach, I., Corbin, B., McNamara, O., Stark, S., & Warne, T. (2002). Towards an uncertain politic of professionalism: Teacher and nurse identities in flux. *Journal of Educational Policy, 17*(1), 109–138.

Taylor, P. (1999). *Making sense of academic life: Academics, universities and change.* Buckingham: The Society for Research into Higher Education (SRHE) and Open University Press.

Taylor, J., & Machado, M. L. (2006). Higher education leadership and management: From conflict to interdependence through strategic plan. *Tertiary Education and Management, 12*(1), 137–160.

Teichler, U., & Yagci, Y. (2009). Changing challenges of academic work: Concepts and observations. In V. L. Meek, U. Teichler, & M.-L. Kearney (Eds.), *Higher education, research and innovation: Changing dynamics* (pp. 85–145). Report on the UNESCO Forum on Higher Education, Research and Knowledge 2001–2009. Kassel: International Centre for Higher Education Research Kassel (INCHER-Kassel).

UNDP. (2002). UNESCO Brings together South-East Europe ministers to step up cooperation in education, science and culture. http://portal.unesco.org/es/ev.php-URL_ID=3108&URL_DO=DO_PRINTPAGE&URL_SECTION=201.html.

van. Damme, D., (2002). Higher education in the age of globalization. In S. Uvalic-Trumbiced (Ed.), *Globalization and the market in higher education. Quality, accreditation and qualifications* (pp. 21–33). Paris: UNESCO/IAU/Economica.

Watts, C. (2000). Issues of professionalism in higher education. In T. Bourner, T. Katz, & D. Watson (Eds.), *New directions in professional higher education* (pp. 11–18). Buckingham: The Society for Research into Higher Education (SRHE) and Open University Press.

Wielemans, W., & Roth-van-der-Werf, G. J. M. (1995). Onderwijsbeleid in de landen van die Europese Unie. Feiten, tendenzen en kritische interpretatie. Centrum voor |Comparatieve Pedagogiek, K. U. Leuven & Open Universiteit, Heerlen.

Wilson, L. (1980). Dialectic aspects of recent changes in academe. *Annals of the American Academy of Political and Social Science, 448,* 15–24.

Electronic References

Report of the World Summit on Sustainable Development. http://www.johannesburgsummit.org/html/documents/summit_docs/131302_wssd_report_reissued.pdf. Accessed 5 June 2003.

http://www.globalschoolnet.org/index.cfm. GlobalSchoolNet. 2007. Accessed 27 Nov 2007.

http://www.nea.org/he/tanda.html. Web site of the National Education Association. Here you can find the journal of NEA "Thought & Action".

http://www.gse.harvard.edu/~hpfa/. The Project on Faculty Appointments at Harvard University.

http://www.nea.org/he/heupdate/index.html. HEA Higher Education Research Center Update.

http://www.aaup.org/. American Association of University Professors.

http://www.ec.europa.eu/growthandjobs/pdf/1206_annual_report_ro.pdf. A modern Europe that Encourages Innovation, COM (2006) 589. Accessed 12 Oct 2006.

http://www.europarl.europa.eu/meetdocs/2004_2009/.../ad/715/.../715254ro.pdf. To put the knowledge into practice: A vast strategy on what concerns innovation in EU, COM (2006) 502. 13 Sep 2006.

http://www.europa.eu.int/eracareers/europeancharter. EU (2005) The European Charter for Researchers.

Facing New Expectations—Integrating Third Mission Activities into the University

Bojana Ćulum, Nena Rončević and Jasminka Ledić

1 Extending Teaching and Research—New Conditions and Challenges for Universities and the Academic Profession

Throughout history, universities have been providing society with new ideas, knowledge and specific skills as institutions of advanced education and research. Furthermore, they have played critical roles as agents of social change. Bearing in mind the remark of Rosenthal and Wittrock (1993) that the university is the second oldest institution with a continuous history in the Western world, right after the Roman Catholic Church, one would expect strong stability from such longevity. However, several major shifts in higher education have occurred (Stephens et al. 2008). In the late nineteenth century, the first change was largely introduced within the modern Humboldtian university—the development of the modern research university whose mission was to pursue scientific knowledge (Scott 2006). The primary and, for several centuries, intact purpose of (medieval) university at that moment expanded from merely preserving and transmitting knowledge to creating it (Etzkowitz 2001; Scott 2006). Industrial Age then expanded the role beyond the transmission and research to advanced training of professionals, as was demanded by industrialisation (Scott 1992, 2006).

For the sake of the knowledge-economy and society, rising demands for knowledge and highly skilled labour, have changed universities remarkably in the last two or three decades. Much of the recent literature on the university's roles draws attention to those significant changes that higher education has undergone in most parts of the world. It has expanded drastically, become increasingly differentiated and appears to be driven by different external forces (Teichler 1996; Brennan 2007; Altbach 2008). The scale of expectations has increased exponentially and a much

B. Ćulum (✉) · N. Rončević · J. Ledić
Department of Education, University of Rijeka,
Rijeka, Croatia
e-mail: kehm@incher.uni-kassel.de

B. M. Kehm, U. Teichler (eds.), *The Academic Profession in Europe: New Tasks and New Challenges,* The Changing Academy – The Changing Academic Profession in International Comparative Perspective 5, DOI 10.1007/978-94-007-4614-5_9, © Springer Science+Business Media Dordrecht 2013

wider range of stakeholders place their demands upon universities today (Jongbloed et al. 2008). Those include the governments, students, the industry and the civil society (Göransson et al. 2009). Governments demand education for an increasing number of students; the students seek for job relevance in academic curricula; the industry is focused on highly specialised skills and demands innovation and research relevance; civil society looks for guidance and assistance in addressing all sorts of relevant issues which affect both the local and global community.

Over the last decade, many national and international reports argue that higher education has become subjected to various pressures, which include: greater managerialism, greater instrumentalism, greater competition, new forms of control and growing demands for accountability, relevance and employability, competitive globalisation, growing bureaucratisation, centralised accumulation of decision making power, constraints on federal resources, and, above all, the infiltration of corporate culture (Checkoway 2001; Brennan et al. 2004; Mac Labhrainn 2005; Schoen et al. 2006; Kogan and Teichler 2007; Brennan 2007; Locke and Teichler 2007; Altbach 2008). The latest shift was to the discourse of for-profit activities. This shift, with its primary focus on output and productivity, creates additional pressure for higher education (and academics in particular) to produce practical knowledge for the knowledge-based society (Etzkowitz et al. 1998).

However, in the last decade, the governments all around the world have come to regard a large or growing higher education system as essential for economic development emphasising its economic pay-off (Brennan et al. 2004). Brennan (2007) argues that there is something behind the knowledge-based society. He claims that actually the needs of the economy and industry lay behind. In other words, the needs that are generally putting pressure on universities to be more relevant. Ordorika (2009) claims that the idea of universities being broad cultural societal projects or institutions focused on the production of public goods has moved into a marginal or solely discursive realm. These notions have been substituted by a renewed emphasis on the links between higher education and the market. According to different authors, they were substituted by a schema of entrepreneurial university (Clark 1998; Etzkowitz et al. 2000); by notions of excellence (Readings 1996); by the centrality of managerial concepts and goals, such as 'productivity' or 'efficiency'; and by the increasing privatisation of education supply and financing (Slaughter and Leslie 1997, in Ordorika 2009). Some even speculate that this will lead to a change that would make participation in the process of economic development a core university value (Gibbons 1999 cited in Stephens et al. 2008).

According to Nayyar (2008, in Escrigas and Lobera 2009) markets and globalisation are beginning to influence universities and shape education in terms of what is taught and researched. Universities are introducing new courses, which are in demand in the market, and the markets are influencing research agendas of universities. The universities which follow such a paradigm might be initiators of innovation but Enders and Jongbloed (Jongbloed et al. 2008) anticipate, on the other hand, a strong possibility of placing the 'private good' character of higher education above the 'public good'. Escrigas and Lobera (2009) therefore note that higher education institutions have reached a critical moment in their long evolution as disseminators and producers of knowledge. They are, at the same time, facing global challenges, including the rapid development of science and technology; demands related to the creation of knowledge-societies; and the growing competition dominated by market forces. Universities are challenged to fulfil multiple roles, and their attempts in doing so, make their mission disperse, and the quality of their academic activities, as Altbach (2008) warns, often diminished.

Universities have frequently been regarded as key institutions involved in the process of both economic and social change and development. Therefore, the ongoing pressures put on higher education for greater responsiveness are not only limited to the economic sphere. They simply cannot be separated from the political one or from the network of institutions, which constitute civil society (Brennan et al. 2004). A disturbing increase in warning analyses and a series of researches related to the current trends and patterns of resource-use, followed by a rapid technological change as well as rapidly changing and complex societal structure, are all stressing the impact they have on society in critical and, above all, unsustainable ways (Cifrić 1997; IPCC 2007; Stephens et al. 2008). It is not surprising to find an impressive set of documents, declarations and protocols which indicate existing problems in our society and recognise the importance of higher education and academic involvement in delivering possible solutions, as well as promoting civic engagement and sustainable development.[1]

It is also important in this context to point out recent research studies which systematically deal with low level of citizens' political participation on the one hand, and the increase of the level of political apathy and alienation on the other, as well as indicators of a growing mistrust in political institutions and structures (Šalaj 2002). The results, which show that opinions about political institutions (in this case in Europe and EU institutions) are not more positive among civil society activists than among average population, prove the seriousness of the situation (Maloney and van Deth 2008). What is even more distressing is the lack of youth interest for social and political engagement. Both in Europe and USA—almost equally—the

---

[1] Besides the latest and, as Lindberg (2010) pointed out, extremely relevant for universities all over the world—The Bonn Declaration (2009) adopted at the UNESCO World Conference on Education for Sustainable Development, then the most influential, the UNESCO World Conference on Higher Education in 1998 and The UNESCO World Declaration on Higher Education for the Twenty-first Century: Vision and Action, some of the most relevant documents related to the contemporary role of universities and academics are: The UN Millennium Declaration and the United Nations Millennium Developmental Goals; Kyoto protocol; Education for All; Food for All; the UN Decade of Education for Sustainable Development 2005–2014; High-level Group Report on the Alliance of Civilizations, etc. Additional selection of international declarations also emphasising the role of universities and higher education in society (in the field of environmental protection, sustainable development and cultural understanding) offer the following relevant documents: The Stockholm Declaration, Sweden (1972); The Talloires Declaration, France (1990); The Halifax Declaration, Canada (1991); The Rio Declaration, Brazil (1992); Agenda 21 (1992); The Swansea Declaration, Wales (1993); the Copernicus Charter (1993); The Barbados Declaration (1994); Learning: The Treasure Within, UNESCO (1996); The Thessaloniki Declaration (1997); The Earth Charter (2000); The Luneburg Declaration, Germany (2001); Alliance of Civilization (2005); and Communiqué of the 34th session on the UNESCO General Conference (2007).

youth find no interest in the public sphere and politics, have no confidence in state institutions nor the politicians, are rarely willing to volunteer (long-term), and the percentage of youth voters is diminishing (European Commission 2007; Checkoway 2000; National Commission on Civic Renewal 1998; Putnam 1995). Different researches warn that students leave universities without knowing democratic principles. They usually lack the knowledge and skills necessary for their role as active citizens in the community and for democratic development. Regardless of their higher education surrounding, they stay detached from the needs of civil society as well as from the possibility to contribute to the community development. It seems that our students leave university without the sense of social responsibility for community needs and problems.[2] Considering its expected role in society, it is perfectly understandable to actually expect from the academic community to make the necessary changes.

The social context in which universities operate today strongly emphasises its economic, instead of its broader societal, relevance. Also, the focus of academics on core activities of teaching and research has intensely diminished with their struggle and aspiration to become market-oriented, and their work market-relevant (Clark 2004; Geiger 2004; Altbach 2008). Introducing more market-like processes and money-making opportunities into higher education and all of the above mentioned changes has brought tremendous challenges for the traditional roles of the academics (Morshidi et al. 2007). As core staff in the institutions of higher education, academics are evidently affected by the changes around and within higher education (Locke and Teichler 2007) and faced with major challenges concerning its structures and values (Vabø 2007). The faculty is challenged to teach more, collaborate more inside and outside the academia, to be fundraisers and adopt greater administrative and managerial roles and to engage in (third mission/service) activities for which the traditional faculty reward structures have had little regard (Schroeder 1999; Golde and Pribenow 2000; O'Meara et al. 2003; Ledić 2007).

On top of innovative teaching and research, universities and academics are confronted with a new set of roles, with the emphasis on promoting the usefulness of knowledge and the scholarship of application (Sirat 2007). By raising the level of professionalisation of educational programmes and research, by departmentalisation (Lucas 1994; Checkoway 2001) and professionalising the role of academics (Kogan and Teichler 2007; Locke and Teichler 2007), it is obvious that the academic community is adjusting to its market surroundings. The increasing involvement of universities in various activities, brought by the changes described above, as Cummings (2006) argues, results in a potential diversification of the academic role. Along with teaching and research at the university, professors engage in various off-

---

[2] According to a comparative research conducted in eight EU member states "EUYOUPART—Political Participation of Young People in Europe: Development of indicators for Comparative Research in the European Union" 63 % of youth does not show any interest for the public sphere. The research was conducted in Italy, Austria, Germany, France, Great Britain, Slovakia, Finland and Estonia between 2003 and 2005 on the population of youth from 15 to 25 years of age. The Austrian Institute for Social Research and Analysis conducted the research. More information available at: http://www.sora.at/de/start.asp?b=14.

campus activities. However, it rather seems that new assignments are simply being added to the existing load (Cummings 2006). The increasing demands on academics are distracting them from traditional teaching and research.[3]

Because of the before mentioned reasons, higher education has become a target for critics who claim several things. First of all, students (successfully) leave universities without developing active citizen's competencies. Secondly, academic research does not respond to community needs. Lastly, universities, by being completely insensitive to the problems and preoccupations of contemporary society, have lost their civic purpose[4] (Bender 1997; Hollander and Saltmarsh 2000; Ehrlich 2000; Checkoway 2000, 2001; Harkavy 2006). Taylor (2008) believes that universities should contribute more to social development by educating socially responsible and active citizens, promoting and developing the concept of sustainable development, promoting civic engagement and directing and facilitating active participation of citizens in the community.[5]

Stephens et al. (2008) claim that institutions of higher education and academics have a particularly interesting potential in society to facilitate societal responses to the plethora of sustainability challenges facing communities around the world. That presupposes, emphasises Escrigas (2008), a powerful wish, first of all, to change the current individual and competitive university paradigm into a social and collaborative one. The change should include the shift of focus from content to applicability of content and values; from educating productive professionals to educating socially responsible citizens who are professional in what they do; from a dominant market-orientation to a social one. Finally, higher education as a public good should be based on the contribution of professional citizens to public and common good and the development of human and social capital, and not on individual status and producing rich individual professionals and supporting economic development.

As contemporary society faces challenges associated with rapid technological advancements, environmental changes, resource scarcity, increasing inequality, injustice and democratic deficit, new demands are being placed upon universities with various opportunities for higher education and academics emerging (Stephens et al. 2008). Universities and academics should be engaged in delivering solutions for these complex problems in innovative ways, opening the space of traditional teaching and research functions. In addition, Calhoun (2006) argues that academics

---

[3] The international comparative analysis on the academic profession reveals that the time spent on service activities by university professors varied according to country from 6 to 12 % (Teichler 1996).

[4] Parker and Jary (1995) warn about how the current changes have transformed universities in *McUniversity*—widely available and standardized service.

[5] Jongbloed et al. (2008) reminded on the OECD-CHERI edition *The University and the Community: The Problems of Changing Relationships* from 1982, where universities were called upon to assume a public service function, i.e. make a contribution to solve major problems the local community and society at large were faced with, and participate directly in the process of social change. They continue by stressing the relevance of this 27 years old call in today's discussions on the role of the university.

have the responsibility to be relevant—to take knowledge beyond the walls of the academia into the public domain.

Literature analysis suggests that it is the issue of the third mission that thoroughly explores how universities interact with the public domain Calhoun (2006) talks about—meeting the needs of society at large. Presenting and analysing various concepts and interpretations of the third mission activities set the platform for further analysis of broadening core academic activities (teaching and research). However, this paper focuses on the two following segments: (I) university civic mission and (II) education for sustainable development, with double focus: (I) as issues "pushing" higher education and academics towards a more deliberate social engagement and (II) as potential answers to the pressures universities and academics are faced with to become more relevant to society's complexity and needs, in addition to the traditional settings of teaching and research.

2   University Third Mission

2.1   An Introduction

Universities are asked to take on an important role concerning issues of economic growth, self-financing (by engaging in commercial activities), transferring research results to technology and industry, creating insights of direct relevance to social as well as sustainable development and better forms of political organisation and governance (Göransson et al. 2009). As Bennani (2008, in Escrigas and Lobera 2009) notes, such challenges require the world's educational systems to adopt new roles and readjust their traditional mission of both teaching and research.

There is an on-going debate about the need to develop a broader view of scholarship, especially regarded to the third mission or 'service' (see Boyer 1990; Paulsen and Feldman 1995; MacFarlane 2005; Greenbank 2006; Karlsson et al. 2007; Ledić 2007; Göransson et al. 2009). The debate makes it obvious that universities have to find a balance between a wide range of different roles and responsibilities. Teaching and research activities are central tasks, but universities and academics have been increasingly called upon to play a direct role in supporting regional and national economic development as well as to have a direct impact on society.

Universities have always contributed both directly and indirectly to the wider society. These tasks are thus not innovative in that sense. However, what differs in recent years is the intensified focus on the third mission activities in the context of extending traditional university settings of teaching and research for the purpose of local, regional and national development. An OECD report, The Response of Higher Education Institutions to Regional Needs (1999) identified a "new regionalism" as part of an emergent third role (mission) for higher education institutions. But what do we understand by 'university third mission'? Generally, it is the relationship between higher education and society beyond the first (teaching) and second (research) missions, and the "new" role of universities as entrepreneurs and contributors to social and economic development.[6] The third mission issues explore the response of universities to this challenging call of answering different needs of various stakeholders and being in a far more relevant and deeper interaction with society. This call is, as Göransson et al. (2009) have illustrated, the result of mounting external and internal pressures on universities to re-define themselves in an increasingly competitive and globalizing world.

The discourse on university third mission takes on many directions. The main ones will be presented in detail in the subsequent chapters. There are three basic models currently elaborated in the literature: (I) third mission as an exclusive university contribution to economic development (dominated in literature as economic or technological third mission, strongly related to the innovations development), (II) third mission as university-community civic relationship (dominated in terminology as civic mission) and (III) third mission as an integrated concept making all three sectors—public, private, and non-profit relevant for the cooperation. These models can further differ regarding the placement of the third mission activities as the ones that are: (I) in addition to teaching and research, (II) tied and integrated within teaching and research or (III) a combination of the previous two. In addition, there is a division regarding partners with whom universities can perform third mission activities. Two main stakeholders arise—the societal partners and the ones from business/industry.

The implementation of the education for sustainable development in higher education institutions, regarded as one of the specific third mission aspect, is analysed within the discourse on sustainable university, and will be explained in more detail later on. It offers two basic models: (I) universities as institutions which need to address sustainable development issues—this involves their institutional change (characteristics of the sustainable university) and (II) universities as agents of change (known as the "whole-of-university" approach to sustainability). Both approaches emphasize the necessity for a curriculum change to address sustainability, which is one of the most important indicators of expanding research and teaching, since it is expected from academics to change the way they traditionally work.[7]

Having in mind the complex phenomenon of the third mission and how the integration of various third stream activities reflects upon the academics, it is important to 'find a proper place' for the issue of extending teaching and research within

---

[6] Jongbloed et al. (2008) point out the university mission overload stating how contemporary universities suffer from an acute case of mission confusion.

[7] The integration of sustainability within higher education implies a shift from transmissive learning to learning through discovery; from teacher-centered approach to learner-centered approach; from individual learning to collaborative learning; from learning dominated by theory to praxis-oriented learning which links theory and experience; from a focus on accumulating knowledge and a content orientation to a focus on self-regulative learning and real issue orientations; the emphasis on cognitive objectives only to cognitive, affective and skill-related objective; from institutional staff-based teaching/learning to learning with and from outsiders; from low-level cognitive learning to higher-level cognitive learning (Van den Bor et al. 2000, in Sterling 2004).

distinctive concepts of third mission, especially civic mission and education for sustainable development.

2.2   University Third Mission—Illuminating the Concept

With teaching and research as the two core and honoured activities, the 'third mission' becomes a rather illusive and fuzzy concept covering basically all other activities beyond the first two. The concept itself is strongly connected with the emerging regional development agenda (Chatterton and Goddard 2003). It requires university regional engagement to be formally recognized as a "third role" for universities, not only sitting alongside, but also fully integrated with the university pillars, teaching and research.

An often-used definition is that third mission activities represent those, which are concerned with the generation, use, application and exploitation of knowledge and other university capabilities outside the academic environments. "In other words, the Third Stream (Mission) is about the interaction between universities and the rest of society" (Molas-Gallart et al. 2002, p. iii). The most controversial issue of university third mission, as will be introduced later in more detail, is to whom or to what 'the rest of society' actually refers to or, in other words, whose needs should the universities and academics address?

Within the PRIME project of an "Observatory of the European University" (OEU), the university's third mission encompasses the relations between a university and its non-academic partners. It is multifaceted, as it examines several issues of both the economic and societal dimensions of universities. It supersedes the sole transfer of knowledge towards economic actors (patents, licenses, spin-offs…) and public bodies, as well as university involvement in social and cultural life (Schoen et al. 2006, p. 129).

In "Engagement as a Core Value for the University," a consultation document released by the Association of Commonwealth Universities (ACU; 2001) points that university engagement with the non-university world implies "strenuous, thoughtful and argumentative interaction in at least four spheres: (I) setting universities' aims, purposes and priorities, (II) relating teaching and learning to the wider world, (III) dialogue between researchers and practitioners and (IV) taking on wider responsibilities as neighbours and citizens" (ACU 2001, p. i).

The analysis of the contemporary context in which universities operate, taking into account various countries with different economic, political and geographic features, led Göransson et al. (2009) to reveal an increasing demand for such activities, particularly with regard to technology transfer, but also to civil society in more general terms. However, there is little consensus on how to perform third mission activities and the interpretation of cooperative outreach functions varies considerably. Laredo (2007) points out that the third mission should be taken differently, depending on the configuration of university activities, upon its embedding in its geographical territory, and upon the country's institutional framework. The third mission is vaguely defined and has been an on-going process (Bortagaray 2009), still searching for the broader and more intensive scientific discourse on how to find the appropriate balance between demands put upon universities.

University third mission, university third stream, university third revolution, university civic mission, extension, outreach, knowledge transfer, knowledge application, knowledge transmission, knowledge diffusion, service, community service, service to the society, community engagement, engaged university, community engaged university, university third task, or university third leg, are all different names (and concepts) actually pointing out the same—university reaching out to society at large through various kinds of linkages.

It was Boyer who opened the field of an on-going debate about the 'service' in his insightful call for the scholarship of service (Boyer 1990). A number of scholars who follow his work have been emerging both in the United States and in Europe (Checkoway 2001; Ostrander 2004; Macfarlane 2005; Harkavy 2006; Greenbank 2006; Karlsson 2007; Ledić 2007). Still, no consensus has been reached upon the question of serving whom?[8] The contribution of service to society is a complex phenomenon and not easy to pinpoint (Gregersen et al. 2009). It involves different stakeholders, a wide range of direct and indirect activities, and takes into account both direct and indirect effects of the third mission, as Gregersen et al. (2009) continue, its definition as well as the answer to the question of serving the needs of various stakeholders are even more blurred. Therefore, a coexistence of broader and narrowly defined approaches can be observed in the present discourse, since the third mission activities are perceived and implemented in different ways, depending on both internal and external factors influencing the university.

What the third role highlights is the increasing embeddedness of universities in their regions and their duty as responsible local, as well as national and international agents of change. For this reason, it is very important and relevant to analyse and compare how the third mission activities are explained and carried out as an input to needed clarification.

2.3   Third Mission Discourse and Models

2.3.1   Third Mission—University's Exclusive Relationship with Business/Industry

Although it is becoming more and more obvious that both the societal as well as the enterprise and technological (third) mission are highly relevant for university development, third mission is more often equated with knowledge transfer directly linked with the commercialisation of research (Thorn and Soo 2009; Krücken et al. 2009) related to the direct contributions of universities to economic development.

---

[8] For detailed and interesting observations on the issue, read Graham, G. (2002). *Universities: the recovery of an idea*. Charlottesville: Imprint Academic.

The international debate on the concept of the third mission, by Abramson et al. (1997, in Göransson et al. 2009) is mostly dominated by the US paradigm. Their spin-off enterprises and strong research commercialisation imply a real economic boom and the Bayh-Dole Act aims at an improved economic use of university knowledge through increased university patenting. The expected role of university as the main brain behind economic development is well elucidated in national policies[9] and important reports, such as the OECD report (2007) and the Communications from the European Commission (2003). New models are therefore being proposed to guide universities on their new path. They range from one labelled as Mode 2 knowledge production (Gibbons et al. 1994) to triple helix models involving private–public partnerships (Etzkowitz and Leydesdorff 1997) and the creation of entrepreneurial universities (Etzkowitz et al. 2000) more in line with supporting economic development of a country. Nevertheless, there is no universal model. Most of them ultimately suggest that the universities should move towards a technology-oriented third mission, making a closer interaction with enterprises.

The collaboration between university and industry has improved worldwide[10] (Mwamila and Diyamett 2009). There is a growing number of academics considering third mission activities exclusively as their contribution to innovation and economic growth, i.e. transfer of knowledge and technology through different modes of interacting and creating 'money-making' opportunities with the industry (Maculan and Carvalho de Mello 2009; Gokhberg et al. 2009; Krücken et al. 2009; Palsson et al. 2009; Etzkowitz and Leydesdorff 1997). The governments have prioritized and encouraged university–business cooperation, as an important step in building a knowledge-based economy. Largely in response to this policy orientation, universities have begun to take more focused actions to pursue industry linkages, spurred also by the need for additional resources (Wang and Zhou 2009; Fiskovica et al. 2009; Laredo 2007). Göransson et al. (2009) found the same while analysing the issue of third mission in 12 countries[11]: "…in many countries the official political documents ask for a closer connection of the universities with society, and in more detailed implementation rules it becomes obvious that the government is exclusively looking at more intensive technology transfer" (Göransson et al. 2009, p. 162).

Altbach (2008) warns that the market-oriented academic tendencies of the twenty-first century and the more popular corporate mission are reasons for concern because of the influences that contemporary changes have on university mission. By aiming at a closer collaboration with the industry and economy and by invest-

---

[9] According to Laredo (2007), a pilot study conducted by OECD at the end of the 1990s demonstrated that nearly all OECD countries have developed specific policies to nurture the creation of firms and promote their development: science or technology parks, incubators, incentives for academic staff to engage in commercial activities, etc.

[10] Faced with financing challenges, mostly because of the lack of state investments, universities are forced to find models of sustainability, making the tuition costs and public-private partnerships to rise (OECD 2004). Buchbinder (1993) warns about the financial reality and the surroundings in which universities operate, and shows a trend of survival by adjusting to the political economy characterized by global competition, contract business and efficiency.

[11] For further details see: Göransson et al. 2009.

ing more in serving the society though various sponsored research, universities are faced with new challenges in norms and values of the academic life.

2.3.2   Third Mission—University Civic Links with the Community

Universities have a wide range of roles, responsibilities, and activities and cut across different economic, political and social networks. There is no doubt that they make contributions to the government as well as the private sector. Nevertheless, contributions to civil society must not slip out. Universities not only add value to the economic performance but also help to improve the quality of life in communities and the effectiveness of public services. Any approach to university 'third stream' activities, which focus purely on university linkages with industry and commercial activities, argue Molas-Gallart et al. (2002) "is likely to miss large and important parts of the picture".

The social segment of the third mission, in literature usually called 'civic mission', articulates various university activities and academic civic engagement in local communities. There is a group of authors who claim that civic mission is actually the one and only university third mission (Harkavy 2006; Ostrander 2004; Checkoway 2001). Advocates of such a model emphasize that educating students to be constructive citizens in the democratic society, is essential for the development and preservation of democracy (Checkoway 2001; Harkavy 2006) and that universities should aim to improve the living conditions in local communities and develop democracy and civil society (Ostrander 2004).

Requests are being made to bring university teachers and practitioners into closer relationships, expecting academic knowledge to directly improve living conditions in local communities and affect democracy and civil society development (Ostrander 2004). Students should acquire knowledge, develop skills and opinions through active participation/civic engagement, which in turn develops their sense of social responsibility, as well their engagement on community-related issues. Pursuing that, academics turn to the academic service-learning model, as well as to variations of internships (e.g. social internship) or work placements (for example, in public and non-profit/civic work surroundings).

Most authors, academics and practitioners, agree that the purpose of student civic engagement is to educate them to be responsible and active citizens in the future, and engaged in all segments of everyday life. Professional knowledge and skills they acquire during their education is very important, for them personally, but also for the development of society, although by far not sufficient enough. They are (at least they should be) additionally expected to have certain values, motivation and commitment to the community and the enhancement of living conditions (Jacoby 2009). The authors agree that it is the purpose of university civic mission to enable the development of this ideal.

While ties with the industry are mostly worthwhile, at least indirectly through research funding, Krücken et al. (2009) note that links to civil society remain largely unrewarded in academia. As links to civil society cannot be mapped by standard indicators, which dominate in measuring scientific excellence (such as peer-reviewed publications), there is a trend of avoiding 'distracting' activities (especially among the young scientists), such as this segment of the third mission appears to be (Krücken et al. 2009; Göransson et al. 2009; Ledić 2007). Macfarlane's (2005) findings suggested that third mission, or 'service' as he refers to it, is not regarded as something that gives professional credit—"There was a keen awareness among academics that service work suffers both a lack of status, and further, won't get you tenure, promotion or a pay rise" (Macfarlane 2005, p. 173).

2.3.3 Third Mission—Two Sides of the Same Coin

While there is a certain tension between the social and the economic (commercial) role of the university third mission, they should be treated as two sides of the same coin, since both are based on the need to communicate and cooperate more extensively with stakeholders beyond the academic community (Fiskovica et al. 2009). Although it is obvious that both the social as well as the commercial (technological) third mission are highly relevant, there is little consensus on how to perform third mission activities. Göransson et al. (2009) distinguish, for example, transfer and extension activities. The economic one relates to knowledge and research activities commercialised for the technology/industry sector. The second relates to various activities of social character.

For Krücken et al. (2009), the third mission activities refer to university direct contribution to economic development through the transfer of technology to industry, while they label heterogeneous ties to civic society as extension activities. Having in mind that university third mission in general covers activities focused on non-academic community, for Montesinos et al. (2008) it has at least three dimensions: (I) a non-profit—social approach, (II) an entrepreneurial focus and (III) an innovative approximation. While researching the issues of economic and social roles of universities in Latvia, Fiskovica et al. (2009) found that the third mission is treated differently by the exact and social scientists (with the distinction being made along the lines of the disciplinary particularities of "hard" and "soft" sciences featuring a certain bias towards either commercial or social aspects). The exact scientists refer to innovation, knowledge and technology transfer, commercialisation of research results and orientation towards the needs of the business sector. The social scientists are more in tune with the education of the nation, general culture function, influence on society and people's minds and a vision of the university to contribute to the enlightenment of the public and raising its educational and cultural level (Fiskovica et al. 2009).

It is important to notice that economic and social segments of the third mission activities do not always enjoy the same intensity. This intensity largely depends on the government and university strategy as well as clear policy framework. That is the reason the universities which aspire to develop stronger integration (and institutionalisation) of the third mission are faced with big challenges. In fact, the possibility of university teachers to adjust their roles to elements of third mission activities has serious conceptual and practical problems considering that this task is constant-ly and unsuccessfully competing with the (primary) role of university professors as teachers and researchers (Bloomgarden and O'Meara 2007). Many projects have therefore been devoted to the identification, delineation and management of activi-ties that are a part of the third mission (Molas-Gallart et al. 2002). A recent review project (Schoen et al. 2006) has proposed to gather third mission activities around eight dimensions—four economic and four social. In their report, Molas-Gallart et al. (2002) emphasize university's contribution to social and economic develop-ment through a wide range of activities that fall outside the direct commercialisa-tion of university's research results. That is the reason the holistic approach to the assessment of third stream activities, aiming at considering the total contribution of universities to society rather than relying only on narrow indicators of commerciali-sation, is strongly advocated (Karlsson et al. 2007; Ledić 2007; Bloomgarden and O'Meara 2007; Greenbank 2006; Molas-Gallart et al. 2002; Boyer 1990).

2.3.4 Third Mission Activities—In Addition to or in Symbiosis with Teaching and Research?

The concept of the third mission, claim Göransson et al. (2009), encapsulates many of the raising demands put before the university and encompasses all university activities not covered by the first two missions—teaching and research. Having in mind the dominant thought that teaching and research are the only two roles the academic staff performs (Karlsson et al. 2007), it comes as no surprise that there is a great confusion among academics about what the third mission actually is.

According to Macfarlane (2005), there are five different interpretations among academics of what third mission activities are: (I) administration—taken negatively in general, with third mission activities seen as growing burdens on academics, (II) customer service for students and business organisations, (III) collegial virtue—as a moral obligation in supporting colleagues, (IV) civic duty as doing voluntary work or outreach for the benefit of the local community, not necessarily connected with scholarly expertise, and (V) integrated learning which connects academic study work and community based projects and internships, carried out by students and not the academic staff (e.g. academic service learning, social internships).

The placement of third mission activities in addition to teaching and research dominates the debate. There is a great number of authors contributing to this set of interpretations claiming that service to the society is practice-oriented engagement and cooperation with the surrounding community where all the activities must be performed outside the traditional box of teaching and research (Ngoc Ca 2009; Gre-gersen et al. 2009; Karlsson et al. 2007; Thorn and Soo 2009).

On the other side, there are authors talking about the importance of integrat-ing this "holy trinity"[12] (Ledić 2007; Harkavy 2006; Ostrander 2004; Checkoway 2001). Laredo (2007), for example, questions the very notion of third mission

---

[12] For further details see: Göransson et al. 2009.

claiming that there exists a certain irony in discussing the need for universities to connect to the community, and in particular to the economy. The central role of universities, he continues, has long been to train students and to prepare them for professional activities they will later deploy. There is thus no logic in connecting entrepreneurial university with third mission. Instead of that, the connection should be made with the ability of scholars to develop new original teaching curricula and research projects, and to integrate them.

Bortagaray (2009) sees the role of the third mission in narrowing and blurring the boundaries between the inside and outside, between teaching and research. Greenbank (2006) argues for the integration of teaching, research and service as interconnected scholarly activities. A very interesting point has been raised by Karlsson (2007) who does not perceive service as a contribution solely executed in one way—from university to the community (as has been primarily advocated in the debate). What he wants to highlight is an urgent need for a holistic view of this scholarship to be developed, where the integration of collaboration, teaching and research would be seen as interdependent, rather than in hierarchy to one another.

In their final report to the Russell Group of Universities, Molas-Gallart et al. (2002) raised one additional issue, claiming that cooperation with non-academic community is what actually makes a set of third mission activities. They consider all three as core activities (teaching, research and communication of results) as well as possible third stream activities, if they are developed in cooperation with the non-academic actors. Jongbloed et al. (2008) talk about the mission overlap as being the basic problem of the third mission analysis. They claim that the third mission is not so much a mission of its own but rather a reflection of the unique stakeholders that fall outside of the traditional purview. In addition, they emphasize the difficulty of separating third mission activities from traditional teaching and research claiming they cannot be separated.

3   University Civic Mission

3.1   Background

Even though always up to date, it seems that the question of the basic purpose of the university has lately become the focal point of academic and professional debates all around the world. Some authors claim that universities have closed themselves too much, separated themselves from the community in which they function and from the problems that surround them. Their criticism goes so far to warn universities about their need to think about their common purpose and deal with main contemporary issues in order not to become socially irrelevant (Boyer 1990). Rapidly growing number of titles which reflect sharp criticism and public concern regarding university responsibility speak of a time that has come, a time of serious negotiations about the role universities have in society. They need to embrace their social responsibility and commitments that their total work make relevant in the attempt to resolve current social problems (Edwards and Marullo 1999; Marullo et al. 2003; Escrigas 2008). They appeal to universities to take their intense preoccupation with the market, financial (self-)sustainability, enrolment quotas, rash publications, benchmarking policies, test and ranking and change it with the commitment to resolve real problems of the community, encourage education of socially sensitive and responsible students as well as to contribute to the development of civil society and democracy. Escrigas and Lobera (2009) are also very explicit in their vision and mission for the role of higher education in the future—"one needs to be clearly reoriented towards society's challenges, beyond the paradigm of the 'ivory-tower' or the market-oriented university, to reinvent an innovative and socially committed response that anticipates and adds value to the process of social transformation" (p. 7).

Along with the concern for the intensive market-orientation, critics draw attention to the issue of democratic deficit most of the countries, including the EU, are faced with. Educating students to be responsible and active citizens (Checkoway 2001; Harkavy 2006) and active citizenship is the ideal contemporary society should aspire to (McLaughlin 1995; Griffith 1998; Wilkins 1999; Heater 1999; Faulks 2000). Escrigas (2008) reminds that universities educate citizens of the future, who will build the social system for the future generations to inherit. Having in mind that the current education system is based on training competitive human resources, according to Escrigas and Lobera (2009) "it is appropriate to raise its evolution towards a system that could educate global citizens to be builders of inclusive, just and fair social systems, with ethical criteria, who can understand the reality from a holistic perspective and be prepared to act under trust and collaboration patterns" (p. 11). Universities therefore have to intensify their contribution to social development by educating active citizens who will be knowledgeable about the human and social condition, with ethical awareness and civic commitment (Ehrlich 2000; Escrigas 2008; Taylor 2008; Escrigas and Lobera 2009).

3.2 The Issue of University Civic Mission

Analysts and critics of higher education, as well as academics, have been giving more attention to the idea of university civic mission since the early 1980s. The debate about defining roles and relationships between the university and the community is as old as the first European (medieval) universities. However, the vast literature we have today still does not provide a clear, accurate and concise definition of the university civic mission. It is in fact an elusive concept, a concept that is often used in literature and practice, which is ambiguous and, as such, subject to subjective interpretation, which is why it is often equated with everything that has the prefix civil: civil society, civil sector, civic engagement. It is not uncommon to find this term used as a synonym for political and social component of the university, often in comparison with the moral and ethical values. In fact, the literature (mainly from the U.S. academic community) often states that encouraging civic engagement positively affects the moral development of students. Even though this is very important for youth development, Ostrander (2004) warns that encouraging greater integration of the university civic mission in the core academic activities does not rest on the important role of the university, which is to discover and create new knowledge and teaching students. She claims that defining university civic engagement only in the area of ethical, moral development of students means condemning civic mission to a marginalised position. For the university civic engagement activities to be fully integrated, institutionalised and sustainable, they must be built on stable intellectual arguments, which will, within the university civic mission, define a strong educational role in the development of a new generation of moral, socially responsible and active citizens.

Ostrander (2004) believes that in the constellation of relations between universities and communities, university civic mission should be observed through: (I) teaching and learning, (II) curriculum transformation, (III) research priorities defined in cooperation with the community and based on current social problems and (IV) the production of new knowledge. Teaching students and their learning, besides the basic concepts of science, concerns the segment of student social responsibility and their engagement in the community. Curriculum transformation should follow this requirement and provide content and educational opportunities for learning and acquiring competence for active citizenship.

Harkavy (2006) points out that the definition of university civic mission is crucial, and educating students to be democratic, creative, caring, and constructive citizens of a democratic society is necessary for developing and preserving democracy. According to Ledić (2007), university civic mission presents efforts of the academic community conducted through research, teaching and active involvement of its members in the community, and directed towards improving the quality of life in the community and educating active and socially responsible citizens. For Checkoway (2001), the university civic mission includes, apart from preparing students for active participation in democracy and developing their knowledge for the improvement of community and society in general, the reflection and action on public dimensions of education. Ostrander (2004) sees the civic mission in basing academic knowledge on real-life conditions, connecting knowledge with practice, connecting the academic community with practice, improving the living conditions of local communities and developing democracy and civil society. He concludes by saying there is no correct definition of the civic mission. It depends on many factors: university tradition, specific problems in the community where the university operates and rapid institutional changes, to name just a few.

3.3   Civic Mission Integration—Challenges for the Academic Profession

The relationship between the traditional roles of university professors as researchers and teachers has become more complex in the past decade. This is due to a strong wave of described university third mission initiatives. Studies mainly indicate that university professors, regardless of affiliation to scientific discipline, recognize the need for integration and synergy of their roles (Colbeck 1998, 2002; Neumann 1992, 1996). Achieving the balance of these roles frequently becomes the subject of research (Bess 1998; Menges 1999; Bloomgarden and O'Meara 2007; Kogan and Teichler 2007; Locke and Teichler 2007). The dynamic and changing demands university teachers are trying to respond to affect the distribution of their activities and basic tasks, at the same time demanding their increasing engagement (Rice et al. 2000; Kogan and Teichler 2007). University professors often carry out activities in addition to their regular workload, and perform roles, which, it seems, are neither formally employed nor responsible for, but which may also affect (important) dimensions of their (academic and professional) achievements (Bloomgarden and O'Meara 2007).

Several authors suggest that the institutionalisation of university civic mission and the contribution to the development of sustainable partnerships with the community requires a strong and long-term research as well as teaching connected with the community (Bringle and Hatcher 2000; Furco 2001; Lombardi 2001). Encouraging university professors to develop these activities requires the development of new and customized educational programmes with the emphasis on appropriate work methods as well as thinking about research projects based on community's needs. Today, all the more relevant encouragement of the strengthening of university social responsibility and integrating civic engagement of university professors and students within the basic tasks of teaching and research is an additional challenge universities must respond to (Ward 2003). When responding to them, the studies that point to serious compatibility of multidimensional roles and increased workload should certainly be taken into account (Bess 1998; Milem et al. 2000; Rice et al. 2000; Kogan and Teichler 2007; Locke and Teichler 2007).

The activities of the academic community in the segment of community work and encouraging civic engagement represent, among other things, a great organisational challenge (Holland 1999). Preparing, implementing and evaluating such teaching and research activities that meet multiple community as well as university needs, require specific knowledge and skills and, above all, the commitment of university professors. The expectations are more than purely broadening teaching and research. Academics who wish to integrate community service into their regular teaching and research activities are in fact expected to establish and manage partner (research) projects in the community. It is their responsibility to design and prepare unconventional teaching programmes, assignments and fieldwork activities that stimulate learning related to discipline, but also address problems in the community. Proper evaluation and documentation of their own work, and in particular the work of students and their progress, comes along as well. Parallel, academics should be thinking about rights, obligations and responsibilities of everyone involved in such a way that the benefits from the activities be equally distributed. This form of work requires fulfilling both the academic goals (of specific disciplines and university excellence criteria in all areas) and community goals in a way that could (or does not always have to) match the professional skills, personal priorities nor the priorities of scientific disciplines, departments and the parent institution. This way often promotes interdisciplinary work.

The complexity of this way of understanding the role of university professors and acting in accordance with the described principles should be adequately evaluated as well. Boyer (1990) stresses that never before in history did the universities had to work on strengthening their connection with the community as they do today. He also emphasizes that the prerequisites for the advancement of university teachers, which he considers exceptionally inadequate, should be one of the mechanisms that would encourage such a shift. In fact, if through the advancement system and set prerequisites for tenure election only the traditional academic and scientific results are prioritized, compared to the usual results of activities of community service (reports, evaluations, presentations, situation analysis, public policy analysis, new curricula, plans for personal and professional development, project proposals, etc.), it is not realistic to believe that the university professors will be involved in such activities and generally promote university civic engagement (Boyer 1990; Braxton et al. 2002; Lynton 1995; O'Meara 2002). The authors therefore warn about the autonomy of university professors and emphasize that the decision about civic engagement depends mostly on their perception of the importance given to this activity in terms of their own academic advancement (Bloomgarden and O'Meara 2007; Ledić 2007).

4 New Demands Put Before the Academic Profession: Education for Sustainable Development

4.1 Short Overview on History and Approaches

Even though sustainable development as a paradigm causes controversy among scientists, and we can talk about several dozen different definitions of sustainable development, it is evident that our society needs adjustments for the world to develop in a sustainable direction. We see an increase in troublesome and warning scientific analyses from all over the world, which do not leave a lot of room for doubt when it comes to the necessity of fundamental changes in our society today (Cifrić 1997; IPCC 2007; Stephens et al. 2008). We can say that sustainable development in general represents a modified and responsible relationship towards the environment and society because it respects the needs of generations to come. For a serious understanding of the importance of the education for sustainable development we need a favourable social climate, and the knowledge of education for sustainable development deficit presupposes changes in the attitude not only in education policies but the whole society (Cifrić 2005). However, the educational system still does not accept ecological and social challenges, what can cause educational incompetence in the long run, as well as more serious consequences for future generations (Cifrić 2005). Therefore, pressures on higher education derive from part of the society concerned with sustainable development, because universities and academics have a special responsibility for future development. The last two decades in particular show a continuity in publishing several documents and declarations on the national, European and international level, last being the Bonn Declaration (2009)—extremely relevant for universities all over the world (Lindberg 2010). It is necessary to encourage and implement education for sustainable development in the core academic activities and universities in general. Universities are also seen as agents in promoting these principles within society, and as institutions in need of a change themselves. In any case, universities and academics should and will in the future inevitably play crucial roles in promoting sustainability as well as the third mission activities through their core activities—teaching and research.

Education for sustainable development[13] was defined in 1992 on a UN conference in Rio de Janeiro when the Program for Action for Sustainable Development and the Agenda 21 were adopted. Agenda 21 involves three priorities: expansion of basic education to all children; reorientation of current education to embrace the concept of sustainable development and raising public awareness (Geiser 2006, p. 31). Since 1992, all UN conferences agreed that education was the driving force to achieve the necessary changes. The UNESCO report "Education for sustainability—from Rio to Johannesburg" gives an overview of lessons learned about the education for sustainable development (ESD) over a decade (1992–2002; UNESCO 2002).[14] The United Nations Decade of Education for Sustainable Development started in 2005, for which UNESCO is the lead agency. In the same year, the Economic Commission for Europe adopted the UNECE "Strategy for Education for Sustainable Development" in Vilnius, on a high-level meeting of Environment and Education Ministries.[15] The Article 19 of the Strategy states that "ESD is a lifelong

---

[13] A recommendation was given to expand the concept of "environment" ("environmental protection") to the concept of "sustainable development".

[14] The key lessons that have been learned about education for sustainable development: "Education for sustainable development is an emerging but dynamic concept that encompasses a new vision of education that seeks to empower people of all ages to assume responsibility for creating a sustainable future. Basic education provides the foundation for all future education and is a contribution to sustainable development in its own right. There is a need to refocus many existing education policies, programmes and practices so that they build the concepts, skills, motivation and commitment needed for sustainable development. Education is the key to rural transformation and is essential to ensuring the economic, cultural and ecological vitality of rural areas and communities. Lifelong learning, including adult and community education, appropriate technical and vocational education, higher education and teacher education are all vital ingredients of capacity building for a sustainable future" (UNESCO 2002, pp. 5–6).

[15] From UNECE Strategy for Education for Sustainable Development: "Education, in addition to being a human right, is a prerequisite for achieving sustainable development and an essential tool for good governance, informed decision-making and the promotion of democracy. Therefore, education for sustainable development can help translate our vision into reality. Education for sustainable development develops and strengthens the capacity of individuals, groups, communities, organizations and countries to make judgments and choices in favor of sustainable development. It can promote a shift in people's mindsets and in so doing enable them to make our world safer, healthier and more prosperous, thereby improving the quality of life. Education for sustainable development can provide critical reflection and greater awareness and empowerment so that new visions and concepts can be explored and new methods and tools developed" (UNECE Strategy for Education for Sustainable Development 2005, p. 1).

process from early childhood to higher and adult education and goes beyond formal education. Since learning takes place as we take on different roles in our lives, ESD has to be considered as a 'life-wide' process. It should permeate learning programmes at all levels, including vocational education, training for educators, and continuing education for professionals and decision makers" (UNECE Strategy 2005, p. 4).

Education for sustainable development becomes a priority, which requires curriculum changes, not only the transfer of knowledge. The increase of interest for this topic is visible from the analysis of the ERIC database where the results of a bibliometric study showed a total of 1,497 articles (in English) dealing with the education for sustainable development from more than a thousand authors from 304 institutions in 23 countries from 1990 to 2005 (Wright and Pullen 2007).

4.2   The Debate About the Term Education for Sustainable Development

There is much debate about the term sustainable development and education for sustainable development in the existing literature. Without the need to make a final and complete list it is possible to point out four terminological versions: (I) education for sustainable development, (II) education for a transition to sustainability, (III) sustainable education, and (IV) higher education for sustainability.

Education for sustainable development seeks to: increase environmental literacy; integrate social, economic and environmental values; focus globally and internationally; raise awareness of environmental limits and threats; build skills and capacity for analyses and intervention (Geiser 2006, p. 32). However, Geiser argues that ESD is mostly implemented in programmes that have remained campus-based and focused on college-enrolled students, so ESD has to move forward to education for a transition to sustainability that has to be integrated into the daily needs of professionals and activists. Education for a transition to sustainability is focused on the learner within the context of current and ongoing work and struggle. In other words, universities have the obligation to, by reaching out to currently active practitioners and activists, make available the resources of higher education institutions to those who need skills and knowledge because their daily struggles starkly reveal their need to know (Geiser 2006, p. 40).

The aims of sustainable education are directed towards the following (Salite 2002 in Slahova et al. 2007, p. 143): an ecological human being; retention of identity, culture and the environment; cognition of the world; awareness of sustainable development; education of a responsible and co-evolutionary character; and harmony in relationships. Higher education for sustainability, on the other hand, is not without strong foundations, as it draws on various disciplines including environmental education, policy analysis, higher education, management theory, sociology, ecology, psychology and philosophy (Wright 2007). Higher education for sustainability (HES) research[16] differs from these traditional fields in two major ways.

HES research focuses on transcending disciplinary boundaries and integrating research from many sources and disciplines, interprets, adds context to, and explains research results from a new interdisciplinary perspective. Furthermore, HES research is applied and action-oriented, service related, combining theory and practice, and including both applied research and outreach (Wright 2007, p. 35). The results of a Delphi exercise used at the Halifax Consultation in which 35 experts representing 17 countries gathered to develop research priorities for the emerging field of higher education for sustainability showed 19 research theme areas, and at the end ten themes were thought to be the most important to further HES research:

- impacts of teaching and learning methods,
- university and community linkages,
- mainstreaming sustainability,
- institutional culture and organisational/governance structures,
- evaluating educational approaches,
- case study analysis,
- legitimizing HES research and practice, leadership and management,
- transformative learning,
- philosophy and epistemology in HES,
- disciplinarity, transdisciplinarity and interdisciplinarity (Wright 2007).

Finally, all the approaches mentioned demand and expect from the academics to change and expand their own approach to teaching and research to adequately respond to the social demands.

4.3 The Role of Higher Education in the Education for Sustainable Development

Education for sustainable development is a great challenge for universities and the academic profession, both with a great responsibility for the society and urged to answer these particular social needs. The role of higher education institutions in encouraging education for sustainable development is evidently crucial, because it educates people who will soon make new development decisions, and people who will soon educate younger generations. Sustainability is relevant for

---

[16] The published HES literature has focused on sustainability education; curriculum development; physical operations; HES policy analysis; assessment methodologies for HES initiatives; the development of theory; developing key competencies and learning outcomes (see Wright 2007 who provides extensive literature on these topics).

universities in many regards and at many levels: both at the micro-level and at the macro-level. At the micro-level, universities as sociotopic constructions with political implications and the macro-level looks at the higher education system as a political construct with sociotopic implications (Kehm and Pasternack 2000, p. 207, in Adomssent et al. 2008). Higher education is important to sustainable development for three main reasons: "one is the immediate interface with employers which allows students go where the sustainability issues faced by society are met on a daily basis (...) The second reason is the unique research remit of higher education institutions (...) The third reason is based on the premise that higher education institutions have direct links with business and the community where research could be disseminated, connections made, and social change brought about—all of which will be crucial to help society transform itself" (UNESCO 2009, p. 91).

Main directions of the discourse on sustainable university can be summed around two basic models: universities as institutions that need to address sustainable development issues and involve institutional change (characteristics of the "sustainable university") or universities as agents of change ("whole-of-university" approach to sustainability).

The first approach can be found in the work of Ferrer-Balas et al. (2008) and Svanstrom et al. (2008). For example, Ferrer-Balas et al. (2008), strongly support the approach in which universities need to address sustainable development issues in a way that institutional change is needed. Such "sustainable university" has the following characteristics: the emphasis is put on transformative education; a strong emphasis on effectively conducting interdisciplinary and transdisciplinary research and science; societal problem-solving orientation in education and research through an interaction of multiple stakeholders to be pertinent to societal goals; networks that can tap into varied expertise around the campus to efficiently and meaningfully share resources; leadership and vision that promotes needed change accompanied by proper assignment of responsibility and rewards, who are committed to a long-term transformation of the university and are willing to be responsive to society's changing needs (p. 296).

Furthermore, in parallel with the making of the Agenda 21, conferences on the sustainability issue were taking place. Also, different declarations that many universities have signed[17] have been developed. Those include: Talloires in 1990, Halifax

---

[17] Svanstrom et al. (2008) discussed the commonalities that can be found in learning outcomes for education for sustainable development in the context of the Tbilisi and Barcelona declarations. The commonalities include systemic or holistic thinking, the integration of different perspectives, skills such as critical thinking, change agent abilities and communication, and finally different attitudes and values.

in 1991, Copernicus[18] in 1994[19], Lüneburg in 2001, Graz in 2005[20], and Bonn in 2007. All these declarations have two things in common—universities need to address sustainable development issues and that will have to include institutional change. Scott and Gough (2007) relate such a change particularly to:

- how the university presents its role through vision and mission statements;
- how its estates and resource are managed;
- what (and how) it teaches its students;
- how that teaching is managed.

The second approach can be found in the work of McMillin and Dyball (2009) and Stephens et al. (2008). McMillin and Dyball (2009) argue that universities can optimize their role as agents of change with regard to sustainability by adopting a "whole-of-university" approach to sustainability. This approach explicitly links research, educational, operational and outreach activities and engages students in each. The benefits arising from pursuing a whole-systems approach to institutional sustainability are threefold: pedagogical, operational/reputational and capacity building. This can result in many positive benefits: including raising the profile of university's sustainability initiatives; providing solutions to sustainability problems; building trust among students, managers and academics; and providing meaningful learning experiences for students (McMillin and Dyball 2009). Escrigas (2008) also believes that it is necessary to articulate a sustainable model of university development, but not one which will nurture only the economical, or often misunderstood, ecological segment of social development, but a model which will need to equally take in consideration the human, social, cultural and economic aspects of democratic communities. Similar to the on-going debate, Gough and Scott's (2007, p. 1) main concern is a "proper place of sustainable development in what a university

---

[18] The Copernicus Declaration contains an action plan, which sums up the role of universities in ten principles: (1) institutional commitment; (2) environmental ethics; (3) education of university employees; (4) programmes in environmental education; (5) interdisciplinarity; (6) dissemination of knowledge; (7) networking; (8) partnerships; (9) continuing education programmes; (10) technology transfer.

[19] Very interesting analysis on the implementation of the Copernicus declaration in Aalborg University was written by Christensen et al. (2009), which stated that when seen from a present perspective, it seems that this policy was never really implemented. The reason for this is probably twofold: (1) the university never made sure that the proper policies and management system were in place to secure the involvement of all interested parties and communication only took place internally in the committee. (2) Environmentalism has been on the decline in Danish society for some years adding to the fact that it has been difficult to keep up the spirits in such activities (p. 16).

[20] This Declaration calls for the universities to allocate a fundamental status to sustainable development within their strategies and activities, promoting creative development and implementing comprehensive and integrated sustainable actions in relation to learning and teaching, research, and both internal and external societal responsibility. Furthermore, universities should cooperate with other higher education institutions and communities (Glavič and Lukman 2007, p. 104).

does, rather than the role of universities in implementing (any particular conception of) sustainable development". They propose a range of steps that universities can initiate and implement:

1. innovative, context-sensitive pedagogies;
2. cross-disciplinary research linked, when appropriate, to teaching and learning;
3. purposive design and management of network;
4. management of institutions that tolerates and encourages divergent approaches;
5. connective middle management "sustainable" forms of assessment (p. 169).

4.4 Drivers and Barriers in the Transformation of University and Academic Work

Ferrer-Balas et al. (2008), in their paper "An international comparative analysis of sustainability transformation across seven universities", identified, by comparing the strategies of seven universities world-wide, the key aspects of the transformation of universities towards sustainability as well as the drivers and barriers in the transformation. We can find different identifications of key characteristics in the literature (cited by Ferrer-Balas et al. 2008), as there are many barriers to transforming institutions into sustainable universities.

Potential barriers (internal and external) are recognized in the following:

- freedom of individual faculty members;
- incentive structure (salaries, promotions, and granting of tenure) that does not recognize faculty contributions to sustainable development;
- lack of desire to change, and
- pressure from society (Ferrer-Balas et al. 2008, p. 297).

On the other side, certain drivers (internal and external) are likely to emerge:

- internal: visionary leadership; sustainability champions, often seen as "lone wolves" or "innovators" (Lozano 2006) at their universities, can be important agents of change; connectors refer to existing networks of people such as inter-disciplinary research groups that reach across the university to include a critical mass of campus actors; size (small universities, less than 10,000), the existence of a coordination unit or project for the sustainability transformation.
- External: pressure from peer institutions or top-tier universities can serve as examples to promote change; sources of funding and employment availability (Ferrer-Balas et al. 2008).

The UK Higher Education Academy also lists barriers and solutions for a successful implementation of ESD in many disciplines in higher education (HEA 2005, p. 5). An overcrowded curriculum can be overcome with creation of space through a rigorous review of existing curricula. The perceived irrelevance by academic staff can be altered with development of credible teaching materials, which are fully contextualised and relevant to each subject area.

Some approaches and strategies to overcome the typical barriers to change are also presented by Lozano (2006) and can be grouped into three levels: (1) resistance to the idea of SD itself; (2) resistance to involving deeper issues; and (3) deeply embedded resistance to change (in Lozano-Garcia et al. 2008). Therefore, efforts of higher education institutions to respond to challenges of sustainability must begin "with an honest institutional assessment of the obstacles they face": what is a necessary first step toward the change and a way of assessing the limits of institution to respond to the challenge of sustainability? (Viederman 2006, pp. 20–21). For university to change its profile of teaching and research in accordance with sustainable development, two prerequisites must be met. The teacher must be willing to modify his/her area of expertise in relation to ecological issues and principles of sustainable development what represents a change in the way they design, teach and assess and it is necessary to establish new jobs, define job descriptions differently and create incentives for research and education in the area (Kuckartz 1997, p. 18; de la Harpe and Thomas 2009). Recent research of de la Harpe and Thomas (2009) on academic attitudes showed conditions needed to be met to influence curriculum change at universities:

- Identify a core group of staff willing to work together to lead and oversee the curriculum development and change initiative and to convince others that change is necessary;
- work with others to ensure that a vision was agreed collaboratively or that a project or programme brief was developed to guide the intended change;
- sufficient resources available;
- implementation strategy;
- staff's professional development;
- administrative systems and structures;
- a monitoring programme communicated often and rewarded along the way (p. 83).

Many universities are trying to implement curriculum change. However, up to date reports suggest that broad-ranging curriculum change has not been yet achieved by any university as there are many barriers to transforming institutions into sustainable universities (cf. de la Harpe and Thomas 2009, p. 76). A possible reason why universities do not encourage or implement ESD can be found in the following: the culture of universities makes it difficult for fundamentally different views to prevail or even be fully addressed (Viederman 2006). Since ESD implies interdisciplinary and/or transdisciplinary approaches, many academics find it hard to see "outside the box" and feel more comfortable to stay within the boundaries of their own discipline. In education this means that institutions of higher learning must move beyond the narrowly defined, discipline-specific model that has characterized the modern university over the last 150 years (Koester et al. 2006, p. 41).

5   Key Challenges and Research Questions

As universities are called upon to become more relevant to the society, more in tune with contemporary problems, socially relevant and accountable to the public, they face an increased scale of expectations from a various range of stakeholders. Those stakeholders place new demands upon universities, creating a pressure on higher education institutions and academics to contribute more to the economic development and to have a stronger impact on society. In an attempt to answer those pressures, universities and academics are broadening their settings and engaging in various (off-campus) activities. Those activities have brought tremendous challenges for the traditional roles of the academics, structures of their activities, and values. Contemporary universities face a great challenge of finding a balance between a wide range of different expectations, roles and responsibilities.

We have analysed teaching and research extension phenomena within the discourse on the university third mission and have tried to indicate its complexity by presenting the concepts developed so far, focusing on two particularities—university civic mission and education for sustainable development. Between the concept of being the mission of its own and the concept of being a reflection of various stakeholders' expectations set before the traditional teaching and research, third mission phenomena face many conceptual challenges.

Bearing in mind the importance of establishing deeper interactions with society, implementing (third mission) activities is found crucial for contemporary universities (Göransson et al. 2009). However, the ideas and concepts about the third mission that vary considerably, warnings about the mission overlap (Laredo 2007; Jongbloed et al. 2008), the confusion among the academics about what the third mission actually stands for (Macfarlane 2005), warnings about the additional work that has been put on the academics (Cummings 2006), and last, but not least, the absolute absence of a rewarding structure for engaging in such activities (Boyer 1990; Bloomgarden and O'Meara 2007; Ledić 2007), all call for re-framing of existing (presented) concepts as well as for the development of new ones for future study on broadening teaching and research.

In order to further explore the concepts presented here and to empirically investigate the tendencies suggested in this paper, research questions are proposed for tackling some of the emerging issues of the third mission (civic mission in particular and education for sustainable development).

1. How do academics relate to the current (internal and external) pressures associated with extending of the traditional teaching and research? Do they accept the new expectations or resist them by thinking it questions the core academic activities?
2. Do academics prioritize different stakeholders in their regions, and their expectations? If so, which stakeholders do they personally prioritize—economic or public? How do they perceive and differentiate the demands from private/economic and public/civic stakeholders?

3. Do academics place the extending activities in addition to teaching and research (third mission) or advocate the integration and readjustment of the traditional teaching and research?
4. Does the current rewarding structure recognize extended (third mission/service) activities?
5. What are the functional and structural stimuli that higher education institutions may create to promote university civic engagement, integration of the concept of civic mission and the education for sustainable development?

By identifying these research questions we hope to contribute to the future systematic research on the university linkages and deeper interaction with the community and society at large. We are aware of the need for more research in this important area, especially having in mind strong criticism and continuous rising of expectations put before universities.

References

Abramson, H. N., Encarnação, J., Reid, P. P., & Schmoch, U. (1997). *Technology transfer systems in the United States and Germany – lessons and perspectives*. Washington, D.C.: National academy press.

Adomssent, M., Godemann, J., & Michelsen, G. (2008). *Sustainable university—empirical evidence and strategic recommendations for holistic transformation approaches to sustainability in higher education institutions*. Proceedings of the 4th International Barcelona Conference on Higher Education (Vol. 7). Higher education for sustainable development. Barcelona: GUNI. http://www.guni-rmies.net.

Altbach, P. (2008). *The complex roles of universities in the period of globalization. In Global University Network for Innovation (GUNI), Higher Education in the World 3. Higher education: new challenges and emerging roles for human and social development* (pp. 5–14). Basingstoke: Palgrave Macmillan.

Association of Commonwealth Universities (ACU). (2001). *Engagement as a core value for the university: a consultation document*. London: ACU.

Bender, T. (1997). *Intellect and public life: essays on the social history of academic intellectuals in the United States*. Baltimore: Johns Hopkins University Press.

Bess, J. L. (1998). Teaching well: do you have to be schizophrenic? *The Review of Higher Education, 22*(1), 1–15.

Bloomgarden, A. H., & O'Meara, K. A. (2007). Faculty role integration and community engagement: harmony or cacophony? *Michigan Journal of Community Service Learning, 13*(2), 5–18.

Bortagaray, I. (2009). Bridging university and society in Uruguay: perceptions and expectations. *Science and Public Policy, 36*(2), 115–119.

Boyer, E. L. (1990). *Scholarship reconsider: priorities of the professoriate*. Stanford: The Carnegie Foundation for the Advancement of Teaching.

Braxton, J., Luckey, W., & Helland, P. (Eds.). (2002). *Institutionalizing a broader view of scholarship through Boyer's four domains* (ASHE-ERIC Higher Education Report, 29(2)). San Francisco: Jossey-Bass.

Brennan, J. (2006). *The changing academic profession: the driving forces.Reports of changing academic profession project workshop on quality, relevance, and governance in the changing academia: international perspectives* (pp. 37–44). Hiroshima: Research Institute for Higher Education, Hiroshima University.

Brennan, J., King, R., & Lebeau, Y. (2004). *The role of universities in the transformation of societies*. London: Association of Commonwealth Universities and Centre for Higher Education Research and Information.

Bringle, R. G., & Hatcher, J. A. (2000). Institutionalization of service learning in higher education. *The Journal of Higher Education, 71*(3), 273–290.

Buchbinder, H. (1993). The market oriented university and the changing role of knowledge. *Higher Education, 26*(3), 331–347.

Calhoun, C. (2006). The university and the public good. *Thesis Eleven, 84*(1), 7–43.

Chatterton, P., & Goddard, J. B. (2003). The response of higher education institutions to regional needs. In R. Rutten, F. Boekama, & E. Kuijpers (Eds.), *Economic geography of higher education: knowledge, infrastructure and learning regions* (pp. 19–41). London: Routledge.

Checkoway, B. (2000). Public service: our new mission. *Academe, 86*(4), 24–28.

Checkoway, B. (2001). Renewing the civic mission of the American Research University. *The Journal of Higher Education, 72*(2), 125–147.

Christensen, P., Thrane, M., Herreborg Jørgensen, T., & Lehmann, M. (2009). Sustainable development. Assessing the gap between preaching and practice at Aalborg University. *The International Journal of Sustainability in Higher Education, 10*(1), 4–20.

Cifrić, I. (1997). *Napredak i Opstanak*. Zagreb: Hrvatsko Sociološko Društvo—Zavod za Sociologiju Filozofskog Fakulteta Sveučilišta u Zagrebu.

Cifrić, I. (2005). Ekološka edukacija. *Filozofska istraživanja, 25*(2), 327–344.

Clark, B. R. (1998). *Creating Entrepreneurial Universities: Organizational pathways of transformation. Issues in higher education*. New York: Elsevier Science Regional Sales.

Clark, B. R. (2004). *Sustaining change in universities: continuities in case studies and concepts*. Maidenhead: Open University Press.

Colbeck, C. L. (1998). Merging in a seamless blend: how faculty integrate teaching and research. *The Journal of Higher Education, 69*(6), 647–671.

Colbeck, C. L. (2002). Integration: evaluating faculty work as a whole. *New Directions for Institutional Research, 114*, 43–52.

Cummings, W. K. (2006). *The third revolution of higher education: becoming more relevant. Reports of changing academic profession project workshop on quality, relevance, and governance in the changing academia: international perspectives* (pp. 209–222). Hiroshima: Research Institute for Higher Education, Hiroshima University.

Harpe, B. de la, & Thomas, I. (2009). Curriculum change in universities: conditions that facilitate education for sustainable development. *The Journal of Education for Sustainable Development, 3*(1), 75–85. http://jsd.sagepub.com. Accessed 13 Oct 2009.

Edwards, B., & Marullo, S. (1999). Editors' introduction: universities in troubled times—institutional responses. *American Behavioral Scientist, 42*(5), 754–765.

Ehrlich, T. (Ed.). (2000). *Civic responsibility and higher education*. Westport: American Council on Education/Oryx Press.

Escrigas, C. (2008). *Foreword. Global University Network for Innovation (GUNI), Higher education in the World 3. Higher education: new challenges and emerging roles for human and social development* (pp. xxviii–xxxi). Basingstoke: Palgrave Macmillan.

Escrigas, C., & Lobera, J. (2009). *Introduction: new dynamics for social responsibility. Global University Network for Innovation (GUNI), Higher education at a time of transformation—new dynamics for social responsibility* (pp. 1–19). New York: Palgrave Macmillan.

Etzkowitz, H. (2001). The second academic revolution and the rise of entrepreneurial science. *Technology and Society Magazine, IEEE, 20*(2), 18–29.

Etzkowitz, H., & Leydesdorff, L. (Eds.). (1997). *Universities and the global knowledge economy: a triple-helix of university-industry-government relations*. London: Cassell Academic.

Etzkowitz, H., Webster, A., & Healey, P. (1998). *Capitalizing knowledge: new intersections of industry and academia*. New York: State University of New York Press.

Etzkowitz, H., Webster, A., Gebhardt, C., & Terra, B. (2000). The future of the university and the university of the future: evolution of ivory tower to entrepreneurial paradigm. *Research Policy, 29*(2), 313–330.

European Commission (EC). (2003). The role of the universities in the Europe of knowledge. Communication from the Commission, Brussels, 05 Feb 2003, COM, 58 final.

European Commission (EC). (2007). Promoting young people's full participation in education, employment and society. Communication from the Commission, Brussels, 5 Sept 2007, COM, 498 final.

Faulks, K. (2000). *Citizenship*. London: RoutledgeFalmer.

Ferrer-Balas, D., Adachi, J., Banas, S., Davidson, C. I., Hoshikoshi, A., Mishra, A., Motodoa, Y., Onga, M., & Ostwald, M. (2008). An international comparative analysis of sustainability transformation across seven universities. *The International Journal of Sustainability in Higher Education, 9*(3), 295–316.

Fiskovica Adamsone, A., Kristapsons, J., Tjunina, E., & Ulnicane-Ozolina, I. (2009). Moving beyond teaching and research: economic and social tasks of universities in Latvia. *Science and Public Policy, 36*(2), 133–137.

Furco, A. (2001). Advancing service learning at research universities. *New Directions for Higher Education, 114*, 67–78.

Geiger, R. L. (2004). *Knowledge and money: research universities and the paradox of the marketplace*. Stanford: Stanford University Press.

Geiser, K. (2006). Education for a transition to sustainability. In R. Forrant & L. Silka (Eds.), *Inside and out: universities and education for sustainable development* (pp. 29–40). New York: Baywood.

Gibbons, M. (1999). Science's new social contract with society. *Nature, 402*(6761), C81–C84.

Gibbons, M., Limoges, C., Nowotny, H., Schwartmann, S., Scott, P., & Trow, M. (1994). *The new production of knowledge: the dynamics of science and research in contemporary societies*. London: Sage.

Glavič, P., & Lukman, R. (2007.) Review of sustainability terms and their definitions. *Journal of Cleaner Production, 15*(18), 1875–1885. http://www.sciencedirect.com/. Accessed 15 Oct 2009.

Gokhberg, L., Kuznetsova, T., & Zaichenko, S. (2009). Towards a new role of universities in Russia: prospects and limitations. *Science and Public Policy, 36*(2), 121–126.

Golde, C. M., & Pribbenow, D. A. (2000). Understanding faculty involvement in residential learning communities. *Journal of College Student Development, 41*(1), 27–40.

Göransson, B., Maharajh, R., & Schmoch, U. (2009). New activities of universities in transfer and extension: multiple requirements and manifold solutions. *Science and Public Policy, 36*(2), 157–164.

Gough, S., & Scott, W. (2007). *Higher education and sustainable development: paradox and possibility*. London: Routledge.

Graham, G. (2002). *Universities: the recovery of an idea*. Charlottesville: Imprint Academic.

Greenbank, P. (2006). The academic's role: the need for a re-evaluation? *Teaching in Higher Education, 11*(1), 107–112.

Gregersen, B., Tved Linde, L., & Gulddahal Rasmussen, J. (2009). Linking between Danish Universities and Society. *Science and Public Policy, 36*(2), 151–156.

Griffith, R. (1998). *Educational citizenship and independent learning*. London: Jessica Kingsley.

Harkavy, I. (2006). The role of universities in advancing citizenship and social justice in the 21st century. *Education, Citizenship and Social Justice, 1*(1), 5–37.

Heater, D. (1999). *What is citizenship?* Cambridge: Polity.

Higher Education Academy. (2005). *Sustainable development in higher education: current practice and future development*. New York: Higher Education Academy.

Holland, B. A. (1999). Factors and strategies that influence faculty involvement in public service. *Journal of Public Service and Outreach, 4*(1), 37–43.

Hollander, E. L., & Saltmarsh, J. (2000). The engaged university. *Academe, 86*(4), 29–32.

IPCC. (2007). IPCC Fourth Assessment Report: Climate Change 2007: Synthesis Report. http://www.ipcc.ch/pdf/assessment-report/ar4/syr/ar4_syr.pdf. Accessed 26 Nov 2008.

Jacoby, B. (2009). *Civic engagement in higher education: concepts and practices*. San Francisco: Jossey-Bass.

Jongbloed, B., Enders, J., & Salerno, C. (2008). Higher education and its communities: interconnections, interdependencies and a research agenda. *Higher Education, 56*(3), 303–324.

Karlsson, J. (2007). Service as collaboration—an integrated process in teaching and research: a response to Greenbank. *Teaching in Higher Education, 12*(2), 281–287.

Karlsson, J., Booth, S., & Odenrick, P. (2007). Academics' strategies and obstacles in achieving collaboration between universities and SMEs. *Tertiary Education and Management, 13*(3), 187–201.

Kehm, B. M., & Pasternack, P. (2000). *Hochschulentwicklung als Komplexitätsproblem. Fallstudien des Wandels*. Weinheim: Beltz.

Koester, R. J., Eflin, J., & Vann, J. (2006). Greening of the campus: a whole-systems approach. *Journal of Cleaner Production, 14*(9/11), 769–779.

Kogan, M., & Teichler, U. (Eds.). (2007). *Key challenges to the academic profession* (Werkstattberichte, Vol. 65). Kassel: International Centre for Higher Education Research Kassel (INCHER Kassel) and UNESCO Forum on Higher Education, Research and Knowledge.

Krücken, G., Meier, F., & Müller, A. (2009). Linkages to the society as "Leisure Time Activities"? Experiences at German universities. *Science and Public Policy, 36*(2), 139–144.

Kuckartz, U. (1997). Ekologizacija Visokog Školstva. *Socijalna ekologija, 6*(1–2), 1–22.

Laredo, P. (2007). Revisiting the third mission of universities: toward a renewed categorization of university activities? *Higher Education Policy, 20*(4), 441–456.

Ledić, J. (2007). U Potrazi za Civilnom Misijom Hrvatskih Sveučilišta. In V. Previšić, N. N. Šoljan, & N. Hrvatić (Eds.), *Pedagogija—Prema Cjeloživotnom Obrazovanju i Društvu Znanja* (pp. 123–134). Zagreb: Hrvatsko Pedagogijsko Društvo.

Lindberg, C. (2010). Universities are key agents for promoting sustainable development. GUNI Newsletter. http://web.guni2005.upc.es/interviews/detail.php?chlang=en&id=1522. Accessed 24 Feb 2010.

Locke, W., & Teichler, U. (Eds.). (2007). *The changing conditions for academic work and careers in select countries* (Werkstattberichte, Vol. 66). Kassel: International Centre for Higher Education Research Kassel (INCHER-Kassel).

Lombardi, J. (2001). Quality engines: the strategic principles for competitive universities in the twenty-first century. The Center Reports. http://jvlone.com/UCV_ENG_1a.pdf. Accessed 03 Feb 2009.

Lozano, R. (2006). Incorporation and institutionalization of SD into universities: breaking through barriers to change. *Journal of Cleaner Production, 14*(9–11), 787–796. http://www.sciencedirect.com/. Accessed 02 Nov 2009.

Lozano-Garcia, F. J., Gandara, G., Perrni, O., Manzano, M., Hern, D. E., & Huisingh, D. (2008). Capacity building: a course on sustainable development to educate the educators. *The International Journal of Sustainability in Higher Education, 9*(3), 257–281. http://www.esmeraldinsight.com/1467-6370. Accessed 24 Oct 2009.

Lucas, C. J. (1994). *American higher education*. New York: St. Martin's Griffin.

Lynton, E. (1995). *Making the case for professional service*. Washington, DC: American Association for Higher Education.

Mac Labhrainn, I. (2005). *Reinvigorating the civic mission of the university*. Galway: Centre for Excellence in Learning and Teaching, National University of Ireland.

Macfarlane, B. (2005). Placing service in academic life. In R. Barnett (Ed.), *Reshaping the university: new relations between research, scholarship and teaching* (pp. 165–177). Berkshire: Open University Press.

Maculan, A. M., & Carvalho de Mello, J. M. (2009). University start-ups breaking lock-ins of the Brazilian economy. *Science and Public Policy, 36*(2), 109–114.

Maloney, W. A., & Deth, J. van. (Eds.). (2008). *Civil society and governance in Europe: from national to international linkages*. Cheltenham: Edward Elgar.

Marullo, S., Cooke, D., Willis, J., Rollins, A., Burke, J., Bonilla, P., & Waldref, V. (2003). Community-based research assessments: some principles and practices. *Michigan Journal of Community Service Learning, (Spring), 9*(3) 57–68.

McLaughlin, M. (1995). *Employability skills profile: what are employers looking for?* Report 81-92-E. Ottawa: Conference Board of Canada. http://www.ericdigests.org/1997-2/sills.htm. Accessed 25 Mar 2008.

McMillin, J., & Dyball, R. (2009). Developing a whole-of-university approach to educating for sustainability: linking curriculum, research and sustainable campus operations. *Journal of Education for Sustainable Development, 3*(1), 55–64. http://jsd.sagepub.com. Accessed 13 Oct 2009.

Menges, R. J. (Eds.). (1999). *Faculty in new jobs: a guide to settling in, becoming established, and building institutional support.* San Francisco: Jossey-Bass.

Milem, J. F., Berger, J. B., & Dey, E. L. (2000). Faculty time allocation. *The Journal of Higher Education, 71*(4), 454–475.

Molas-Gallart, J., Salter, A., Patel, P., Scott, A., & Duran, X. (2002). *Measuring third stream activities.* Final Report to the Russell Group of Universities, SPRU, University of Sussex.

Montesinos, P., Carot, J. M., Martinez, J. M., & Mora, F. (2008). Third mission ranking for world class universities: beyond teaching and research. *Higher Education in Europe, 33*(2/3), 259–271.

Morshidi, S., Zain, A. N. M., & Yunus, A. S. M., et al. (2007). Malaysia: New and diversified roles and responsibilities for academics. In W. Locke & U. Teichler (ed.). *The changing conditions for academic work and careers in selected countries* (pp. 147–162). Kassel: International Centre for Higher Education Research Kassel, University of Kassel.

Mwamila, B. L. M., & Diyamett, B. D. (2009). Universities and socio-economic development in Tanzania: public perceptions and realities on the ground. *Science and Public Policy, 36*(2), 85–90.

National Commission on Civic Renewal. (1998). A nation of spectators: how civic disengagement weakens America and what we can do about it—final report. http://www.puaf.umd.edu/Affiliates/CivicRenewal. Accessed 14 Jan 2009.

Nayyar, D. (2008). Globalization: what does it mean for higher education? In L. E. Weber & J. D. Duderstadt (Eds.), *The globalization of higher education* (pp. 3–14). Paris: Economica.

Neumann, R. (1992). Perceptions of the teaching-research nexus: a framework for analysis. *Higher Education, 23*(2), 159–171.

Neumann, R. (1996). Researching the teaching-research nexus: a critical review. *Australian Journal of Education, 40*(1), 5–18.

Ngoc Ca, T. (2009). Reaching out to society: Vietnamese universities in transition. *Science and Public Policy, 36*(2), 91–95.

OECD. (2004). *Public-private partnerships for research and innovation: an evaluation of the Dutch experience.* Paris: OECD. http://www.oecd.org/dataoecd/49/18/25717044.pdf. Accessed 16 Jan 2009.

OECD. (2007). *Higher education and regions: globally competitive, locally engaged.* Paris: OECD.

O'Meara, K. A. (2002). Uncovering the values in faculty evaluation of service as scholarship. *Review of Higher Education, 26*(1), 57–80.

O'Meara, K., Kaufman, R. R., & Kuntz, A. M. (2003). Faculty work in challenging times: trends, consequences and implications. *Liberal Education, 89*(4), 16–23. http://www.aacu.org/liberal-education/le-fa03/le-fa03feature2.cfm. Accessed 03 Feb 2009.

Ordorika, I. (2009). *Commitment to society: contemporary challenges for public research universities. Global University Network for Innovation (GUNI), Higher education at a time of transformation—new dynamics for social responsibility* (pp. 72–74). New York: Palgrave Macmillan.

Ostrander, S. (2004). Democracy, civic participation, and the university: a comparative study of civic engagement on five universities. *Nonprofit and Voluntary Sector Quarterly, 33*(1), 74–93.

Palsson, C. M., Göransson, B., & Brundenius, C. (2009). Vitalizing the Swedish university system: implementation of the third mission. *Science and Public Policy, 36*(2), 145–150.

Parker, M., & Jary, D. (1995). The McUniversity: organisations, management and academic subjectivity. *Organization, 2*(2), 319–338.

Paulsen, M., & Feldman, K. (1995). Towards a reconceptualization of scholarship. A human action system with functional imperatives. *The Journal of Higher Education, 66*(6), 615–640.

Putnam, R. D. (1995). Bowling alone: America's declining social capital. *Journal of Democracy, 6*(1), 65–78.

Readings, B. (1996). *The university in ruins*. Massachusetts: Harvard University Press.

Rice, E. R., Sorcinelli, M. D., & Austin, A. (2000). *Heeding new voices: academic careers for a new generation. New pathways: faculty careers and employment for the 21st century, inquiry #7*. Washington, DC: American Association for Higher Education.

Rosenthal, R., & Wittrock, B. (1993). *The European and American universities since 1800: historical and sociological essays*. Cambridge: Cambridge University Press.

Šalaj, B. (2002). Modeli Političkoga Obrazovanja u Skolskim Šustavima. Unpublished master thesis, Fakultet političkih znanosti Sveučilišta u Zagrebu, Zagreb.

Schoen, A. (Ed.). (2006). Strategic Management of University Research Activities, Methodological Guide—PRIME Project 'Observatory of the European University.' http://www.enid-europe.org/PRIME/documents/OEU_guide.pdf. Accessed 09 Nov 2009.

Schroeder, C. C. (1999). Partnerships: an imperative for enhancing student learning and institutional effectiveness. *New Directions for Student Services, 87*, 5–18.

Scott, J. C. (1992). *The influence of the Medieval University on the Latin Church and Secular Government Politics*. San Francisco: Mellen Research University Press.

Scott, J. C. (2006). The mission of the university: medieval to postmodern transformations. *The Journal of Higher Education, 77*(1), 1–39.

Scott, W., & Gough, S. (2007). Universities and sustainable development: the necessity for barriers to change. *Perspectives: Policy and Practice in Higher Education, 11*(4), 107–115. http://search.ebscohost.com/. Accessed 23 Jan 2010.

Sirat, M. (2007). Forging university-industry links: implications for knowledge transfer in developing countries. *Updates on Global Higher Education, Institut Penyelidikan Pendidikan Tinggi Negra (iPPTN)*, No. 11, July 14, 2007.

Slahova, A., Savvina, J., Cacka, M., & Volonte, I. (2007). Creative activity in conception of sustainable development education. *The International Journal of Sustainability in Higher Education, 8*(2), 142–154. http://www.esmeraldinsight.com/1467-6370. Accessed 24 Oct 2009.

Slaughter, S., & Leslie, L. L. (1997). *Academic capitalism: politics, policies, and the entrepreneurial university*. Baltimore: Johns Hopkins University Press.

Stephens, J. C., Hernandez, M. E., Roman, M., Graham, A. C., & Scholz, R.W. (2008). Higher education as a change agent for sustainability in different cultures and contexts. *The International Journal of Sustainability in Higher Education, 9*(3), 317–338. http://www.ebscohost.com. Accessed 24 Oct 2009.

Sterling, S. (2004). An analysis of the development of sustainability education internationally: evolution, interpretation and transformative potential. In J. Blewitt & C. Cullingford (Eds.), *The sustainability curriculum—the challenge for higher education* (pp. 43–62). UK: Earthscan.

Svanstrom, M., Lozano-Garcia, F. J., & Rowe, D. (2008). Learning outcomes sustainable development in higher education. *International Journal of Sustainability is in Higher Education, 9*(3), 339–351. http://www.sciencedirect.com/. Accessed 24 Oct 2009.

Taylor, P. (2008). Higher education curriculum for human and social development: filling a pail, or lighting a fire? http://www.slideshare.net/guni_rmies/session-1-peter-taylor. Accessed 23 Jan 2009.

Teichler, U. (1996). The conditions of the academic profession—an international, comparative analysis of the academic profession in Western Europe, Japan and the USA. In P. A. M. Maassen & F. A. Vught van (Eds.), *Inside academia—new challenges for the academic profession* (pp. 15–65). Utrecht: De Tijdstroom.

Thorn, K., & Soo, M. (2009). Latin American universities and the third mission: trends, challenges and policy options, World Bank Policy Research, Working Paper 4002.

UNECE. (2005). UNECE strategy for education for sustainable development. http://www.unece.org/env/documents/2005/cep/ac.13/cep.ac.13.2005.3.rev.1.e.pdf. Accessed 10 Oct 2006.

UNESCO. (2002). Education for sustainability from Rio to Johannesburg: lessons learnt from a decade of commitment. http://unesdoc.unesco.org/images/0012/001271/127100e.pdf. Accessed 24 Oct 2009.

UNESCO. (2009). World Conference on Education for Sustainable Development: 31 March–2 April 2009, Bonn, Germany Proceedings. http://www.esd-world-conference-2009.org/fileadmin/download/ESD2009ProceedingsEnglishFINAL.pdf. Accessed 24 Feb 2010.

Vabø, A. (2007). Challenges of internalization for the academic profession in Norway. In M. Kogan & U. Teichler (Eds.), *Key challenges to the academic profession* (Werkstattberichte, Vol. 65, pp. 99–107). Kassel: International Centre for Higher Education Research Kassel (INCHER Kassel) and UNESCO Forum on Higher Education, Research and Knowledge.

Van den Bor, W., Holen, P., Wals, A., & Filho, W. (2000). *Integrating concepts of sustainability into education for agriculture and rural development*. Lang: Frankfurt.

Viederman, S. (2006). Can universities contribute to sustainable development? In R. Forrant & L. Silka (Eds.), *Inside and out: universities and education for sustainable development* (pp. 17–28). Amityville: Baywood.

Wang, H., & Zhou, Y. (2009). University-owned enterprises as entry point to the knowledge economy in China. *Science and Public Policy, 36*(2), 103–108.

Ward, K. (2003). *Faculty service roles and the scholarship of engagement* (ASHE-ERIC Higher Education Report, 29(5)). San Francisco: Jossey-Bass.

Wilkins, C. (1999). Making "Good Citizens": the social and political attitudes of PGCE students. *Oxford Review of Education, 25*(1/2), 217–230.

Wright, T. S. A. (2007). Developing research priorities with a cohort of higher education for sustainability experts. *International Journal of Sustainability in Higher Education, 8*(1), 34–43. http://www.esmeraldinsight.com/1467-6370. Accessed 24 Oct 2009.

Wright, T., & Pullen, P. (2007). Examining the literature: a bibliometric study of ESD journal articles in the Education Resources Information Center Database. *Journal of Education for Sustainable Development, 1*(1), 77–90. http://jsd.sagepub.com. Accessed 10 Nov 2007.

Index

B. M. Kehm, U. Teichler (eds.), *The Academic Profession in Europe: New Tasks and New Challenges,* The Changing Academy – The Changing Academic Profession in International Comparative Perspective 5, DOI 10.1007/978-94-007-4614-5, © Springer Science+Business Media Dordrecht 2013

16691976R00123

Printed in Great Britain
by Amazon